Roy Wagner

The Innovation
of Meaning
in Daribi Religion

The University of Chicago Press
Chicago and London

The University of Chicago Press, Chicago 60637
The University of Chicago Press, Ltd., London
©1972 by The University of Chicago
All rights reserved. Published 1972
Printed in the United States of America
International Standard Book Number:
 0-226-86972-5
Library of Congress Catalog Card Number:
 75-188236

To Sue and Erika
with love

Contents

Illustrations

Preface

The preparation of this study took place in the context of my efforts to conceive a plausible theory of cultural meaning, and although it may be far from obvious, the approach presented here amounts to an extension of certain ideas found in my earlier book, *The Curse of Souw*. Necessary criticism has perhaps rendered my appreciation of Lévi-Strauss's *The Savage Mind* less apparent than it might be, and the critical examination of other, less directly relevant approaches has been omitted for the sake of brevity. The original idea of this work emerged from a study of Daribi magic and dream interpretation, and was paralleled and augmented by the insights of Mr. J. David Cole. Mr. Cole has chosen to develop his ideas in a different direction, however, and I must assume responsibility for the theory presented here. Discussions with my colleague, Dr. Johannes Fabian, were an important asset during the final stages of the formulation. The influence of Dr. David M. Schneider is perhaps not apparent beyond the first two chapters, but it is present at the very core of my idea of what anthropology can and should be, and indispensable to the position taken here.

This study is based on a total of over two years' fieldwork among the Daribi people. The first period of fieldwork, from November 1963 to February 1965, was carried out on a grant from the New Guinea Native Religions Project, of the University of Washington, under the direction of Drs. James B. Watson and Kenneth E. Read. Funds for the project were provided by the Bollingen Foundation and the University of Washington. The second period of fieldwork, from July 1968 to May 1969, was facilitated by a Faculty Research Grant from the Social Science Research Council of New York City.

I am grateful to the Administration of the Territory of Papua–New Guinea for its continued cooperation and assistance. Patrol officers Norman Wilson and James Aitken warmly extended the hospitality and consideration that has become traditional at Karimui and in their service generally. Extended stays in the bush were brightened by the enjoyable visits of Mr. Don Vincin, of Regional Leprosy Control, as well as, on occasion, those of Dr. Douglas Russell.

The warmth and friendship of the Mesplays of Karepa Mission Station has been a sustaining force throughout my work at Karimui. Through their keen interest in, and consideration for the native culture, Ken and Roselyn—and Christy, Lisa, Kent Philip, and Ian—Mesplay can be said to "belong" to Karimui in the deepest sense of the word. My wife and I would like to express our deep gratitude to them all, and to Miss Donna Luedtke and Miss Johanna Florek. Mr. and Mrs. Jack Frame of Goroka have given generously of their hospitality.

The people of Karimui are profoundly courteous and considerate. All of those who have given freely of their time and energy to help me understand their culture, or to make sure that my stay among them was pleasant and comfortable, are too numerous to list. I must however express my most heartfelt thanks to Kagoiano, a true friend who acted as field assistant, and his clanmates Suabe, Hanari, Tạre, Obe, and Homu. Yapenugiai shared his arcane knowledge of Daribi culture. Other important informants include Ebinugiai of Karuwabu, Kaware of Iuro, Sạri of Kilibali, Bai' of Tiligi', Wạu of Noru, Ogwane, Kiru, and Waro of Hagani, and Ba'nugiai of Soạri. Geroai of Dobu, our cook and general assistant, created for us a new and more intense meaning of the word "devotion." The small children everywhere we visited, particularly Maruwe and Jon at Kurube, and little Wabo at Hagani, helped as much as anything to make our stay at Karimui a pleasant one.

I should not neglect to mention Mr. Ian Hughes, of the Department of Human Geography, Australian National University, who provided companionship and intellectual stimulation during our patrol to Lake Tebera, and Mr. Ian Willis, a student of the early history of the highlands, whose company and hospitality were most appreciated. A pleasant afternoon with Mr. Michael J. Leahy of Zenag helped to round out my picture of the early history of Karimui.

Finally, special thanks are due to my wife Sue, who made a difficult adjustment to field conditions with apparent ease, and later diligently and carefully typed this manuscript with the anonymous moral support of our daughter Erika.

Introduction:
The Masks of
Meaning

There is an old legend told among the peoples of the Near East to the effect that God, on the day of judgment, will summon forth all the artists who have attempted the representation of the creatures of the world and challenge them to breathe life into their creations. Most certainly this parable realizes and celebrates an ingrained Byzantine and Islamic tradition of iconoclasm, but beyond this it dramatizes the essential *hubris* of all artistic representation. In the act of creation, which must be accomplished through his own skills, talents, and personality, the artist or artisan effectively preempts the role of the divinity—for he sets his own works beside those of the latter—whereby his art becomes a species of anticreation.

Nothing could be more foreign to our contemporary view of reality than the absolute, deistic conception of the world as "creation," yet this fact can scarcely diminish the philosophical implications of our parable. For when the artist or scientist attempts to represent a subject, whether through the medium of painting, poetry, scientific regularities, or formulas, his representation implies a comparison with the subject itself. The degree to which he achieves a plausible representation is a measure of his skills, talents, and personality, as well as of his understanding of the subject. If indeed it is not God but rather man through his culture, collectively or individually, who "creates" the world, then the problem of *hubris* is still with us, for it is still this creation that the anthropologist, as humanist or scientist, strives to represent.

In this respect the task of the anthropologist involves a very special kind of *hubris*, for he undertakes to represent the creativity of a subject-culture through the analytic processes of his science, and hence through the creativity of his own culture. But all too often the modes of analysis that he employs can only bring about a representation of the subject-culture as a fixed, unchanging, "logical" order or a "closed" system of timeless determinants. While the rules and techniques of science allow the anthropologist to be creative in the enterprise of deciphering the meanings of a native culture and formulating them in terms of a model, this model, as the static artifact of his analysis, seldom makes provision for creativity within the culture that it purports to represent. Thus the

3

scientist preempts creativity as a property of his own culture and denies it to that of the native, entailing a *hubris* not unlike that of the artist who usurps the forms of divine creation for use within his own designs.

The notion of "hot" and "cold" societies fostered by some contemporary structuralists provides a convenient *apologia* for this procedure by objectifying the roles of "analyst" and "system" as definitive properties, respectively, of the anthropologist's and the native's cultures. In this view "hot" societies, such as our own, are semantically oriented toward the production of events, whereas "cold" societies, including most "tribal" peoples, tend to ritualize events and assimilate them to a set of static paradigms. Whatever truth or usefulness this typology may contain, it succeeds admirably in providing a rationale for the kind of reductionism that the structuralist approach promotes. Much of the argument hangs upon the distinction between "ritual" and "event," and it is not evident that western society could not as easily be described in "ritual" terms or "tribal" societies be treated in terms of "event."

Representation in itself defines a form of creativity, for it involves the presentation of elements, objects, ideas, or images in some meaningful way, that is, through the mediation of words, pictorial styles, or other symbolic resources of a culture. In a sense these representational forms are the "masks" that any meaningful expression must assume, and the *hubris* of the artist or scientist springs from an all-too-thorough "masking" of his subject, an expressive use of his culture's forms to conceal rather than to dramatize the subject's inner life. The special *hubris* of the anthropologist who analyzes cultural meaning is a consequence of his concern with the representation of representation, the problem of illuminating another creativity through the medium of his own. Since this problem devolves upon the nature of meaning itself, let us now turn to this more basic issue.

Meaning in human cultures is contingent upon symbolic, or representational, forms and can only be invoked or dealt with through symbols. Symbols are based on the principle of signification, according to which a sound, figure, gesture, or some sequence of these is said to "stand for," "denote," or "designate" some other element. Because signification uses one thing to stand for another, it implies a necessary contrast between the signifier itself and the thing signified. This contrast amounts to the difference between a word, for instance, and the thing or things to which it refers; it is necessary to the symbolic expression of meaning, though as we shall see it is not the only thing that is necessary to it.

The words defined in a dictionary are all based on the principle of signification, and in most cases their signification is what is called *lexical*, that is, each word refers to one or more specific elements (which may be objects, actions, attitudes, ideas, or many other things). In such cases the relation between the word and the things to which it refers is established by definition or precedent (usage) alone, and is otherwise arbitrary. Thus we use the letter "A" to signify certain sounds because

this is a convention of our culture, and not because there is some necessary connection between the shape of this letter and the sounds themselves. (It is true that the "ancestor" of our letter "A" may once have had
a pictorial significance, but that significance does not directly concern
our use of the letter.) Definition merely tells us that a certain word
conventionally signifies certain elements; it does this, optimally, by
specifying those elements through the combination of other, more
general words, that is, by *classifying* them.

Because their signification is based on definition alone, and is otherwise arbitrary, lexical signifiers, as well as the classificatory systems
built upon them, can embody only a tautologous meaning. Although
they may enter into meaningful constructs (by assuming figurative
significances), their sole effect, when taken literally, is to repeat the
terms of their definitions. At most such signifiers can be invoked in an
appropriate grammatical format to reiterate trivial and tautologous
propositions such as "this is a dog," used in reference to an animal that
is, according to the accepted criteria, classifiable as a dog. Such a statement merely classifies; it provides, in the presence of a signified element,
the word that is used to signify that element, and hence repeats the
terms of the definition.

Nontautologous meaning can only be produced through the innovative extension of signifiers into metaphors, that is, the formation of
symbols whose contrast with the element signified is supplemented by
a relation of similarity, or analogy, with that element. Thus although
lexical signification is characterized by an arbitrary relationship between
signifier and signified, metaphorical signification involves a nonarbitrary and determinate relationship between signifier and signified. The
key to this difference is the fact of relationship itself; a metaphor brings
the element signified into relation with the system of meanings in a
culture, whereas lexical signification merely registers its conventions
of labeling. A lexical "coding" signifies an isolated element, but a metaphor signifies a relation.

As an example, let us consider the instance, cited by Geertz in his
essay "Religion as a Cultural System," of the Bororo man who says "I am
a parakeet."[1] The man has selected a word that already has a lexical
reference, to a kind of bird, as a signifier for himself, and thus the word
"parakeet" comes to signify a relation between the bird and the man.
This is because the contrast between "man" and "parakeet," which is
set up by the fact of signification, is supplemented by an analogy, and
hence a relation, between the two that constitutes the meaning of the
expression. The signifiers "man" (implicit in the context) and "parakeet" effectively "bracket" this analogy without actually stating it, and
so, in metaphoric formulations of this sort, words (or other forms) may

---

1. Clifford Geertz, "Religion as a Cultural System," in ASA Monograph No. 3, *Anthropological Approaches to the Study of Religion*, ed. Michael Banton (London: Tavistock,
1968), pp. 37-38.

be used to convey more than is included in their lexical definitions, and thus to extend arbitrary codings into meaningful constructs. What the Bororo intends to say is "As a man, I am a parakeet," and so identify himself "totemically."

Much has been written on the subject of metaphor, and the term has many particular denotations and connotations. Some of these define it very generally, others form a contrast between metaphor as the direct substitution of analogous terms, and such variant forms as *simile*, in which the comparison of terms is mediated by "as" or "like," or *metonymy*, in which a recognized part of an element is taken to represent or metaphorize the whole. Such classificatory nuances may be necessary to certain approaches; for our purposes, since we are concerned very broadly with cultural symbolism, all of these subtypes will be grouped together under the heading of "metaphor" as symbols implying a determinate relationship to the thing symbolized.

Metaphor constitutes the dynamic expression of a meaningful relation in a culture; through its combination of contrast and analogy it generates relations of opposition in which elements remain distinct from one another and are yet interdependent. The Bororo in our example metaphorized his identity as that of a parakeet among men, forming a relation that emphasized both his distinctiveness from other men and his similarity to them. The metaphor *extends* the notions of "man" and "parakeet" by drawing them into a new relation and a new meaning; it is an *innovation* upon the meanings of the culture.

The significance of this kind of innovation can be better appreciated when viewed in another perspective. The continual formation of metaphors has the effect of bringing "established" signifiers into new meaningful relations, of "extending" them, but the continued use or repetition of any particular metaphor leads to its "decay" into a lexical signifier as the analogic link between signifier and signified, the relation to which it refers, comes to be both ignored and taken for granted. Thus meaning is a function of change as well as of form; every creation of meaning alters the formal constitution of a culture, yet this alteration must take place if the formal elements (words, etc.) are to be used in a meaningful way, because these forms can only achieve meaning by entering into figurative constructs. As long as an expression continues to signify a relation, and hence retains its metaphoric properties, we may speak of its use as "innovation," because it operates upon other signifiers to draw them into a new relation. When it loses its metaphoric properties, the expression turns into a simple lexical signifier, though it often bears traces of its former metaphorical significance (as do most of the words of our language, for instance).

Every meaning in a culture is generated through metaphorical opposition, but not all the meaningful relationships of a culture are those of opposition. The metaphors that combine to make up a set of consistent meanings do not oppose *each other;* such metaphors exist in a *comple-*

mentary relationship to one another. I will call such a set of complementary metaphors an *ideology*. Each of the component metaphors of an
ideology involves a different aspect of the same whole, and thus they
neither overlap nor innovate upon one another. An ideology corresponds
to a particular cultural domain, and embodies the range of linked
concepts that make it meaningful. Daribi social ideology, which we
shall presently examine, includes the series of meanings, and their
elaborations and corollaries, pertaining to Daribi social relations and
"institutions."

Since ideologies are made up of metaphors, any metaphoric innovations made upon them in effect metaphorize what is already a metaphor.
And yet, since ideologies express the central propositions or tenets of a
culture, the most significant innovations in the culture will take the
form of metaphors involving them. When a metaphor is used in the
formation of another metaphor in this way, the *relation* signified by the
former is employed as a context for the latter. This use of a relation to
produce another relation brings about a dialectical interaction between
the meanings involved. Because of the contrast implicit in the fact of
signifying, the metaphors remain distinct, but because of the analogic
"link" of similarity implicit in the nature of a metaphor, they depend
upon each other; each uses the relation signified by the other as its own
context. In our earlier example, the Bororo identified himself as against
the notion of "man" by metaphorizing himself as a parakeet, but "man,"
too, is a metaphoric concept (involving the notions of procreation, kinship role, etc.), and thus the two metaphors are dovetailed; each is a
metaphorization of the other. When a Bororo wishes to marry someone
who is identified perhaps as a "toucan," he is obliged to make his
action meaningful through the generalizing metaphors of kinship (procreation, etc. – things that one does as a "man"), which are formed upon
his identity as a parakeet, as innovations. Marriage, in other words,
amounts to a declaration that, as a parakeet, he is a man, and a denial of
his "parakeet" status, for parakeets do not mate with toucans.

The ordinary process by which metaphors "decay" into lexical signifiers is contained and turned inward upon itself in a dialectic of this sort;
the innovative emphasis of one metaphor in such a situation occurs at
the expense of the relation signified by the other. As a result, the
opposed metaphors or ideologies that make up the dialectic form a
stable axis across which the change necessary to the formation of
meaning takes place, and the consequent meanings stand in a relationship of serial contradiction to each other.

Let us sum up the model that has been presented thus far: meaning
is created by the formation of metaphors involving the formal elements
of a culture. The relationship among specific metaphors within a culture
can be either one of complementarity (consistency) or of innovation
(contradiction). A set of complementary metaphors, whose meanings
are consistent, constitutes an ideology, but the distinct ideologies of a

culture stand in an innovative relationship to one another, that is, they achieve their meaning by metaphorizing, and hence contradicting, one another. The following chapters of this book will provide examples taken from Daribi culture to illustrate this thesis.

The importance of innovative extension cannot be overstressed. Meaning is intimately involved in every conscious cultural act, and cannot justifiably be detached from the events and actions through which it is constituted, or from the modes of its production. Eventless meanings are as inconceivable in a cultural context as meaningless events. The creation of meaning shares the rhythm of man's active and productive life; it neither forms nor presupposes a "closed" system because, like the life of a society, it is "open-ended" and ongoing. Human actions are additive, serial, and cumulative; each individual act stands in a particular relationship to the life of the individual or the group, and it also "adds" something, in a literal or figurative sense, to these continuities and to the situation itself. Thus every act, however habitual or repetitious, *extends* the culture of the actor in a certain sense.

An analogy with conversation may help to clarify this proposition. Each successive statement that is made in the course of a conversation should add something "new" to the conversation, in the form of information, opinion, or reaction, and yet this addition must be addressed to the subject at hand. Statements, in other words, should be relevant to the context, but they should also innovate upon that context, for it is senseless to add material that bears no relation to the subject, pointless to repeat that which is already known. Thus a conversation allows the participants to exchange and interpret information or views in an innovative sequence. In a general way, then, a conversation is no different from a scientific enterprise, for whereas scientific "laws" or theories form a context for the metaphoric interpretation of "new" phenomena, the only phenomena worth interpreting, from an experimental point of view, are those that "test" the implications of the laws or theories. In both cases innovation, based on contrast and similarity, is a necessary part of the undertaking; the "exploratory" nature of the conversation or scientific investigation requires the extension of "given" knowledge through the creation of new relations.

The necessity to innovate is not limited to conversation and scientific investigation alone; it is characteristic of all cultural activity. It amounts to the cultural necessity to attribute meaning to every successive act, event, and element, and to formulate that meaning in terms of already known referents or contexts. The metaphor may be one that has been repeated millions of times before, or it may be a completely original creation, but in either case it achieves its expressive force through the contrast that it presents and the analogy that this contrast elicits.

The source of this force is the special impetus or illumination, or the force of conviction, that attends upon every creation of meaning, and every solution to a problem or a riddle. Identity embodies the force that results from the creation of meaning for personal or group individuality; for instance, moral force is concomitant with the performance of an act that is meaningful in terms of the social collectivity, and "magical" or spiritual efficacy coincides with innovation upon established techniques of production or dogmas about man's existence.

The ultimate dogma, known to all cultures, is that of mortality, the inevitability of personal death, and it follows that the most powerful innovative constructs will be those that achieve their force against this kind of human limitation. Hence it is that ghosts, gods, and other religious creations are so often represented as being omnipotent, omniscient, and immortal. Insofar as these beings are constituted as innovations upon a universal state of man, they are of necessity represented anthropomorphically, as metaphorical people who share man's active, causational capacity but not his mortality or his other limitations. Most effectively, they take the form of innovations upon living human beings, and achieve their metaphoric status through acts of impersonation, the metaphorization of social role, whereby a person is "extended" into the role of a ghost or deity. Man's life-course can be seen as the ultimate social role, which subsumes all others, and it is at this level of generality, that of man as a whole being, that religious impersonation as a form of innovation takes place.

Impersonation involves the assumption of a being's identity not merely by assuming its name, but by adopting its appearance, mimicking its mannerisms, and in general taking on, in an imitative fashion, culturally significant aspects of its role. Impersonation achieves meaning through the analogy elicited by the contrasting roles or identities, that of the impersonator and that of the being (person, ghost, deity, etc.) whom he has chosen to impersonate. The impersonator derives his advantage (the "force" of his innovation) through the "external" capacities that impersonation adds to his own; by assuming the identity and role of another being, he also assumes its special powers and adds them to his. Thus we can speak of a ghost, which always appears as the impersonation of some particular medium, as an innovation upon his particular limitations, and of ghosts in general as innovations upon man's mortality.

This is the significance of the shaman who incorporates within his own person the souls of people or animals during his performances, of the priest who "is" Christ during the services, and of masked dancers and mediums in all cultures. Impersonation is simply another form of metaphorization, representing people or objects in the form of other known cultural elements to extend the given, literal forms of culture into meaningful relations. Indeed, the distinction drawn between metaphor and impersonation is a mere convenience of expression; the Bororo who "is" a parakeet can be said to impersonate a parakeet in some sense, if only through his name, and all the words, forms, images, and gestures that are utilized in metaphorization can be viewed as "masks" that are assumed in the countless acts of impersonation through which meaning is created.

Because the production of meaning is dependent upon *extensive* acts of this kind, we can say that culture lives on the difference between its formal means of expression and what it wants to say. The formation of metaphors takes place as a part of the normal course of events in a culture, and the contrasting meanings that these expressions elicit appear to us as paradoxes (that a man is a man and also a parakeet; that men must die, but that they live on after death). But these contradictions only assume the form of paradoxes when we think of them as simultaneously "valid" corollaries of a consistent "belief-system," and thus ignore their dialectical relationship. And this, in turn, suggests that the conceptual basis of a culture can never be adequately summed up as a logical ordering or a closed system of internally consistent propositions.

In the chapters that follow I will explore, in terms of the concepts introduced here, the consistencies and contradictions of Daribi culture. In Chapter 1 Daribi social ideology is analyzed via its articulation through mythical forms, and in Chapter 2 it is explicated as a complex of metaphors involving food and exchange. Chapter 3 introduces the notion of metaphoric innovation as against ideology, and explores three significant "styles" of innovation involving the creation of "power" or advantage. In Chapter 4 identity is analyzed as a product of innovation against social ideology. Chapter 5 considers the ideological theme of mortality as it is expressed in conjunction with cosmological ideas and the conceptualization of space. In Chapter 6 the concept of impersonation, the embodiment of an innovative relation by a human being, is introduced, and the styles of ghost impersonation found among the Daribi are reviewed. Chapter 7 presents the collective rite of mourning, as the ideological realization of mortality, and goes on to develop the significance of the *habu* ceremony as an impersonative innovation against this ideology. In Chapter 8 the conceptual basis of my argument is briefly recapitulated and concluded.

I would like to emphasize that this book is not in any way addressed to the issue of how society "operates" as a "mechanism," of "what makes it tick," an approach that, as the metaphor suggests, has achieved its greatest success in dealing with the products of our own technology. Although statistics, charts, and other evidential materials appear, these are intended mainly as descriptive and exploratory examples, and my major concern is with the understanding of Daribi culture as a system of meanings. Such an understanding is only attainable through an act of interpretation[2], which involves the anthropologist, in all of his personal and professional capacities, as much as his informants and the culture that they represent.

---

2. My position in this respect coincides with the views developed by Johannes Fabian in his studies of African religious movements.

A comprehensive descriptive introduction to the Daribi people can be found in Chapter 1 of *The Curse of Souw;* here I shall attempt only a brief sketch. About 4,000 Daribi inhabit the volcanic plateau skirting Mount Karimui to the north and west as well as the adjacent limestone valleys; several hundred more occupy a similar plateau south of Mount Suaru, nearby.[3] These areas are included, respectively, in the Karimui, Daribi, and Bomai census divisions, which are administered from Karimui Patrol Post, now located in the Chimbu District of the Territory of Papua–New Guinea. A pocket of over 1,000 Pawaia-speakers, who are bilingual with Daribi, live immediately to the east of them in the valley of the Sena River. Other bilinguals can be found among the Foraba, or Polopa-speakers of Lake Tebera and the lower Erave (Bore) River.

The Daribi language, known as "Mikaru" to members of the Summer Institute of Linguistics, is a member of the Mikaruan language family, which extends southward and southwestward into the Gulf District.[4] Daribi shares between 30 percent and 40 percent cognacy with most languages of the family. The southward tendency manifested in Daribi linguistic relationships is also reflected in their blood-group frequencies, which show a raised B frequency characteristic of south coastal populations and quite untypical of central highlanders.[5] Strong similarities in cultural conception and usage are shared by the Daribi with the linguistically related peoples to the southwest, the speakers of the remotely related Wiru language of Pangia, to the west,[6] and the speakers of the virtually unrelated Pawaia language, with whom they marry and live in close contiguity at Karimui.

Daribi clans, which include an average of eighty to ninety members, are defined through exchanges made on behalf of their members with external kinsmen of the latter. Members of a clan hold a territory in common, generally including between .16 and .5-square-mile of cultivable land as well as considerably more "peripheral" or bush land for hunting or sago-growing. Two to four allied clans are often found living together as a *community,* averaging between two hundred and two hundred fifty residents; the territory of such a community is strictly apportioned among its constituent clans, although common gardens were sometimes made in the past.

Gardening takes place, and long-term residence occurs, between 2,500 and 4,500 feet above sea level, although excursions into lower country for sago growing or into higher country for hunting are com-

3. Demographic figures represent the situation as of March 1969; these and other data, based on recent observations and revised interpretations, should be considered to supersede earlier published information in the event of contradiction.

4. Karl J. Franklin, "Languages of the Gulf District: A Preview," in *Pacific Linguistics*, Series A, No. 16 (1968), pp. 25-26.

5. Dr. P. B. Booth has kindly made available to me serological data collected by Dr. Roy Simmons in connection with leprosy research at Karimui.

6. Andrew Strathern, personal communication, 1969. Strathern estimates a linguistic cognacy of 10.6 percent between the Daribi and Wiru languages.

mon. The staple of sweet potato is cultivated under a system of bush-fallowing or swidden horticulture. Other important food crops include taro, bananas, yams, maize, sweet manioc, edible leaves, sugarcane, pitpit, and pandanus fruit. Pigs, dogs, and chickens are kept, though not in large quantities. Except for gardens or areas of recent cultivation, the whole region is covered with dense rain forest. Although overcast and a high degree of humidity are common, the climate avoids the extremes of temperature found in the highlands and on the coast.

The Daribi have probably been a distinct people for some hundreds of years at least; the natives to the south speak of them as "Hawari-Hwẹ," the "Tua River people," and examination of Daribi traditions as well as other evidence indicates that the society once inhabited the deep valley of this river, to the west of its present area of settlement. Beyond this, their history presents a kaleidoscopic array of blurred boundaries and transformed identities. A group of Wiru clans is said to have settled the western portion of the Daribi area, at Hweabi, much as the present-day Daribi live in association with the Pawaia. The Wiru were driven out, but the present Nekapo line traces its ancestry to them, much as Masi and Di'be trace theirs to the Pawaia. The question of who is Daribi, who Wiru, and who Pawaia is, of course, incidental to our interests and probably misleading in itself, but the issue it evokes is precisely to the point. Tribal identity, like any other kind of identity, and like any other kind of meaning, is a function of change. We delude ourselves to imagine that the peoples of New Guinea existed in a sort of frozen stasis until the advent of the Europeans brought history and change to them.

The point is made even better by the recent "cult" history of the Daribi. The first white men to reach Karimui were hailed and cele-brated as returning creators of the world, although they were in fact tired and lost travelers. The second encounter, with Mr. Ivan Champion, although it lasted only a few days, led to subsequent warfare and other interpretive extremes whose extent is now impossible to measure. In these encounters it was not the westerner, transient, unassuming, and objective as he was, who instigated change, but rather the natives, who seized upon these events as the occasions for epochal innovations of their own. This tendency toward spontaneous, capricious enthusiasm and action is a familiar experience to anyone who has lived in a Daribi village for some time, and an unfailing source of frustration for the field-worker. Nevertheless, I am convinced that although it varies with time, place, and people, it is a characteristic of all human society.

What we might speak of as the religion of the Daribi people stands in an innovative relationship to other aspects of their culture. Like the latter, it comprises an ever-changing assemblage of forms and practices whose attendant meanings undergo a continual metamorphosis under the impress of successive events. It would be futile to try to reduce such phenomena to some sort of "inventory" of universal practices or con-

ceptions, although in fact the usages themselves are not radically different from those found in other tribal societies. Almost all of the activities
described here were in actual performance during the periods of my
fieldwork; the spells were recited, the dreams were dreamed, *sogoyezibidi* practiced their craft, and the *habu* and *gerua* ceremonials were
carried on.

This was so in spite of the presence, since 1961, of Lutheran and
Seventh Day Adventist missionary groups at Karimui. Although the
presence and activities of the missionaries and native "evangelists"
were always conspicuous, it was difficult to discover any trace of Christian influence in the native religious conceptualization and practice. It
could well be argued, I believe, that this situation results from the fact
that mission ideology bears a unique innovative relationship to Daribi
culture (when it is understood, or interpreted, at all); the contrasts
presented are simply too great to permit any consistent metaphorization
in terms analogous to native religion, and the "message" of the missions
is not perceived to be in conflict with the latter.

In spite of this, at times religious usage has been a difficult matter to
discuss with the Daribi. Although Daribi religious conceptualization is
largely impervious to the influences of western ideology, their religious
practices have sometimes been the target of mission (or other outside)
condemnation. This situation is quite common in New Guinea, and
stems from fanciful presumptions on the part of outsiders regarding the
nature of native religion. The latter is often felt to be "backward" and
"primitive" in relation to rationalism and the various mission religions,
although in point of fact it seems to share a good many points of similarity with these aspects of western culture, excepting of course their
sense of evangelical vocation. But the anthropologist, too, has certain
expectations regarding the significance of native religion, for indeed if
he had not he would scarcely choose to study it, and I hope that my
own expectations will be made clear in the course of this book.

This book is not intended as an ethnography, although the detailed
explication required by its theoretical argument might prove helpful to
those interested in New Guinea as a specific area. Every ethnography
has its "theory," no matter how diffuse, insipid, or matter-of-fact this
may be, just as every theory has its ethnography. The theory presented
here has been developed in conjunction with my efforts to understand
Daribi culture, and is articulated in the context of its forms.

1

Ideology and Innovation

1 / Origins

ORIGIN MYTHS

Accounts relating to the origins of the universe, of man, or of man's condition are not uncommon among human societies. Often they involve lengthy, highly articulate, and even introspective efforts, some are by contrast pithy and terse, and there are others that represent the results of sophisticated mathematical and physical operations. Whatever their esthetic or scientific preoccupations, however, all accounts of this sort effectively translate some kind of systemic paradigm or proposition into a series of temporal events, a sequence of archetypical incidents that serve as a precedent, or set the conditions, for the present situation.

Perhaps all stories can be considered as "origin myths" in some sense, insofar as they are seen to represent archetypical relations or situations, and in fact the Daribi people recognize a wide range of stories as *po page*, the "speech bases" of groups, objects, or institutions. In some cases there may be conflicting or alternate versions of an account, and the issue becomes a matter of doctrine, as in the totemic debates that Bateson describes among the Iatmul,[1] or the controversies surrounding modern cosmology, so that the status of a myth is by no means easily predictable from a consideration of its contents alone.

Myths and stories, again, are something more than "systems," for in the act of "reducing" a narrative to a set of relations we exclude the very associations and elaborations which lend it conceptual elegance and plausibility in the eyes of its creators; by the same token, of course, the marvelous and delicate systemic cosmologies produced by our more analytic culture lose something of their elegance through being reduced to simplistic sequences, such as the explosion of a proto-atom. Quite apart from esthetic considerations, however, it is the systemic "core" of an origin account that provides its explanatory or ideological value, its validity, and its relationship to the major concerns of its culture.

If the systematic nature of an origin myth emerges as its most important didactic characteristic, it also poses a limitation to which all accounts of this sort are subject: very simply, the explanatory powers of the myth

1. Gregory Bateson, *Naven* (Stanford: Stanford University Press, 1958), pp. 126–28.

are in all cases confined to an expounding of the paradigm that it dramatizes. Beyond this, when the initial state postulated by the system is
reached, the world peopled by immortals and the primordial sea or
hydrogen-cloud, the proto-atom, and all other resources for explanation
have been exhausted, no further discussion is possible. In this sense
the difference between the creation epics of early civilizations and
tribal societies and the cosmologies of modern physicists becomes a
purely relative one, for an initial step from nonexistence to a hydrogen-
cloud is no less inconceivable than that from nothingness to a tropical
glade.

It is not, therefore, the "objective" validity of an origin myth that
compels the interest of the social scientist so much as its cultural
"validity," the degree to which the system that it expounds expresses
and articulates the ideals of a particular culture. It is this ideological
aspect, of course, that involves doctrinaire interest and discussion among
members of a culture, so that a major shift in the ideal orientation of a
culture may incorporate a corresponding change in its ideology of origins.
As an illustration of this let us consider the shift from sacred to naturalistic ideology that accompanied the gradual secularization of Western
society beginning in the seventeenth century. Prior to this period, the
origins of man and the universe, as presented in the Book of Genesis,
were held to have resulted from acts of the Divine Will, a cultural order
whose mundane equivalent was represented in ecclesiastical law, much
as man himself, as a cultural being, represented the "image" of God.
Clerical or national ideology of the period, as exemplified in the notion
of the divine right of rulers, was merely an extension of this dogma.
With the rise of natural philosophy, and the notion of "natural man"
propounded by Locke and accepted by Rousseau, the force of the earlier
system was blunted, though it was not until Darwin's hypothesis of the
animal origins of man and its consequences that the issue was finally
resolved. The result, of course, was a complete reversal; the modern,
naturalistic view regards man and his culture as the complex products
of evolution from an earlier, natural order. As the earlier ideology
reinforced the special position of the church as a mediator in both sacred
and secular affairs, so the later system reflects our post-Enlightenment
concern with nature, natural law, science, and rational solutions.
Schneider's treatment of modern American kinship provides a coherent
example of the pervasiveness of these categories in our system of
thought.[2]

As much as it bears out a system of cultural distinctions, an origin
myth also participates in a literary or folk tradition with themes, narrative forms, and styles of its own. A given text may well represent the
local version of a widely diffused motif; a myth may in fact owe its
external form to the kind of exoticism that led Europeans to revel in the

2. David M. Schneider, *American Kinship: A Cultural Account* (Englewood Cliffs, N. J.:
Prentice-Hall, 1968); see especially chap. 2.

names and events of the Old Testament, and later, when the emphasis shifted, to seek models of rationality among the ancient Greeks. It is important, therefore, in approaching literary expressions of the order of origin myths, to become acquainted with the traditions in which they occur. In the remainder of this chapter I would like to introduce the distinctions characteristic of Daribi social ideology as they appear in various origin stories, and to do this effectively it will first be necessary to consider a larger tradition in which many of these myths participate. Of course, this treatment is not intended to be exhaustive, and the emphasis throughout will be on the expression of cultural themes.

PAPUAN "HERO TALES"

The tradition or series of myths known as "Papuan hero tales" is among the most impressive features reported for the flamboyant coastal cultures lying between the Purari Delta and the Kumbe River in West New Guinea. Many ethnographers dealing with the area have commented on the legends, and a number of texts are available, but it is unlikely that the anthropological literature represents anything but an irregular sampling, geographically as well as textually, of the total complex. It is in fact difficult to set precise limits, or to speak of a specific "tradition," for much of the adjacent area is unknown ethnographically, and quite analogous themes and mythic cycles have been found in other parts of Melanesia as well as in Australia. I will therefore restrict my discussion to a number of tales whose major emphases are discernibly similar and probably homologous.

Wherever these texts have been recorded, they seem to have had an unusual significance in the local culture, and, in many places, they had been preserved as secrets;[3] the Gope texts were related to Austen as stories told to initiates,[4] and the Sosom myth is associated with an initiatory cult among the Marind-Anim.[5] At Kiwai Island, where the hero Sido had wanted to renew his life, or return from the grave,[6] Landtman's informants told him that Sido was "all same Jesus Christ,"[7] whereas my informants at Karimui, where the significant feature of the story is Souw's curse of mankind, declared that "you call him God, we call him Souw."

An important feature of these myths is that the hero is generally portrayed as journeying across the known world in some significant way,

---

3. The Daribi Souw stories were deliberately withheld from the early patrol officers at Karimui who enquired into native origin-traditions, because, as my informants admitted, they were afraid that the sexual aspects of the story would upset them, particularly since Souw was traditionally light-skinned. They were also withheld from me at first, but were finally told to me "because you keep asking, and since we are sorry for you because you don't have a wife."

4. Leo Austen, "Legends of Hido," *Oceania* 2, No. 4 (1932): 468.

5. J. van Baal, *Dema* (The Hague: Martinus Nijhoff, 1966), p. 267.

6. Gunnar Landtman, *The Folk Tales of the Kiwai Papuans,* Acta Societatis Scientiarum Fennicae 47 (Helsingfors: Printing Office of the Finnish Society of Literature, 1917): 109–10.

7. Landtman, p. 116.

and that this movement is linked to the major action of the plot; he travels across the sea seeking women and bringing vegetable food, or journeys to the land of the dead, or flees from a pursuing woman with whom he has shamed himself. Landmarks and curious features along his route are often linked to his passage, and at Karimui he is said to have created many of the prominent landforms. Frequently the hero is supposed to have originated in the territory of a neighboring people, like Sida, in the Torres Strait version, who came from "...Sadoa, where the Togeri men come from,"[8] or Sosom, among the Marind-Anim (the so-called Togeri), who in one version is said to come from Australian territory (i.e., the direction of Torres Strait), and often he vanishes into the territory of another group.[9] My Daribi informants told me "we know the story up to the Sazabage [a local ridge], if you want to know what happened afterward, ask the people at Iuro." The total effect is one of a series of linked myths, continued from one society to the next, or, in the native view, the continued adventures of a single wandering hero. Map 1 records a number of these journeys as plotted geographically across some four hundred miles of Papuan coast.

In their continuative aspect, these stories form a striking parallel to the series of myths involving a "traveling creator" reported from northern Australia. There too the activities of the hero are frequently associated with special landmarks, and the hero is often identified or connected with a snake,[10] as is the case in many of the Papuan stories. It is therefore not unlikely that the Papuan tradition we have been discussing draws upon a mythic complex of much greater extent that is widely ramified through Papua and Australia.

Similar as many of the Papuan legends are, there is no justification for regarding them as mutilated or imperfectly transcribed versions of the same story; not only are they involved locally with numerous additional themes, but their general configurations change considerably from place to place, so that the same thematic material is often "recombined" to form different plots. We can trace a number of homologous elements in these stories, and although in some cases their omission may have been a result of accident or oversight, a close examination reveals that interpretive "selection" is also involved.

Among the Marind-Anim of West New Guinea the Dema Sosom is linked to a homosexual initiatory cult for boys; he is said to come from the east during the east monsoon and make a cyclical tour of the villages east of the Kumbe River (Map 1, routes 1, 2) "fertilizing man and soil."[11]

8. W. H. R. Rivers, *Reports of the Cambridge Anthropological Expedition to Torres Straits* 5 (Cambridge, 1904): 31.

9. Van Baal, p. 267.

10. See W. Arndt, "The Dreaming of Kunukban," *Oceania* 35, No. 4 (1965): 241–59. The Black Cuckoo or Koel *(Eudynamis orientalis)* who saves Kunukban (pp. 242–43) is either identical with or closely related to the *kauweri* that cries out in the Souw story, thinking Souw's penis a snake.

11. Van Baal, p. 267.

His "presence" doubtless coincides with the celebration of the rites, and the sound of the bullroarer is said to be his voice. His size is compared to a coconut tree, and "...it is also said that his body is made of stone and that he is so big that he can stand astride the Maro River, one foot on either bank."[12] Van Baal makes a good case for Sosom's having a long penis,[13] and a myth describes how this organ was severed by the mother of a being from whose body he was unable to free it, leaving a mutilated remnant that could only be used to sodomize.[14] If we regard the exaggerated organ as a representation of the Dema's sexual and fertilizing capacities, then this myth provides a unique but ideologically relevant transformation of the motif, for it celebrates the abrogation of normal (i.e., heterosexual) intercourse through the severing of that organ.

The series of myths concerning Sida, Said, Soida, or Soido, from the islands of Torres Strait, and from Kiwai Island in the estuary of the Fly River are likewise constructed around an association of sexuality with fertility. Generally the hero is said to have made a tour of various islands, and in the Torres Strait versions he comes from the far west and goes on to Kiwai Island (Map 1, routes 3, 4). According to Haddon, "...in the eastern as well as the western islands, Sida was regarded as a great benefactor: he instructed people in language, he stocked reefs with the valuable cone-shell, and notably he introduced plants useful to man."[15] The various stories recorded by Rivers, Haddon, and Landtman form a number of transformations on a theme involving the bestowal of vegetable food in return for the giving of a woman. In a number of the stories the hero's penis, as the mediating element in the sexual act, becomes the agent whereby the first food plants are introduced; in Landtman's version the vegetable food eaten by the hero Soido passes directly into his penis, which is enlarged, and after he arrives in the barren Murray Islands these are shaken out as he attempts to have intercourse.[16] In other versions the hero's semen, released in intercourse, causes food plants to spring up, or food plants are simply given to inhabitants of the different islands according to the attractiveness of the women they have provided for the hero. In a further transformation, the woman herself gives rise to food plants after intercourse; she "bears" them with a child,[17] or they spring up from her body after she has been killed.[18]

With the Sido story, which Landtman, who recorded it at Kiwai Island, distinguishes from the Soido texts,[19] an important change of emphasis

12. Van Baal, p. 267.
13. Van Baal, pp. 273, 664, 759.
14. Van Baal, p. 268.
15. A. C. Haddon, *Reports of the Cambridge Anthropological Expedition to Torres Straits* 6 (Cambridge, 1908): 22.
16. Landtman, pp. 119–21.
17. Landtman, p. 123, version E.
18. Landtman, p. 119.
19. Landtman, p. 123.

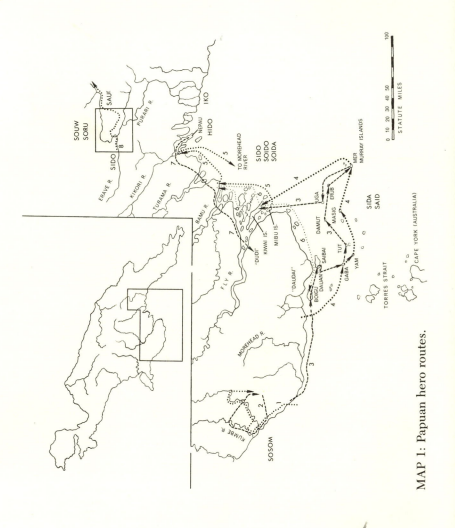

MAP 1: Papuan hero routes.

takes place, one that distinguishes the hero tales occurring to the north and east of that point. The sexual motif, heretofore an aspect of the wandering hero, now involves him in a compromising or shaming situation, which provides the impetus for the journey and forms the basis for an epic of human mortality. Landtman's Sido text represents the longest and best articulated legend in this tradition. Like Faust or Gilgamesh, Sido is presented as a kind of paragon or idealization of human ability and achievement; he is born of his father's connection with the ground, and therefore "belongs to all people."[20] According to Landtman's informant, "...whatever Sido did everyone since then does in the same way. At first people did not know of death, Sido was the first man who died, and since his death all must die."[21] Following a quarrel over the distribution of fish, in which Sido inadvertently gives his wife Sagaru a piece with a bone in it, she runs off and is lifted into the sky by a giant tree. As a final result of his efforts to recover her, Sido is killed, and commences his long journey, via canoe, to the land of the dead (Map 1, route 6). As his body proceeds, the spirit goes along beforehand warning everyone not to take the body and bury it, for this would condemn all people to die. Sido's intention is to regenerate himself, by splitting and shedding his skin, as a snake does,[22] but he is continually frustrated. Following a final attempt to regenerate himself, he is shamed when two "mothers" offer him a drink from his own skull, and he arrives at the land of the dead, which he prepares for all who are to follow.

The legends involving Hido, which Austen recorded among the Gope, one of a number of groups "of Kiwai extraction"[23] between the mouths of the Bamu and Kikori rivers, are clearly variants of Landtman's Sido story. In the first of these Hido (or Waea) is seduced by his sister Hiwabu and shamed, whereupon he leaves and begins a journey to the land of the dead (Map 1, route 7). After four days Hiwabu follows, and Hido takes a number of precautions to avoid detection, including shedding his skin like a snake.[24] Finally, however, both arrive at "Dudi," the land of the dead, where they live happily. A second version involves a restatement of the "tree" motif of the Sido story, and a trip from Mibu Island to "Neuri," then to the Morehead River (Map 1, route 5), but this text glosses over the ideological implications of the action, and seems to have been compromised with episodes involving a different story.[25]

The tradition continues eastward from this point along the coastline of the Papuan Gulf to the Purari Delta, where it is represented in the hero Iko, and it is not unlikely that there are connections to the interior also, linking the legends of the Karimui area to the very similar first Hido text collected by Austen.

20. Landtman, p. 96.
21. Landtman, p. 96.
22. Landtman, p. 110, versions A and F.
23. Austen, p. 468.
24. Austen, p. 470.
25. I.e., the *Aibaru* theme, p. 474.

In this section we have traced a set of homologous mythic elements through a series of transformations, arbitrarily proceeding from west to east (although the hero, in many versions, moves in this direction). In each instance a hero, whose name also seems to undergo regular transformations, becomes involved in a chain of incidents that lend significance to man's present condition. The Sosom myth of the Marind-Anim and the legends from Torres Strait celebrate the regenerative aspects of human sexuality in association with those of nature; in the former instance the hero's penis, as the mediator in heterosexual activity, so often linked with the sexual division of labor in gardening, is cut (by a woman), shifting the locus of regenerative power to the male-oriented Sosom cult, whereas in the latter series the providing of a woman and heterosexual connection lead to the introduction of food plants. In the stories told north and east of Kiwai Island, the significance shifts to the frustration of the hero's regenerative power and its consequences for mankind —namely death, so that the themes of regenerative fertility accompany what is essentially a mortality myth. At Kiwai the association of sexuality with this theme is complex and belabored, but in the first Gope text it is the shame of incest that drives the hero on to the land of the dead. We can recognize a number of points of analogy between this transformation and the story of Souw from Karimui,[26] which represents, nevertheless, a further rearrangement of themes. Let us consider the elements of this major tradition as they are represented in the Karimui area.

SIDO, SOUW, AND SAUr

The series of legends that I recorded among the Daribi and their western and eastern neighbors suggests a kind of microcosm of the range of stories we have been discussing. It includes a set of alternate and sometimes contradictory texts, and some transformations of plot as we pass from one area to the next. Very likely this kind of local variation and fragmentation would be replicated in any other region of comparable size within the compass of our "tradition," as the number and variety of "alternate" versions reported by Landtman and the members of the Torres Strait Expedition will testify.

The stories at Karimui for the most part center around an incident in which the hero is shamed, usually in a sexual attempt, after which he curses mankind with mortality and the motives and techniques for killing. The sister-wife who follows Hido in Austen's text is replaced at Karimui by the hero's daughter, or his cross-cousin, and this following of the man by a female relative, as in the Gope version (but unlike the Kiwai myth), forms an integral part of the plot. Let us examine a number of texts from this series.

The people of Soạri Clan, on the Bore or lower Erave River, located

26. Roy Wagner, The Curse of Souw: Principles of Daribi Clan Definition and Alliance in New Guinea (Chicago: University of Chicago Press, 1967), pp. 38–41.

to the southwest of Mount Karimui, speak both the Daribi language and their own, which they call "Foraba";[27] they belong to a fairly extensive society to which Daribi refer as "Kewa" or "Urubidi." Like the Kiwai Islanders, the Soạri call the hero of their story Sido. Approximately one mile upstream from Soạri village, at Nogidai, the site of Sido's house and a pool of his urine[28] were pointed out to me, and at Wadua,[29] on the opposite bank, I was shown the sago of Sido and a giant *Ficus* tree where the bird cried out on seeing his penis (Map 2, inset); nearby, at Hagarawe, was the house of his son, Abupagai. According to the Soạri,

Sido was born at Nogidai, where his house stood; he had two children, a boy and a girl. Two women were living nearby, a widow and a young girl, who had never married. One day, when they were processing sago at Wadua [an alternative version holds that they were sequestered in a menstruation hut], Sido thought of them and became aroused, and his penis passed beneath the river to Wadua, where a bird saw it and cried out. The women said "The bird has seen an animal" and the widow wanted to go and see, but the young girl went instead. When she saw Sido's penis emerging from the ground, she ran screaming to her house. The widow said "I wouldn't have cried out." Sido was shamed, and wanted to go to Bựmaru; he sent his children to fill some bamboo tubes with water. He gave the boy a whole bamboo, and the girl one that had a hole in it. The boy filled his successfully, but when the girl filled hers, the water ran out. She tried again and again, attempting to patch it with mud. Sido, meanwhile, took his wife and son and left. He left behind a pair of fire-tongs, and his daughter, in her frustration, tried to break these. Sido saw this, and returned for her. As long as Sido lived at Nogidai, people did not die; as he sat in his canoe when leaving he "threw down" the practice of fighting, wooden shields, bark shields, arrows, and then mourning clay and the custom of mourning. Sido went along the Bore in his canoe, and at one point he made it flow underground, so that the women who had shamed him could not follow.

Unlike most of the texts we have been reviewing, this one has a decidedly local character; all of the significant action can be immediately related to the local landmarks mentioned above. As in the Hido text, the hero's sexuality provides the key motivating factor in the plot, but whereas among the Gope shaming is a result of incest, here the aspects of sex and relatedness have become dissociated, so that Sido's children are treated separately in the incident of the bamboo water-containers. Shaming in this case is a matter of what could be called sexual "knowledge," as represented by the alternatives of the experienced woman (who "wouldn't have cried out") and the inexperienced girl; the fright

27. See Karl J. Franklin, "Languages of the Gulf District: A Preview," *Pacific Linguistics,* Series A, No. 16 (1968): 25–26; this clan clearly falls into a language grouping that Franklin calls "Polopa."

28. At the suggestion of Kagoiano, my field assistant, I drank from this pool, which proved somewhat brackish but not otherwise unusual.

29. These place-names appear to be related to a set of names that Daribi recognize as those of Souw's relatives; according to my Daribi informants, Souw's cross-cousins were named Do, Tiarigi, Nobida ("Nogidai"), and Abupagai ("Abugai"); Do's daughter was named Waruai ("Wadua"), and her son was Uru, ancestor of the "Urubidi."

shown by the young girl, her lack of sexual "knowledge," leads, through the shaming of Sido, to another kind of "knowledge," that of death, or mortality, and of the usages connected with it. The loss of one kind of "innocence" is balanced by the loss of another, and this kind of reciprocity between the hero and mankind calls to mind the Sida stories of Torres Strait, in which the inhabitants of an island were rewarded with vegetable food in proportion to the attractiveness of the girl they had presented to Sida. At the conclusion of this text Sido is simply "passed on" to the Daribi.

It does not seem unlikely that the Daribi names for the hero of this story, "Souw," or, occasionally, "Soru," stem from an interpretive phonetic identification of "Sido" with a kind of grass known to the Daribi as sorouw or, in contracted form, souw.[30] The significance that the Daribi attach to the story is indicated by their reaction to the first Europeans to visit their area, who were interpreted in its terms. In some versions of the story, Souw, as he departed eastward along the Tua Valley, promised to return one day. When, in June 1930, Michael J. Leahy and Michael Dwyer approached Karimui, they came from the east, along the river. They were tall men, and were accompanied by large dogs; their coming had already created quite a stir upriver,[31] and Souw was traditionally thought to have had light skin. It is not, therefore, surprising that Daribi understood Leahy and Dwyer to be to nigare bidi, men who had formed the land, or that they interpreted the explorers' form-fitting clothing, which were alien to them, as "the skin of Souw, which he removes at night in order to sleep."[32] Apocalyptic rumors spread, and it was feared that Leahy and Dwyer would go on to the horizon and cut the supports of the sky, which would fall and kill everyone. According to eyewitnesses, crowds visited their campsites, and there was general concern lest an incident occur that would provoke their retribution.

Souw is also integrated into the traditional history of the Daribi; his travels are linked with Bumaru, the extensive grass plain on the Tua where the Daribi claim their ancestors lived. A short text describes how Souw's daughter, here identified as Waburi, meets Bagu, the ancestor of Noru Phratry, as she is cutting a passage through a limestone ridge near the confluence of the Tua and Erave rivers, which her father had made to block off his trail. Inspired by a dream, Bagu digs from one side, Waburi from the other, and they meet halfway. In a number of

30. The name "Sorouw" or "Souw" is still in use among the Daribi, and I found several men so named in 1968–69. In response to my questions, informants replied that the name could be understood as referring either to the variety of grass or to the culture-hero.

31. This and other aspects of the 1930 journey of Leahy and Dwyer are faithfully and comprehensively treated in Ian Willis's excellent study, "An 'Epic' Journey" (subthesis prepared at the University of Papua and New Guinea, Port Moresby, 1969).

32. The skin of Souw was, of course, an aspect of his immortality, since he had only to shed it, "like a snake," to become young again. While attending a seance in a Daribi village in 1968, I referred to the death of a European, and an old woman exclaimed in surprised tones, "We didn't think that you people died!"

genealogies that I collected Waburi was given as the wife of Bagu, establishing Souw in the ancestry of Noru Phratry.

In an earlier study of the Daribi I quoted a fairly extensive text of the
Daribi Souw story,[33] although no attempt was made to analyze it. The
following text represents a somewhat different version, although the
plot remains essentially the same:

> Souw was living on the Bore River with two young girls, one was his
> daughter Yaro and the other was the child of a line called Karoba. Souw
> had a very long penis, and once while the girls were preparing sago it
> became erect and rose from a ravine; a bird called *kauweri* saw it and
> cried out. The girls heard the bird, left their sago, and ran to investigate;
> they saw the penis of Souw, and it tried to enter the Karoba girl. Both
> girls ran away in fright, and returned to their sago-making. At dusk they
> returned home, and the next day they resumed making sago. As they
> were working, Souw gathered firewood and killed two pigs, and then
> by himself he gutted them, one with each hand, and cooked them. He
> put the pigs in his canoe, and took all of his possessions except for an
> *egebe*, or stone knife, which he forgot, and left for Bumaru. When Yaro
> returned from making sago, she found that Souw had gone, and that the
> house was empty except for the *egebe*. She took this and set out to find
> her father; when she came to the top of the mountain called Kiria, she
> called out "I'm coming, wait for me." Souw arrived at Bumaru, ate his
> pigs there, and slept. Then he left all the people there [ancestors of the
> Daribi and other groups] and continued his journey, with Yaro follow-
> ing. When he came to Hweabi, Souw threw down *sia* seeds ["Job's
> tears"], mourning clay, sorcery, warfare, the *kebidibidi*, death, and all
> the evils man is cursed with. He also threw down his own skin. If people
> had taken this skin, they would be immortal, but instead the snakes all
> came together and took it, and now instead of dying they simply shed
> their skins and are young again. When Yaro arrived at Hweabi, she cut
> a rock shelter in the western face with the *egebe* and also cut the pass
> at the top where the road goes through. Meanwhile Souw left Hweabi
> and came to a place outside of Noru where he danced and created a
> lake, and also planted sago there. He then planted *dora'* [*Gnetum
> gnemon*] trees on both sides of the Una River, planted some *sozobi*
> serew pines near Hobe, followed the Ababu River and planted *dora'*
> trees there; he crossed to the Boro River, tested the ground and found
> it firm, and planted sago there. Then he stamped on the ground and
> created the muddy plateau south of Masi, and cut Hweabi away from
> Mount Karimui. When Yaro came to this point she also cut the mountain.
> Then Souw passed south of the mountain, stopping at the Nami River
> to throw down sago flour, causing much sago to grow there, and went
> eastward to the Pawaian people [Map 2, route 1].

This Daribi version is characterized by a certain economy of plot;
the daughter who follows the hero is here identified as one of the
women making sago, and the shame felt by the hero at exposing himself before his own daughter echoes the "incest" theme of Austen's
Gope version and thus reinforces the "sexual knowledge" motif introduced in the Soari myth. The fire-tongs that link father and daughter in
the latter story are replaced here by the stone knife, which Yaro, in her

33. Wagner (1967), pp. 38–41.

pursuit of Souw, uses to help complete the work of forming the landscape. (In the other published version of this story, the "widow" is present as in the Soari story, and the girls are contrasted as being dark-skinned and light-skinned.) Souw's killing, butchering, and eating of the pigs can be seen as a counterpart (exclusively male) to the girls' female activity of processing sago; the fact that Souw fails to share the pigs with the girls (and the fact that their sago is also kept to themselves)[34] parallels the unsatisfactory outcome of his attempt at intercourse, as sexual complementarity is related to the exchange of food and services between men and women. Yaro's pursuit of her father may then be interpreted as an effort to reestablish the relationship abrogated by shaming, as may be her cutting of the ridges, which Souw is said to have created in order to block his path.

The Daribi people who live to the north of Mount Karimui tell a somewhat different version, in which a shift of location of the main action occurs together with a partial transformation of the major theme, so that the story forms a bridge to the Pawaian versions. As the Soari tale concludes at Bumaru, and the legend just quoted has Bumaru as its centerpoint, so this text begins there (Map 2):

Once all men lived at a place called Bumaru, which has no trees, only *kunai* grass. A woman there had two children, one of whom had dark skin, and the other light skin. There was a pig-feast at Bumaru, but when the viscera were distributed, the woman didn't receive any. Souw, the light-skinned brother, left Bumaru and came up around Mount Karimui. The people of Solida[35] followed him, together with the ancestors of the Pawaian and Daribi people. All of these stayed at a place called Teria, near Iuro, after which they went to Orouwa, near the Neru River [Map 2]. Bones of the pig killed at Bumaru were brought along, and those of another pig killed at Orouwa were hung together with them on a tree at Orouwa. The tree has since grown over the bones, but the teeth are still visible. Two women lived at Orouwa, a widow and a young girl. There was a bird in the bush nearby which cried out often, indicating that it had sighted a snake. As long as the widow went into the bush to find the snake, everything was all right. Once, however, the young girl went. She saw a *gura'* snake, and caught its head, but its tail entered her vagina. She cried out, and Souw was ashamed [his semen can still be seen at the spot]. Souw cursed the people at Orouwa; he gave them war, feuding, sorcery, mourning customs, etc., after which they were always burdened with troubles, and went away to the Highlands. At Mengino and Chimbu he left young women, pig bristles, and dog hairs, and as a result these places now have many young women, pigs, and dogs.

The analogous themes of failure to share pork and the young girl's unwillingness to participate in sexual intercourse, which were treated as related aspects of the same situation in the earlier Daribi version,

34. Daribi cuisine regards pork and sago as complementary foods.
35. Solida is a small village near Karimui Patrol Post that includes the remnants of a number of Daribi- and Pawaian-speaking clans that formerly occupied low-lying lands along the Tua River to the east of the present population. Like the Daribi of Bomai Patrol Post, they probably had undergone some acculturation to highland practices.

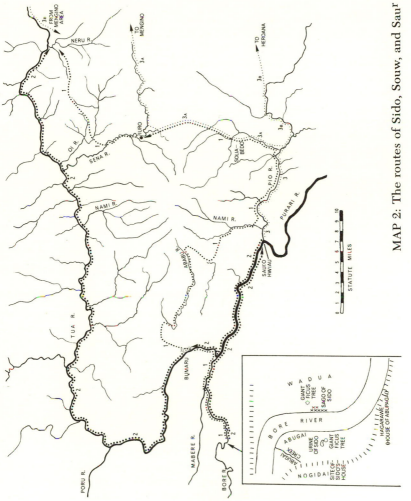

MAP 2: The routes of Sido, Souw, and Saur

are distributed among two analogous situations in this more eclectic version. Since the scene of the "shaming" episode, and the subsequent curse, has been shifted to Orouwa, an "equivalent" theme involving the shaming of Souw's mother through the withholding of pork provides the impetus for the departure from Bụmaru. Very likely this "recapitulation" of the "shaming-and-leaving" theme results from an attempt to associate the Souw motif with two distinct traditional localities, Bụmaru and Orouwa. The element of kin fidelity, represented in the earlier texts by Souw's daughter, is replaced here by Souw's reaction to the shaming of his mother, and the contrasting "dark-skinned" and "light-skinned" daughters become Souw himself and his brother. In this version Souw, who is otherwise merely likened to a snake, appears in the actual form of a snake, and this transformation is by no means uncommon elsewhere.

To the east of the Daribi, the story is taken up by the groups of Tụdawe or Pawaia-speaking people located in the valley of the Sena River north of Mount Karimui, and in that of the Pio River to the south. Like the Foraba, these groups have a history of close association with the Daribi, but unlike the Foraba they belong to a different language family.[36] These people call the hero of the story "Sau^r."[37]

The following text was related to me by a man from the Pio River:

At a place called Sau^{r}o Hwiau, where the Pio River joins the Tua, two women were making sago. One had pendulous breasts, the other had upright breasts. At noon Sau^r arrived, and the woman with pendulous breasts heard the call of a *kaueri;* she wanted to go and see what the bird had sighted, but instead the girl with upright breasts went. She saw Sau^r sitting in the sun; he had white hair. He told her to look for lice in his hair. She stood behind him and searched through his hair; as she did so, he had an erection, and his penis went behind him and entered the woman's vagina. She cried out and ran away; Sau^r was shamed, and to get even he cursed mankind with fighting and death. Sau^r's skin was getting old, and to get rid of it he sloughed it off; the gura' snakes, sago grubs, and eels took it. Man received mourning clay, body shields, arrows, etc., whereas the snakes settled down to a quiet existence. When the woman cried out, the semen of Sau^r spilled all around, creating a lake. If people eat snakes, etc., taken from this water, their teeth fall out.

Like the previous version, this text involves the association of the basic plot with a new locality, and interprets local landmarks in its terms. More than the other variants this one is conceptualized in terms of contrasting oppositions; Sau^r is presented as an old man "with white hair" at the time of his shaming. His curse of mankind and the taking of his skin by the snakes can be seen as complementary events. This dichotomy is balanced by another; that of the woman with pendulous

36. Whereas Franklin assigns both the Daribi and the Foraba to the Mikaruan language family (p. 25), he lists Pawaia as one of two languages in the Pawaian family (p. 24), which continues southward along the Purari.

37. The symbol ^{r} here represents a lightly affricated terminal liquid, similar to an т followed by a Russian "soft" sign.

breasts and the girl with upright breasts; if the former had gone to investigate instead of the latter, Sau^r might not have cursed mankind, and man, rather than the hairless animals, might have been immortal. The elements relating to the sharing of food, the journey, and the hero's female relative are missing from this version.

The versions of the story which I collected at Iuro, in the Sena Valley, demonstrate much more of a continuity with the Daribi sequence of stories than the Pio River text does, and this in turn reflects the traditionally close association between the Iuro people and the Daribi. In these versions the hero's journey is taken up where the Daribi versions leave off; in one version Sau^r continues along the Pio River to Heroana, a settlement of the Gimi speakers to the east, and moves northward, eventually arriving at the Neru River from the east (Map 2, routes 3, 3B) whereas his father's sister's daughter follows the Sena to its source among the Gimi speakers (Map 2, routes 3, 3B), and meets him at the Neru. Alternative routes are given in the text that follows:

Sau^r left the Bore River and went downstream along the Tua until he came to the confluence of the Tua and the Pio. Here he met his father's sister Hawai-Yaro [or Yuaro] and her daughter Yuaro [also called Yuaro-Bawaro], and told them to take Yuaro's huge pig [said to be four feet high at the shoulders] to the Neru River. They left, and as they passed Soliabedo, Yuaro made straight ground for gardening. Sau^r then went back to the Bore, went to Bumaru, then went up-stream along the Tua until he came to the Neru River [Map 2, route 2]. [An alternative mentioned by my informant was that he followed the women directly north from the Pio, as in Map 2, route 1, and stayed for a while at a lake called Kerouwa Sigi near Iuro.] Yuaro and Hawai-Yaro arrived at the Neru, and settled at a place called Tumagiri. Yuaro said "When my cross-cousin arrives, I can kill this pig." When she felt that Sau^r was coming, she went out to look for edible leaves to cook with the pig. She fell asleep on top of a rock, and when Sau^r arrived he saw her sleeping there, with her string skirt tucked behind her back and her genitals exposed. Seeing her thus, he thought it was another woman, and had intercourse with her. She saw who it was, and said "Oh, cross-cousin, you have come; now we can kill the pig and eat it." The pig was killed and they prepared to cook it, but it did not cook well. Hawai-Yaro said to her daughter "You had intercourse first, before the pig was cooked—if you had cooked and eaten the pig first, it would have been all right." Sau^r heard this talk and was shamed and went away. The breast of the pig and the lower jaw were given to Sau^r, he ate the jaw raw, and took the breast meat with him. The jawbone was hung on a tree-limb; the tree has grown over it now so that only the hinges can be seen. Siga', haga, and sago trees can be seen today at Tumagiri. Sau^r followed the Tua north to the highlands, where he put people. He went to Chimbu, and took two women on the other side of Mount Elimbari. At Nomane one of the women cooked taro; she had her period and went to a shelter in the bush, and was left behind. Another woman cooked yams, she went with Sau^r. The woman who had cooked taro searched for Sau^r, but in vain. A man finally found her and married her, and her children became the people of Gumine. The woman who cooked yams followed Sau^r to Karimui, and her children became the Daribi and Pawaia people.

This story represents a radical transformation of the plot that characterizes the other versions; here the elements involving mortality and the snake disappear, and the whole issue is treated in terms of the equivalent themes of sharing food and shameful intercourse. Sau^r hopes to share his cross-cousin's pig, but by mistake he has intercourse with the woman before he recognizes her (sexual relations with a cross-cousin are prohibited at Karimui), and the pig thereupon cooks badly and part of the meat is raw. The connection between these events is pointed out by Hawai-Yaro, and Sau^r, shamed, departs for the highlands. The bond between the hero and his female relative, represented by Sido's daughter in the Foraba myth, and Souw's daughter or mother in the Daribi myths, applies here to Sau^r's cross-cousin, but in this case she is identified also with the sexual partner with whom he is shamed. The expected relationship among cross-cousins, based on sharing, is abrogated by sexual intercourse, and as a result the exchange of cooked meat, representative of their earlier relationship, turns out badly. Sau^r's acceptance of meat from his cross-cousin after having intercourse with her amounts to an act of incest, for he maintains sexual relations as well as those of "sharing" with the same person, and this parallels Souw's departure and refusal to share pork with his daughter, after having exposed himself before her, in the first Daribi text.

The dichotomy of the two highland women, one of whom cooks taro whereas the other cooks yams, serves to contrast the people of Karimui with the highland people, just as the "dark-skinned" and "light-skinned" siblings, or women, in other versions are introduced as the ancestors, respectively, of dark- and light-skinned people at Karimui. With the entry of Sau^r into the highlands, our investigation of this aspect of the tradition reaches its conclusion.

DARIBI SOCIAL IDEOLOGY

Our survey of the Papuan hero tales and of the related subtradition of local stories peculiar to the Karimui area suggests two corresponding levels of thematic generality. The first comprises the set of very generalized elements that define the larger tradition: the recurrent theme of regeneration embodied in its positive aspect, relating to fertility and human reproduction, or its negative form, relating to death and human mortality, or, as in many instances, both aspects considered as alternatives, and the universal significance of the hero, which is conceptualized through the laying-out of his life-course across the known landscape. Frequently these two elements are themselves presented in combined form, as in the annual, cyclical journey of Sosom among the Marind-Anim, associated with the east monsoon, in which he "fertilizes man and soil,"[38] or the westward journey of Sido in the Kiwai version, which becomes the road of all men to the land of the dead, and hence man's mortal destiny.

38. Van Baal, p. 267.

The specific thematic motifs often found in association with these elements, such as that of the exaggerated genitals, the snake's skin, or the creation of landforms, tempting as they may appear to the diffusionist, need not represent anything more than "vehicles" in terms of which the key concepts are introduced or formalized. The apparently random distribution of folkloric details like that of the snake's skin over the whole range of our area from the Marind-Anim to Karimui may in fact signify nothing more than that some narrators choose to activate this particular potentiality, among the total of those that the story suggests, whereas others do not. Again, some tales portray the hero as creating particular landforms or localities, others mention these localities merely as his stopping-places, whereas in still other stories the hero merely travels across the world.

The second level of thematic generality that we have encountered in our survey involves the local interpretation or presentation of the myths, the existence of subtraditions. While the elements discussed above, in their general significance, and with their associated themes, form a coherent tradition, the component myths of this tradition in all cases participate in some subtradition and render the generalities of the major tradition in local linguistic, rhetorical, and ideological forms and in association with local themes and landscape features. Often there is a recombination, inversion, or change of emphasis from one locality or text to another, so that a given ideological distinction undergoes a shift in significance against the more general background. Thus within our larger tradition we have noted contrasts between the fertility tales to the south and west of Kiwai Island and the mortality tales to the north and east, though in each case these in turn resolve into purely local complexes.

While the Daribi tales of Souw may be seen as participating in a number of these traditions or subtraditions, there does not seem to be anything peculiar to Daribi culture or ideology that necessitates explication in terms of the events and features of this or of any other specific origin account, and in fact the Daribi are aware of several other origin myths. It is rather more likely that the tradition we have been reviewing presents a compelling set of possibilities for the articulation of cultural ideology, and that the Daribi, like many other cultures to whom this opportunity has been available, have merely taken advantage of it.

One of the features that distinguish the versions of our tradition known to the Daribi and their neighbors is a tendency to exemplify contrasting or alternative qualities and courses of action in the form of paired opposite characters. Thus the women making sago flour include an experienced widow, or woman with pendulous breasts, and in inexperienced girl, with upright breasts; the former represents sexual knowledge, and a safe course of action, the latter represents ignorance, and spells man's downfall. Man, cursed with perpetual trouble and mortality, is counterbalanced by the snakes and other hairless animals, who manage to appropriate the hero's skin and live an untroubled life. Other contrasts of this sort occupy more peripheral aspects of the stories, such as that, between Sido's son, who is given a good bamboo tube, and his daughter, who receives a defective one, or the two wives of Sau^r, one of whom cooks taro while the other cooks yams.

This balancing of example and counterexample actually represents one of the most recurrent and popular Daribi rhetorical devices; statements like "I came to get this pig, and not for some other purpose," or "He is a good man, not a *kebidibidi*," are heard again and again in ordinary conversation, and traditional folktales feature two stock characters, portrayed as brothers or cross-cousins, the elder of whom is the *bidi-mu* or "true man," who exemplifies forethought, while the younger, or *peraberabidi*, provides an example of negligence.[39]

Discursive or rhetorical paradigms of this sort are of course deeply involved in mythology, but, creative as the effect of this Daribi example may be in terms of plot transformations, it is not ideological in character. As we have just concluded, the essential elements in our major tradition, including the regenerative and universalistic aspects of the hero, do not in themselves disappear in the course of the transformations that they undergo, though they may experience ideological change. Let us, then, look to the circumstances of the plot itself.

We have seen in the preceding section that a major emphasis of the story in the Karimui area is on sexual knowledge; the fright of an inexperienced girl in the face of the hero's advances brings about the shaming of the latter, and his retribution through the curse of mortality, the removal of another kind of innocence. The two kinds of knowledge, that of sex and that of death, are moreover related as the "positive" and "negative" aspects of regeneration, involving a dialectic of the theme itself and its denial. The relationship of these themes is confirmed by the association of the snake with each of them; the penis of Souw is identified, or confused, with a snake, and it is Souw's skin, which could have conferred immortality in spite of the curse, that the snakes take for themselves.

The snake also coincides with the penis of Souw, an enlarged genital organ, and the plot turns on the frustration of the hero's exaggerated sexual capacity and desire. The uncontrolled nature of the hero's desire and his uncanny ability to effect sexual connection may both be likened to bestial characteristics, and Daribi in fact regard snakes with a mixture of exaggerated fear and fascination. Seen in this light, the plot centers on the frustration or tempering of unrestrained desire through the rejection and shaming of the hero. Shame, moreover, is a "social" emotion, the instrument of temperance, and Daribi define it often in the context of marital relationships as "that which you feel in the presence of your wife's father." The other attributes of culture, and of man's condi-

39. Wagner (1967), p. 30.

tion, follow upon this initial "tempering" of sexual desire; the hero, in retribution, terminates man's original idyllic state through the curse of mortality, and his self-regenerating capacity is left to the snakes, representatives of a noncultural existence. The shaming also marks the beginning of the hero's journey, in the course of which the landscape is created or brought into its present state, so that the initial incidents are universalized and extended through the world.

Although the desire originates with the hero, it arises in response to the presence of the women, as intercourse itself is a mediating act. As it is presented in the myth, the hero's penis is a monstrous, uncontrolled, and uncouth organ of mediation, for it can arise seemingly of its own accord and overcome natural obstacles; it represents unrestrained mediation between the sexes, an asocial state. The women are engaged in processing sago flour, a task that Daribi women ordinarily perform; the call of the bird, a signal that it has sighted a snake or animal, provides an excuse whereby the intercourse can take place, for the penis itself is the "snake." But although this excuse is itself phrased in terms of food-getting, for snakes and marsupials are prized sources of meat, hunting is an activity that Daribi reserve for men. The hero's impulsive intrusion into the women's sago-making activity elicits a response that must be excused by a female intrusion into male activity, and the consummation is an act of untempered mediation between man and woman.

This initial mode of male-female mediation, accompanied by anomalous displacements of the sexual division of labor, is terminated by the inexperienced girl's rejection of the penis, which is followed by the hero's butchering of, and his refusal to share, his pigs. An equation is established here between intersexual mediation, including sexual relations, and food. Untempered sexual relations accompany abnormal patterns of sex-specific activity; the abrogation of sexual relations brings about a cessation of food-sharing.

This equation is made most explicit in the Iuro version of the myth, in which Sau^r's impulsive and accidental violation of his cross-cousin, an act of intemperate mediation, results in the pork cooking badly. The girl's mother comments to the effect that they should have cooked this pork first, an allusion to the usual exchange of pigs in marriage. Again, in the second Daribi version quoted above, the refusal of the inhabitants of Bumaru to share pork in itself provides the motive for Souw's leaving. The following text, which was likewise recorded among the Daribi to the north of Mount Karimui, indicates that the refusal to share meat can be substituted *in toto* for the theme of sexual rejection:

There were two cross-cousins; one had light skin and the other dark skin. The dark-skinned man was staying in the bush with his wife; he killed a marsupial and ate the meat himself, not giving any to his cousin. While he was out, his cousin came and told his wife that he, the light-skinned man, was leaving, and wanted to talk to him. That night, when the dark-skinned man came home, his wife did not tell him this. She told him in the morning, and he went to find his cousin, but he had left already. He followed his cousin, and found him at the Tua River. The light-skinned man said "You didn't come to see me yesterday," and his cousin replied that his wife hadn't told him. The light-skinned man said "I'm going now; you take this soot, you take this clay, you take this ax, you take this skin." People took the bows and fought with them, took the axes and made gardens with them, and used the soot and clay in mourning. The dark-skinned man did not, however, take the skin that his cousin had given him; if he had, people would not grow old and die, but he just left it in a tree. The snakes came together and took it, and now snakes do not die as men do, they simply shed their skins and are young again.

The substitution made here is not only applicable in mythology; it also corresponds to the exchange made in Daribi marriage. If shame is definable as that which one feels in the presence of one's wife's father, then meat defines the most appropriate gift to one's wife's father, and it is in this sense that Daribi speak of an exogamous unit as one whose members "eat meat together," for those who share meat may not exchange it.[40] The shame of improper intercourse (including that between cross-cousins, as in the Iuro story) is equivalent to the shame of not sharing meat, where sharing is in order.

The exchange of women corresponds to the exchange of meat among men, but as we have seen, improper intercourse, and the shaming of Souw, involves the mediation between the sexes. This, too, can be understood in terms of food and its sharing, but in this case, as in the Souw stories, the issue involves the allocation and interchange of complementary foods and services between men and women. The relation between "tempered" sexual relations and cultural interaction among men and women is most emphatically illustrated in the following text, which is in many ways an inversion of the Souw story:

Once there was a woman called *Siapagewe;* her skin was covered with tattoos, and her hair was very long. She lived in a good place, and her house and garden were very good. One day a man came and tried to have intercourse with her, but her vagina, which was very large, was hot like a fire, and it burned his penis, causing him to die. This happened again and again, and many men died. Finally a man named Uru [ancestor of the Urubidi] came along; he sharpened a long strip of bamboo, made it into a loop, and fastened it to a fallen tree on the path. As the woman was going to her garden, she passed the fallen tree and the loop cut off her genitals. From then on, whenever she wanted to work in her garden, chop down a tree, plant sweet potatoes, or do some other work, her genitals did it for her. Then the man came to her, and she said "Alright, you have put out the fire. If you want to do work, you can build houses, cut trees for gardening, and build fences. My job is to burn off the garden and to plant food. Now my period has come, I will make a little house in the bush and stay there. If I should have a child, I will make a house like this and bear it there." Then she took some menstrual blood and put it on the nose of the man. Now all Daribi women make this kind of house when they have their periods or bear children.

40. Wagner (1967), p. 145.

Like Souw, Siapagewe has exaggerated genitals, which are hot like a fire, and in fact she refers to them as a "fire."[41] Before the coming of Uru, she is self-sufficient, doing male as well as female work, and intercourse with her is impossible, for it brings death. As in the Souw story, intemperate intercourse is associated with an asocial state in terms of the mediation between man and woman; and just as the Souw story involves the "tempering" of the hero by a woman, so in this story Siapagewe is "tempered" and rendered amenable to ordinary sexual relations and intersexual specialization by Uru's surgery. The two types of story present inverted statements regarding the origin of the present cultural regularities and norms of intersexual mediation; in each case the extreme sexual capacities of one sex are tempered by someone of the opposite sex, rendering "cultural" mediation possible.

The social ideology of the Daribi is based on the subdivision of society into male and female activities, specializations, objects of exchange, and kinds of produce, and on the kinds of mediation that take place, between the sexes as well as among members of the same sex, with regard to these categories. The production, sharing, and exchange of food provides the idiom in terms of which much of this mediation is carried out. In the following chapter we shall consider this ideology in detail.

The myths that we have examined in the course of this chapter by no means exhaust the category of stories that Daribi call *po page*. They are all, however, stories that my informants considered to be important ones with respect to the establishment of human society. There are others relating to the origins of the Daribi people, of human sexual organs, or hairless animals, and of many natural objects and species. Although each of these stories uses folkloric material brilliantly to provide a flash of illumination for some aspect of culture or the world, there can be little hope of ever synthesizing a world-view through a mosaic of such myths, for the explanatory force of such a story rarely transcends the specific incidents of the story itself, except in the very general way that we have encountered here.

41. This detail, and in fact the story as a whole, suggests another mythic tradition, found commonly in the interior of New Guinea. See F. E. Williams, *Natives of Lake Kutubu, Papua,* Oceania Monograph No. 6 (Sydney: The Australian National Research Council, 1940), pp. 149–51, and Colin Simpson, *Plumes and Arrows* (Sydney: Angus and Robertson, 1962), p. 52. This motif may also be related to the form of punishment known as *sia gui,* "fire-genitals," sometimes used with women who are guilty of offenses connected with intemperate sexual relations such as adultery or incest. The woman is staked out on the ground, and a fire is built at her genitals until they are "no good anymore." The effect of this punishment is to "return" the fire connected with intemperate sexuality to the woman.

2/The Ideology of Exchange

MALE AND FEMALE

In an earlier study of the Daribi,[1] I dealt with some aspects of Daribi social ideology in relation to a set of generalized criteria for the comparison of social systems. Because the focus of that study was on some very specific questions of kinship and group definition, I was unable to explore the total significance of this ideology as a system of cultural distinctions. As is often the case in Melanesia, however, kin relationship and group structure do not represent specialized areas of thought and action among the Daribi, but rather they are continuous in operation and conception with the other spheres of activity that make up Daribi social life, and they share the same basic ideology. This ideology, then, serves as the conceptual core for a society that takes on the aspect of a single, undifferentiated, all-encompassing social "institution," and it is this ideology that I would like to explore in the present chapter.

The cultural opposition of male and female has consistently figured among the most significant of those features that characterize Melanesian societies, and, in one form or another, has occupied a preeminent position in most serious studies of the area. The effect of this opposition is so pervasive, even within individual societies, that it often provides a focus for a considerable degree of cultural elaboration as well as basic ideology. An impressive example of this is presented in Bateson's analysis of the ethos and eidos of Iatmul culture on the Sepik River,[2] and Meggitt has provided a description of the richly elaborated sexual ideology of the Mae Enga in the central highlands.[3] Other examples and illustrations can be found in the literature dealing with mythology, ceremonial, initiatory rites, personality, and kinship systems in New Guinea and in the rest of Melanesia.

Even if we restrict ourselves to the more particularistic concerns of

1. Roy Wagner, *The Curse of Souw: Principles of Daribi Clan Definition and Alliance in New Guinea* (Chicago: University of Chicago Press, 1967).
2. Gregory Bateson, *Naven* (Stanford: Stanford University Press, 1958), chaps. 9, 10, 14, 15.
3. Mervyn J. Meggitt, "Male-Female Relationships in the Highlands of Australian New Guinea," in *American Anthropologist* 66, No. 4, Part 2 (1964): 204–24.

social ideology such as those of kinship and marriage rule, the significance of the male-female dichotomy remains evident. In a brief consideration of Melanesian kinship systems, Levi-Strauss observes that "New Guinea and its neighboring regions present, to an extraordinary degree, what Williams has described as 'sex affiliation,' i.e., a differentiation of status between brother and sister, the brother following the paternal line and the sister the maternal line."[4] This particular formulation would seem to represent an involuted version of the more general scheme of affiliation by which men and women are allocated to tangential, but distinct and self-contained social and areal "spaces" within a social unit, so that the adults, the aged, and the older children of each sex form a suprafamilial, and in some cases coresidential, subdivision. The existence of discrete male and female "substance" lines, and the transmission of unit-affiliation through one sex or the other, can also be seen as coherent analogues of this system.

Of course, the delineation and analysis of such themes and their transformations over an area as diverse as Melanesia or even New Guinea taxes to the utmost our expectations of intercultural consistency. Within a particular culture, however, we may justifiably expect a somewhat more rigorous standard of consistency. Let us begin our consideration of Daribi social ideology, then, by examining the basic distinctions that Daribi draw between men and women.

Daribi recognize a major subdivision of adult society into the *wezibi,* the group of women, and the *bidizibi,* or group of men. Children and prepubescent youths are grouped together as the *waiburuba,* which may be further subdivided into the *wegimanezibi,* or group of girls, and the *ogomanezibi,* or group of boys. These categories are quite independent of the reckoning of genealogical ancestry or the partitioning of the society into exogamous units; they may refer to the composition of a single unit, or they may be used in a way that transcends unit boundaries and includes the whole society, for they reflect a set of complementary status distinctions characteristic of the social system as a whole.

In addition to social statuses, the male/female distinction also represents separately transmitted substances, or essences, so that we can also speak of the *wezibi* and *bidizibi* as distinct "lines" or "lineages," with a continuity from generation to generation. Thus Daribi say that the soul of a male child is "given" by the soul of his father, while the soul of a female child is given by that of her mother.

Males and females likewise transmit separate but complementary substances to their offspring[5]; *kawa,* or semen, is given to a child by its

4. Claude Lévi-Strauss, *The Elementary Structures of Kinship,* revised edition, tr. James Harle Bell, John Richard von Sturmer, and Rodney Needham, ed. (Boston: Beacon Press, 1969), pp. 465–66.

5. I am particularly indebted to Hanari, Obe, Yapenugiai, Sumaia, Mina, and informants from Tua Clan for providing me with detailed information regarding the Daribi conceptualization of procreation.

father, and *pagekamine*, maternal blood, is given by its mother (a series of copulations is believed necessary to accumulate sufficient semen for the creation of a child). Each substance plays a separate part in the formation of the body, creating certain organs, and each forms a separate network of vessels within which it is contained. These substances also remain active throughout life, so that "when a man works, the strong substance of his father is operating; when he rests or catches his wind, the blood of his mother is operating."

During the menstrual flow, maternal blood collects in the uterus *(wai' tabi)*, where it creates the beginnings of a child *(wai'-ge,* "embryo"). The male semen introduced in intercourse flows around this and envelops it. The maternal blood forms the bones and internal organs of the child as well as the system of blood vessels, or *kigibidi*, in which it flows. The paternal semen forms the skin, eyes, teeth, fingernails, and hair as well as the tubular system of *agwa bono (agwa*-strands) and *agwa ge (agwa*-nodes) in which it is contained, and which we call the lymphatic system.[6] Thus for Daribi the two kinds of substance correspond to the two major divisions of the body, the external *(tigi,* or "skin") and the internal, and two respective networks, an internal and an external.

After the navel cord *(mosogobe)* has been cut, some of the mother's blood remains in the body, and it flows about the body, strengthening it. In a female child, this blood later causes menstruation. In a male child, some of the father's semen remains in his *agwa* after birth. According to Daribi:

When we cut up our enemies we see that a man has tiny cords all over his body; back, legs, hands, head. His penis goes inside his body, it is not on the surface alone. The little ropes in a man's body all go to his penis; when a man wants to have intercourse, *kawa* comes from all over his body and goes into his penis.

The *agwa* system, however, as well as the *kawa* that it contains, is intimately linked with the eating of meat, for Daribi believe that the fat and juices of meat that is eaten pass into the skin, and into the *agwa*, where they augment the *kawa* already present: "If people didn't eat meat, the blood of the mother would carry away the semen remaining in the body after procreation." A primary distinction is drawn here between meat, the flesh of animals and birds, which remains in the body, and vegetable foods, which pass out of the body as excrement. According to my informants, foods such as bananas, sweet potato, sugarcane, and leafy vegetables serve the body merely by staving off hunger or thirst; they fill the stomach and intestines, then pass out of the body entirely as urine or feces. Once meat has been chewed, however, the fats and juices go to the stomach and then into the *agwa*.

When a child is small, his stomach is filled with mother's milk, and

6. My informant Yapenugiai complained that whereas he had cut up bodies and opened the *agwa*, he had never found any semen inside.

this milk passes into the *agwa*, to join with the *kawa* already there in the case of a male. As the boy grows older, the meat and fat that he eats cause his *agwa* to fill and finally to swell. When a young man's *agwa* have swollen, his skin becomes tight, and he has grown up and begins to feel a desire for women. When a man wants to have intercourse, the flow of *kawa* from all over his body causes an erection in his penis; after it has been ejaculated, according to Daribi, the skin becomes slack. It is for this reason that the flesh of young men is sleek and firm, whereas that of old men hangs loosely on their bones.

As a girl matures, the fluid that has come to fill her *agwa* "has no road" (as has the man's), and it collects in her breasts, which "have many kinds of ropes," and becomes *ame*, or milk. Thus "a pregnant woman says 'my neck is dry,' and her husband brings her meat. She eats this, and it goes into her breasts to form milk." This milk, in turn, is passed to the body of her child, where it enters the *agwa* again.

Although a "kind" of substance is proper to, and is transmitted by, each sex, female substance, or maternal blood, is capable of spontaneous effect, whereas male substance and the parts of the body associated with it must be augmented by the intake of meat. Meat juices and fat are essential for the maturing and the procreative capacity of men, and for proper lactation in women, and they provide a necessary auxiliary to male substance itself. Food is therefore intrinsically involved in the conceptual opposition of male and female, and meat is an essential component of the body.

Simultaneously, a distinction is drawn between two general categories of food; meat, with its special nutritive capabilities, is distinguished from vegetable food, which is considered a mere palliative against hunger. Each of these categories is involved in a different aspect of Daribi social ideology. The production, processing, and consumption of ordinary garden products mediates and integrates the complementary roles of men and women, but it is an everyday affair, concerned with transitory foodstuffs. Meat, on the other hand, is a permanent acquisition of the body, a kind of equivalent of body-substance, and is likewise necessary to procreation. Men exchange meat, as one requisite element in procreation, for women, as another, and for the children that they produce. In more succinct phrasing, men exchange vegetable foods *with* women, whereas they exchange meat, together with other valuables, *for* women. Let us now investigate these systems of exchange.

COMPLEMENTARITY

The notion of a society composed of separate male and female divisions, manifested by separately transmitted "lines" of substance, corresponds to a throughgoing dichotomy of cultural tasks, roles, ceremonial distinctions, styles of life, and spatial allocation. The two subdivisions are in all cases conceived of as being interdependent or complementary, and all the points at which they converge or interact are controlled and tightly constrained by ideology. Apart from ceremonial situations, and barring occasional idle gossip, virtually all interaction between men and women occurs in the context of the production and preparation of food, or in that of sexual relations. Even where sex and food are not directly concerned, they present the most appropriate idiom in terms of which complementary activities may be phrased, and in fact the significances of these two modes of interaction are to some degree interchangeable for Daribi. However complex their manifestation in the details of the culture, the opposed male and female categories, as well as the acts that "mediate" between them, are essentially derivative of the simple paradigm that we encountered in our review of Daribi origin-stories, that of the "tempering" of intersexual relations.

The spatial aspects of the male-female dichotomy among the Daribi have a cosmological significance that will be treated at length in a later chapter; for the moment, let us restrict our concern to the issue of complementarity. Virtually all living spaces are marked off into more or less restricted male and female areas, within which members of the respective sexes sleep, eat, lounge, work, prepare food, converse, and receive visitors. In small bush-shelters, garden- or pig-tending houses, or in the caves that are sometimes occupied, the division may be rudimentary indeed, with separate hearths, sleeping-places, and entrances in the layout, and perhaps a pole laid between. In more substantial dwellings the separation becomes part of the house; men occupy the upper floor of the traditional *sigibe'*, or two-story longhouse, and women the lower, and in the single-story version, or *kerobe'*, a bark-and-pole wall divides the house into a "front" (facing the *be' mesaro*, or "yard," and, ideally, looking eastward), occupied by the men, and a "rear," occupied by the women. The women's quarters, or *aribe'*, are frequently subdivided into small bark rooms on either side of a central passageway, each bordering on a hearth and occupied by a woman and the young children in her charge. A hole in the bark partition of a *kerobe'*, or between floors in a *sigibe'*, the *nai mabo tu̜*, or "food-giving passage," allows the women to pass cooked food to their husbands,[7] and acts as a passage for small children.

When in 1962 the Daribi temporarily abandoned their traditional house-types and constructed makeshift single-family or "line" houses of European inspiration,[8] these were in most cases subdivided by partitions of some sort. Likewise when Daribi began to build outdoor latrines at the instigation of the government, separate "men's" and "ladies'" latrines were built respectively at the front and rear of the houses. In some instances, probably even in aboriginal times, individual dwellings were made for men and women, and the small bush-shelters *(buru-be', temianobe', torianobe')* used by the menstruating or child-

---

7. In some cases cooked food is hauled up into the men's quarters by means of a rope.
8. Fortunately—for the health of the Daribi as well as their self-esteem—enlightened patrol officers permitted a return to the easily built and warmer *kerobe'*, which were being built in large numbers in 1965 and were universal when I returned in 1968.

bearing women of a clan or clan-segment can be seen as an extension of the tendency.

In all instances this subdivision of living spaces manifests nothing more or less than the juxtaposition of two distinct, parallel, and coordinated life-styles, a male and a female. Each living-area forms a nucleus for a specific kind of work, a specific round of activities, and a specific style of socialization, the architectural segregation serving to emphasize a fundamental social separation. Within each house-group, clan, or clan-segment, the men and the women form separate social bodies, with their own friendships, cliques, hostilities, and truces. Women hold discussions, share opinions, and engage in fights just as men do, and where the men organize work-crews and raiding-forces, the women organize parties and assign escorts to assist in such things as childbirth, garden-work and so on.

Characteristically, the Daribi interpret the subdivision of their living spaces as a constraint imposed on male-female relations: "If the house were not divided between men and women, other men would come and see the genitals of the women, and go and have intercourse with them." The physical partition limits and constrains intersexual activity just as the ideology "tempers" it, providing a narrow passage, a "food-giving hole," between the two domains, and screening out nonideological interaction.

Generally, men keep to their own portion of the house, although some will occasionally cross over into the *aribe'* to eat or talk with a woman, and it is against such visits that Daribi say they erect the partitions within the women's quarters, for otherwise a man and his wife's mother might catch sight of one another.[9] Prolonged visiting and conversation with one woman makes the others jealous, according to my informants, and some men will not permit themselves to enter the *aribe'* at all; all must, in any case, sleep in the *bidigibe'*. Women simply do not enter the men's quarters, whereas small children, the *waiburuba,* pass freely between the sections as soon as they can walk, and many tots make a game of running from mother to father and back again. The only exceptions to the general pattern among adults occur at the time of a funeral, when the central divider of a *kerobe'* is removed, or restrictions in a *sigibe'* are lifted, to allow for the mourning of the dead by both sexes, or on the eve of a wedding, when some young men go to the *aribe'* of a bride to participate in a farewell songfest.

The subdivision of living-space, and of social space in general, is continued in the sexual division of labor, and in the allocation of complementary areas of ownership and modes of interaction. The cosmological implications of this dichotomy are likewise realized here: men, who occupy the upper floor of a *sigibe'*, are associated with tree-crops, activities involving the felling and preparation of trees, and with arboreal

9. This relationship entails complete avoidance.

creatures; women, who inhabit the lower floor, are associated with ground-crops, activities involving the clearing and preparation of ground, and with aquatic creatures and insects.

The delegation of tasks in gardening illustrates the way in which these sexual specializations are integrated in the realization of a common project. The men involved first mark out an area by designating where the fence is to be. Later, perhaps in a day or two, the women come and clear the grass or ground-cover up to the mark. Then men come to cut the trees; first the saplings are cleared away, then the larger trees are cut down or ring-barked and left to "dry." When the foliage of the ringbarked tree is dead and "dry," the women come again and gather up the limbs and other debris and heap this material around the base of the dead tree, after which it is set afire. The fire consumes the bark of the tree and burns off the dried foliage. Then the men cut poles, split logs, and fence the garden, after which their work is finished. Finally, the women plant sweet potato stems in holes made three to four feet apart in the unprepared ground; the plots are weeded once before the vines manage to cover the ground. When the garden begins to bear, women will be responsible for harvesting, cleaning, and cooking the tubers.

A similar division of labor is involved in the cultivation of sago. Since it is a tree-crop, men are concerned with the planting and tending of the sago palm. Holes one foot deep by one and a half feet in diameter are dug about ten feet apart in a swampy place; shoots (or "hands") are taken from the base of a "mother" tree and placed, one in each hole, together with pieces of rotten wood. If the young plants do well, the men return later and ringbark trees, allowing the sunlight to penetrate, as in a garden, and surrounding vegetation is cut and heaped on the young plants to provide fertilizer. When the trees finally mature, they are cut by the men, who then construct the *o-sizi*, or sago-processing apparatus, made of poles, leaves, and other parts of the sago palm and of another palm, called *yogo*, which is planted nearby for this purpose. Once the sago-trunk is lying on the ground, it becomes the responsibility of the women, who begin to chop out the fibrous, starch-bearing central pith, collecting it in bark-cloth sheets. When enough pith has accumulated, the women leach it in the funnellike *o-sizi*, pouring water over it and straining it through a woven bag, then letting the starch settle out in a basin. After this, the water is poured off and the starch is taken to the house by the women, who dry it in a large string bag.

In both of these food-production activities, the respective male and female roles are firmly established, and they fit into the appropriate lifestyles and social spaces. The roles represent what are in effect basic sexual specializations, so that women, for example, are put to work clearing the ground in any project, and the men's capacity for working with tree products is extended to house-building, the making of vine-bridges, and any major construction. The ax, formerly of stone, now of steel, is the man's all-purpose tool, as it accompanies his all-purpose specialization, and the woman, likewise, has her own—the digging-stick, the net bag, and a small stone ax for cutting brushwood, or, more recently, the steel bushknife used for this purpose. The part of the men, as well as that of the women, can be played by a single individual, or a small or large group, depending on the magnitude of the job, although usually both men and women prefer to work in groups.

The male and female specializations extend to the cultivation, owner-ship, and processing of food crops. Here, too, men are for the most part concerned with arboreal species, women with terrestrial. Men plant, tend, harvest and cook oil-bearing pandanus, breadfruit, bananas, edible-leaf bearing trees such as *dora' (Gnetum gnemon)*, nut-bearing trees such as *siburu (Pangium edule reinw.)* and *haga*, and also tobacco, cer-tain leaf plants such as *dabiza*, and maize. Upon the death of a man these crops may be transmitted to his brothers or sons; women, too, may inherit them, but forfeit them when they marry and move elsewhere.

Women plant, tend, harvest, and cook sweet potato, taro, yams, pit-pit, manioc, sugar, and many edible-leaf plants. Beans are planted by women and staked by men, and fibers of the paper mulberry, or *ugwa* tree, used for making string bags and bark-cloaks, are cut and processed by women. Hunting is the province of the men, who must like-wise slaughter, butcher, cook, and distribute all meat, including the flesh of pigs, which may be tended by women. Although they may be caught by men, women, or both together, fish, eels, and sago grubs are generally cooked by women.

Just as Daribi recognize two major components of the body, a male and a female, which are transmitted separately, so the Daribi house is subdivided into male and female halves, each with its own ongoing social life, and so every major task, and every major food crop, is recog-nized as being in the province of one of the sexes, or seen as having both male and female components. Although certain details such as the separate male and female "singsings" performed at ceremonies, or the rigid exclusion of males from childbirth and women's menstruation huts, would seem to suggest sexual exclusiveness, in all significant instances the respective "male" and "female" halves, of the body, of the house, of subsistence activities, or of society as a whole, are mutually inter-dependent and complementary. In all cases it is an essential element of culture that has been subdivided; a house, the human body, the labor of subsistence, or the total assemblage of food plants, and the component that each sex provides, a substance, a service, or a kind of food, is essen-tial to the whole because it is needed by all. Thus we may understand the complementarity of male and female activities as a kind of reciprocity in which each sex performs its services in reciprocation for those of the other.

The complementarity of sexual roles and the separation of the sexes are therefore related aspects of the same system. Men and women are parts of the same society, although different parts; the points at which these parts come together, sex, in which their substances are intermingled, and food production, in which their services and products are exchanged, comprise the metaphors of Daribi social ideology. This collective ideology expresses the "tempering" or "constraint" of sexual and gustatory appetites through the reciprocal discipline of complementarity.

The characteristic idiom of complementarity is prepared vegetable food, representing the entire range of reciprocal activities including sexual relations and the division of labor. Unlike sex, which is accomplished privately and seldom discussed in public, the activities of food production, preparation, and consumption are aspects of complementarity that are normally open to discussion and comment and can accommodate few or many participants. Women are the "cooks" for their husbands, preparing the daily staple of sweet potato; at times, the meals of an entire house-group or settlement are steam-cooked together in a single earth-oven, with men as well as women contributing vegetable foods, and on some occasions the communal sharing of cooked food constitutes a ritual.

Just as the subdivision of the society into male and female "parts" or "roles" is an essential feature of Daribi social life and extends to all levels of social grouping from the individual family to the clan, so the complementarity of these parts or roles, as the definitive ideological expression of sociality, is manifested at these levels. Thus a man and his wife can fill the respective roles in gardening, or a group of brothers and their wives may constitute themselves as complementary teams; or, as sometimes happens, all the men and women of a clan may cooperate in preparing a common garden. A more significant illustration of complementarity at these levels, however, is provided by the preparation of food.

A woman is supposed to cook her husband's meals; if a man has several wives, he may consequently receive several "servings" of cooked tubers at mealtimes, some of which he may share among unmarried men or visitors as gifts or gestures of hospitality. Women call attention to grievances against their husbands, or indicate displeasure with them, by cooking their meals badly or omitting them altogether. Thus the accepted excuse for wife-beating is that "She didn't cook food for me" or "She gave me bad food."

The giving of cooked vegetable food by a woman, or its acceptance by a man, is often taken to be synonymous with marital relations, especially in the case of widows, who will use this means as well as sexual seduction to establish claims on young men as potential husbands. Before Kagoiano married, Wabo of Hagani invited him to come and take as a wife a woman formerly married to Kagoiano's patrilateral first cousin Haria, who had lived there. She had two sons, and Wabo offered to take the elder, leaving the younger and the mother to Kagoiano. When

Kagoiano accompanied me to Hagani, the woman sent one of her sons to ask him to come and take some cooked food from her. Kagoiano told the boy to bring it to him, but the boy said "No, you must come." He went, complaining, and the woman gave him the food. He asked her for one of the sons, and she said she would not let the son go without coming herself. Kagoiano said that he might take her. Later Ogwane of Hagani took the woman, as his wife had died, and Kagoiano said "I accepted food from this woman — if someone else wants to take her, he should give me pay." A person who has (an adulterous) sexual interest in someone's spouse will often make his intentions known by throwing a bit of sweet potato at the chest of the desired person; if his intentions are shared, the latter will respond with a similar gesture.

The giving of cooked food also represents the obligation of mutual support within the *zibi* or set of full siblings. A group of brothers share claims on the wealth brought in by their sisters' marriages and by virtue of their sisters' children. The eldest brother, or *gominaibidi*, will often take the responsibility of supporting his younger brothers, and use their share of the wealth to betroth wives for them, or perhaps simply marry the women himself, with the understanding that they will pass to the younger brothers when the latter come of age. While they are living under the *gominaibidi's* protection, his younger brothers are obliged to work for him, and his wives cook food for them, which they should reciprocate by bringing food to the *gominaibidi* after they themselves marry. In these circumstances, as a group of men who cooperate in "male" subsistence activity and who share food prepared by women to whom they have a common claim, the *zibi* becomes a unit of complementarity.

Complementarity also characterizes the clan as the largest distinct and permanent unit in the society; members of a clan share a common obligation to contribute to the bride-prices of clan members, and they therefore share rights to the inheritance of their wives. In addition, clan members usually share a fairly close genealogical relationship, and usually live in close contiguity. Before European contact, clan members frequently inhabited a single house and made a common garden, so that males and females of the whole clan were able to cooperate as complementary groups. One expression of complementarity on the clan level is a small ceremony that takes place several weeks after the initiation of youths.

Boys who are to undergo initiation are forbidden to eat food cooked by their mothers or other women of the clan. This is in addition to a series of specific food taboos, which will be discussed in a later chapter. During the course of the initiation they will be fed various special foods by the men in charge. After the conclusion of the initiation proceedings, perhaps two months after the boys had first entered the initiation house, a feast is held to mark the first time that the initiates, as adult members, can receive and eat food cooked by the women of the clan. The women cook a great deal of sweet potato, and a pig is killed and divided, the head being given to the women, skin and hind legs to the young men, and skin and forelegs to the older men. This custom is said to be very old and to antedate the arrival of the present-day initiation procedure, with its bamboo flutes, from the Gimi speakers to the east. Recently this feast has come to be held for young men returning from contract labor at the coast, following a period after their return during which they too are forbidden to receive food from the women.

A more direct expression of complementarity is a ceremony called *nai tegebo si,* or "food exchange," in which the men and women of a clan or community present each other with large quantities of some characteristic vegetable food, which is prepared, and must be eaten on the spot. This ceremony generally takes place at the climax of the wet season, the *waia si,*[10] when vegetable food is most abundant, and it must be initiated by a challenge. The women will taunt the men, saying "You do not plant *marita* [*Pandanus conoideus*], you plant only wild *karuga* [other *Pandanus* species]," or perhaps the men will taunt the women, "You do not plant sugarcane [*Saccharum officinarum*], you plant only pitpit [*Saccharum edule*],"[11] accusing the other sex of stinginess by associating its efforts with a related, but less desirable, crop. Later the sex that has been challenged harvests a considerable quantity of the desired food, while those of the other sex prepare some characteristic food of their own. At Kurube, in 1964, the men gave pandanus fruit, the women sugarcane; in an earlier ceremony, before contact, the men had given beans, the women, sugarcane.

Separate male and female dances are held on the evening before the exchange, and also on the day of the exchange itself; the men wear plumes, shells, and decorative leaves, and dance with drums, while the women wear only their characteristic net bags, and dance in a modest circle. Meanwhile the food is being prepared and laid out on racks or leaves. At the conclusion of the dancing, members of each sex begin to eat the food presented by the other—they refuse, deprecatingly, to eat any of that provided by their own sex. It is in the spirit of the challenge that the challengers eat "until they vomit"; generally both sides do, and vomiting is met by a derisive chorus of "oooo" from the other side.

The aspects that make this event one of friendly rivalry also accommodate the expression of interclan or intercommunity competitiveness, and a modified form of *nai tegebo* sometimes occurs between clans or communities. Here, however, the motif of complementarity is no longer involved; reciprocation is by delayed exchange. Some months after the challenge, the challengers visit the clan that they have taunted and, after a dance, are given immense quantities of the food in question,

10. The instances that I witnessed were held on 28 March 1964 and 21 February 1965.
11. What they are saying, in effect, is "You might as well be planting pitpit, for all the sugar we are getting from you."

which they must eat "until they vomit." Any vegetable food may be given, and only men are involved. At some later time the former challengers will reciprocate.

Except for these comparatively rare instances when *nai tegebo* occurs between clans or communities, vegetable food does not pass between clans; like the land on which it is grown, vegetable food cannot be exchanged for meat, pearl shells, or any other items in the category *sizibage*, something of value that is given in bridewealth or otherwise exchanged for human beings. *Sizibage* and *tubu nai,* or vegetable food, form exclusive categories;[12] vegetable food is proper to the area of complementarity, the ideological mode by which the separate male and female parts of any social unit are united, and its exchange properly takes place within those units.

Although it provides the mode of integration of male and female roles, and hence the *content* of relations within social units, complementarity has nothing whatever to do with the *definition* of those units, the issue of which men, or groups of men, will enter into complementary relations with which women. The significance of social units, and of individual marriages, is realized via an additional set of metaphors, articulated through the substitution of wealth for people, to which meat and the category of wealth called *sizibage* are proper.

SUBSTITUTION

Complementarity is expressed by the giving of vegetable food, which is transitory in the Daribi view, merely passing through the body when eaten, and which is exchanged, together with a number of services, on a day-to-day basis. The definition of social units, on the other hand, involves the substitution of relatively "permanent" items of wealth for rights in human beings. These items include the category *sizibage* or *sibage* (shell ornaments, axes, bushknives, and Australian currency) as well as meat, represented by live pigs, pork, smoked marsupials, chickens, or tinned meat. As we have learned in an earlier section, meat is a peculiarly appropriate item to be exchanged for female reproductive capacity, insofar as its juices are a necessary concomitant to male reproductive capability.

Since it represents the permanent allocation of people, thus defining the units to which they belong, this set of metaphors is based on non-expendable goods, items of adornment and tools, which can be retained and re-exchanged as a kind of "demographic currency" or "vital wealth," as well as the meat and fat that go to form the fluids of the body itself. Just as complementarity involves the exchange of services and produce, so this system encompasses the exchange of the producers. The inclusion of axes and bushknives in this category is consistent with

12. See Wagner (1967), pp. 27–28; also R. F. Salisbury, *From Stone to Steel* (London: Cambridge University Press, 1962), p. 212; Salisbury treats this dichotomy in utilitarian terms, as a functional "mechanism."

these facts, since such tools are "permanent" requisites of productive activities, and they are counterbalanced by the bark-cloaks and string bags that make up the category of "female wealth" and are relatively "permanent" requirements of female activities as well as products of those activities.

In addition to pearl shells and other objects of adornment, the Daribi exchange-system opposes meat and "male" implements to rights in female productive and reproductive capacity and "female" implements. Although few payments ever consist exclusively of male or female wealth, and such items as pearl shells, trade-cloth, or, nowadays, Australian currency tend to occur in both, the payment given *for* a woman should consist largely of male wealth, and that given *with* a woman should be largely female wealth. Moreover, the individual sibling groups, or *zibi*, which act as wife-givers and wife-takers, should oppose each other strictly in those terms; a *zibi* that has received a wife from a given *zibi* of another clan should not share meat or wealth given by the latter to some other *zibi* of its own clan in return for a woman. The total effect of these usages is to align the statuses of wife-giving and wife-receiving groups in the exchange system with the respective roles of women and men in the system of complementarity.

Daribi reckon the value of an exchange payment in terms of "units" of wealth,[13] each represented by a short "counting stick" in the bundle that will be kept as a record of the payment. Items of wealth are usually evaluated on a fairly rough scale, and there is no attempt to employ fractions or other arithmetic operations. An ax equals one unit, as does a crescent pearl shell, a bushknife, a string bag, a bark-cloak, a blanket, a length of trade-cloth, an Australian two-dollar note, or a pile of (roughly) twenty ten-cent pieces.[14] When such items are exchanged, it is on a unit-for-unit basis, except in the case of what is called *dobu ponabo,* the exchange of items for their exact equivalents. This is a variant of the exchange of wealth for wealth, called *ponabo,* which accompanies all major transactions. When the wealth to be given is laid out in display, members of the receiving clan will approach it holding a pearl shell and "try" their own shell against those displayed, holding it over them; when one is found that exactly matches, they are exchanged. Recently this type of exchange has increasingly involved Australian currency. It allows men to participate in an exchange without getting involved in a "redistribution" — and provides the ethnographer with a convenient

13. There is no Daribi term that expressly denotes such units, which are referred to by the use of object-markers (such as the Pidgin "-*pela*").

14. The two-dollar notes represent a convention initiated by the former one-pound note, whose value was understood to be two dollars in the new currency; the ten-cent piece likewise occupies a position formerly held by the shilling. In 1969 coins of larger or smaller denomination were generally unacceptable to and incapable of being evaluated by most Daribi, although the dollar bill was accepted and understood as the equivalent of the former ten-shilling note. In 1964-65 the conversion of shillings into pounds was not well understood (as it is now), and a pile of perhaps eleven shillings was often accepted as the equivalent of a pound.

way of "making change."

Items of wealth for an exchange payment may be solicited from, or contributed by, all adult male members of the clan of the giver as well as members of other clans in the community or relatives in external clans who are not otherwise involved in the exchange. In most cases the "core" of such a payment is assembled by the man who is presenting it, together with his brothers; a considerable portion is given by others of his clan and a small fraction by those of other clans. Generally clan-mates and others of the community each give one or two units of wealth. The wealth is taken to the house of the receiver, where it is arrayed in a line on bark-cloaks or trade-cloth for display, after which a smaller, reciprocal payment may be given by the receivers, speeches may be made and a ceremony may be held. Somewhat later, the receivers dis-tribute the wealth to the kinsmen involved and those who contributed to the reciprocal payment. Within the clan of the givers, many of the contributors will have to wait until a sister or daughter of the man who raised the payment marries before they can expect a return on their contributions, for clanmates should "share wealth."

All significant exchanges are made with respect to individual per-sons, to "mark" claims on them, to recruit them by giving compensation for the claims of their kinsmen, or to compensate their kinsmen at their deaths. Except in the case of death-compensations, a reciprocal pay-ment, called *sogwarema-mabo*, is generally made by the receivers of the major payment, kinsmen of the person concerned. (The *sogware* payment often includes largely "female" wealth, especially when a betrothal or marriage is involved.) As a result, a major payment, such as a bride-price, consists of two portions. One of these, usually about two-fifths of the total, represents the value of the *sogware* payment and is exchanged for it on a wealth-for-wealth basis; this is called *pona siare*, the part that is "finished by exchange." The other portion, usually the bulk of the payment, is called *oromawai*, and consists of the wealth that is given "nothing" *(oro)*, directly, or without return, for the person in question.

The payments made on behalf of an individual, which normatively determine his clan membership, continue, as do the claims of his kins-men, throughout his life, and should be made at times of life-crises. Taken as a whole, they serve to incorporate the life-course of an indivi-dual, in terms of his major status changes, within the social system; com-pensation is given each time a person's role is "redefined," as it were. The kinsmen to whom such payments are made on behalf of an indivi-dual are his *pagebidi*—the close maternal kinsmen, represented by the mother's brothers, of a pre-pubescent child or of a man, and the close kinsmen, represented by her brothers, of a married woman. The series of payments for a man is, therefore, rather different than that for a woman.

"Recruitment" payments given to the *pagebidi* on behalf of a child

are called *pagehabo* (from the verb *pagehaie,* "to pay the *pagebidi*");
the payment given to the *pagebidi* of a person who has died is called
puiabo (from *puie,* "to make a death-payment," probably derived from
puberaie, "to bury").

The series of payments given during a male's lifetime is as follows:

1. *Pagehabo:* a payment of 10-12 units of wealth, plus perhaps a pig,
   given when the boy is three or four years old. Others of the father's
   clan often contribute.
   Ogwa sogwarema mabo: a payment of three to five units of wealth
   given in return by the *pagebidi;* sometimes the latter holds this payment back, to be given later when the boy wishes to marry.
2. *Pagehabo:* a payment of 10-12 units of wealth, plus perhaps a pig,
   given when the boy is initiated. The clan of the father often con-
   tributes.
   Ogwa sogwarema mabo: sometimes a small return payment is made
   by the *pagebidi,* sometimes, again, he waits until the boy is to marry
   and helps him then.
3. *Idare bidibuma perama sibage hanarubo* (going to the mother's
   place to request wealth): when a youth is assembling his bride-price,
   he may go to his *pagebidi* and request assistance; generally four to
   five units of wealth are given. There is no reciprocal payment.
4. A man "of good understanding" will later select one of his mother's
   brothers as an *awa-mu,* or "true mother's brother," and make small,
   occasional exchanges with him.
5. *Puiabo:* a payment of about ten units of wealth, and perhaps a pig,
   made at a person's death to his *pagebidi.* Others of the clan contribute;
   there is no reciprocal payment.

The series of payments made during a woman's lifetime are as follows:

1. *Pagehabo:* a payment of ten units of wealth, plus perhaps a pig, made
   to her maternal kin when a girl is three or four years old.
   Wegi sogwarema mabo: a payment of four to five units of wealth given
   in return by the *pagebidi.*
2. *Ororobo:* betrothal payment of five to ten units of wealth and a pig,
   made to girl's father and brothers when she is five to ten years old.
   We-sogwarema-mabo: a payment of string bags and bark-cloaks given
   in return by the girl's kin.
3. Occasional gifts of meat are made to the girl's parents by the man
   who has betrothed her; these are reciprocated by gifts of "female
   wealth." A pig is given shortly before, or at the time of, the wedding.
4. *We kẹbo* ("woman-fastening," or "tying"): a total payment of 50 to 80
   units of wealth, made to a woman's father and brothers when she is
   married. A portion of the total, 20 to 30 units of wealth, is reciprocated
   by the return payment.
   We-sogwarema-mabo: a payment of 20 to 30 units of wealth, includ-
   much "female" wealth, given by the clan of the bride to that of her
   husband.
   Apego wegi sibage: a portion of the bride-price, ten or so units of
   wealth, plus perhaps a pig, given to the bride's maternal *pagebidi* to
   mark the changing of her clan membership. Sometimes reciprocated
   with a return payment.
5. Occasional payments are made to a woman's father and brothers by
   her husband when visiting them; these are reciprocated.

6. *Puiabo:* a payment of 10 to 20 units of wealth plus a pig given by a woman's husband to her father and brothers at her death. Her father and brothers pass the payment on to her maternal kin. There is no reciprocal payment.

Should a girl or boy die before marriage, a *puiabo,* consisting of ten units of wealth and a pig, is given to the *pagebidi.* The *pagebidi* has a claim to all children born to his sister, but generally payment is *offered* only for the first two or three, the most being given for the first. If he wishes, the *pagebidi* may request payment for later children, however. If he is not paid, a *pagebidi* may choose to wait and press his claims later, or he may take possession of a child, or negotiate a settlement;[15] as a last resort he may demonstrate to make his wishes known,[16] or curse "his" children.

Payments are also given by members of a clan to the kinsmen of someone who has died on their land; generally these amount to perhaps five to ten units of wealth. A much larger payment, called *boipibo* ("the fight sleeps"), is given in compensation for the killing of a man, during peace-making ceremonies. This payment is equal to a large bride-price, and includes two pigs.[17] In one case the payment also included a woman, who was to bear a child, to be named after the dead man, *before* a bride-price could be given for her.

In all of these instances the major effect of exchanges has been to compensate kinsmen for their claims to human beings, or, in other words, to substitute wealth for human beings. In some cases social usage seems to demand an additional exchange of one human being for another, as in the example of *boipibo* given above, or in the expectation that a *zibi* that has given a woman to some external clan should receive one from them, and that a *zibi* that has received a woman from such a clan should also give one,[18] so that each marriage made by a *zibi* is balanced by another in the opposite direction. Even in the latter cases, however, the reciprocation of one woman for another presupposes that each individual transaction will involve the giving of wealth in return for the woman.

Complementarity and the system of exchange, or substitution, together represent Daribi social ideology. Their interrelationship is expressed in the contrast between vegetable food and meat, or in that between exchanging *with* women and exchanging *for* women. The moral force of this ideology is stressed in the origin myths through the

---

15. See Wagner (1967), pp. 69–70, for some examples of this.

16. In 1968 I attended a gerua-dance at Pelia village; without warning Kagoiano, who was standing beside me, loosed an arrow into a gerua board as it was carried by one of the parucipants. Kagoiano explained later that the man was his sister's son, and that he was "shooting his child" for whom payment had not been given.

17. As these pigs are led to the place of payment, the recipients aim their bows at the men leading them, then slowly swing the arrows downward and shoot the pigs, emphasizing the "substitution" involved.

18. See Wagner (1967), pp. 144, 155–57.

motif of "tempering," wherein the force of individual desires is subdued or bridled by the distributive demands of society. In the act of providing a set of metaphors, or equivalences, by which wealth and pigs may be substituted for a woman, or a man and woman can supplement each other's needs, society supplies the equation by which the tempering and satisfaction of each person's needs can be realized, and thereby continually reenacts the relationships of its myth. In this sense, society itself is the equation, individuals represent specific needs and capacities, and the metaphoric acts by which these are met and discharged are manifest in the overt activity of daily life.

3/The Magic of Metaphor

THE STRUCTURING OF POWER

When we consider the Daribi social system as a mode of continuous individual action rather than a set of interlocking propositions, it takes on the aspect of an inventive or improvisatory style. The activities of everyday life, of subsistence, socialization, and family existence, achieve a moral or normative force through their metaphorization in terms of the exchange of food or other products or implements of sex-specific production. Within the social unit acts and events are represented in terms of sexual role and of vegetable food; interunit transactions involve the substitution of implements and products of sexual specialization (as well as meat) for human beings, as metaphorizations of their general productive "value." In either case the "normatizing" of acts in this way assimilates the actor to a collective "identity"; he assumes the role of a man or a woman, the equivalent of any other man or woman, and that of a member of a group that is the equivalent of any other group. Hence innovative acts that achieve their meaning through such social metaphors are limited to a collective significance for the very reason that the meaning that they create is social; at most, they can distinguish a person as being human and as male or female.

Of course social metaphors of this kind can only realize their meaning in contradistinction to a set of individuating personal or group identities, just as the productive roles that they emphasize are predicated on a range of individual needs, skills, talents, and capacities. Social events such as marriage or initiation must always involve specific individuals and groups, whose identities, as metaphoric constructs, are temporarily suspended through the activation of the collective metaphor. It is in this sense that we can speak of these events as "innovations" upon personal or group identity, for such social, collectivizing acts become the means through which the individual person or group is augmented. Thus although a person or group may realize a separate identity through the designation of some plant or animal, this identity is belied by the metaphor of sex-specific role created when a man receives cooked sweet potato from his wife, or by the exchange of wealth-objects representing equivalent productive capacity through which a wife or child is added to the group. Personal or group identity, therefore, forms the *context* against which the symbols of social ideology achieve their metaphoric value, and hence their meaning; they metaphorize the collectivity or equivalence that is necessary if the interaction of individuals or units is to have any meaning at all. Therefore, we can speak of such metaphors as creating moral or normative force, that particular value that accrues to actions respecting the social collectivity. As we have seen in our discussion of Daribi origin stories, this value is frequently expressed as a "tempering" of individual desires and needs, often through the agency of shame, which plays such a significant role in kin relationships.

Just as individuating identity and capability, or skill, form the context against which social metaphors are realized, so, by the very converse of the dialectical relationship, the metaphors by which identity is established, or personal skill or advantage is obtained, are formed against the context of social ideology. Like names, the special abilities or powers that a person may acquire serve to differentiate him from the collectivity of society as well as to place him in a determinate relation to the latter. The acts of metaphorization through which these abilities acquire their meaning can be understood as innovations upon a person's social role, for they bestow the specific advantages by which influence and other types of social "leverage" are attained. In more concrete terms, the fact that a person is a forceful or convincing talker, a skillful gardener, a good axman, or a clever manipulator may be of great consequence when brought to bear on the social system, for indeed it is precisely such abilities that the system mediates. But capabilities of this kind, if they are to realize their full innovative effect upon the system, must necessarily derive from sources that are external to it. Thus they achieve their full meaning as metaphors against the context of social ideology, bringing extrinsic causal and experiential fields to bear on the activities of gardening, hunting, or procreation, and thus simultaneously augmenting these activities and denying their specifically social orientation.

Of course the acquiring of a particular talent or skill may involve much more in terms of individual practice, observation, or ingenuity than the mere construction of a metaphor, for all that the latter can achieve is a semantic innovation. On the other hand, the significance of this aspect of innovation cannot be overstressed: man does not attempt "meaningless" acts, and however efficient or revolutionary a given application may be, it can only be conceived, realized, understood, and communicated through cultural meaning. The importance of advertising in modern America provides an apt illustration of this; advertising creates meaning in the form of (often illusory) "advantages" attributed to the technological artifacts it is trying to "sell." Typically, this involves the formation of metaphoric constructs linking a bit of scented liquid to an adolescent's insecurities regarding interpersonal relations, for instance, or to the housewife's legendary phobias involving dirt and insects. As every American knows, the product that fails to "differentiate" itself from its competitors through meaning-creation of this sort, regardless of its inherent worth, eventually loses "selling power" and must be removed from the market.

In contradistinction to the institutionalized innovative "industries" of Western society, tribal peoples tend to incorporate such activities in the form of individual mediation. Accounts from the American West recall the feeling among many Indians that the technological superiority of the whites resulted from the revelation of principles like that of firearms or of the steam engine in a series of powerful dreams. These Indians, of course, shared the widespread North American preoccupation with the obtaining of power or efficacy from animal or spirit "helpers" through dreams, visions, or other forms of mediation. The individual acquired his power through the point of articulation that the vision structured between his own world and that of the animal or spirit, whose special abilities were added to those of the person himself. The mediator serves as a kind of "bridge" or "conductor" between two conventionally unrelated systems, bringing them into coordinate action.[1] This view bears a certain resemblance to theories that have been put forth by anthropological writers on the subject of "magic"; let us briefly consider two of them.

Perhaps because it provided a foil for his own outspoken identification with scientism, magic became a perennial problem in the writings of Malinowski. Among many astute observations and anticlimactic "explanations," his realization that "...the effects of magic are something superadded to all the other effects produced by human effort and by natural qualities"[2] falls into line with our own discussion, as does his notion of the "creative metaphor"[3] of magic, which he did not, unfortunately, expand upon or attempt to apply. Malinowski's most famous and characteristic observation, however, deals with the occasions on which magic is practiced: "It is most significant that in the lagoon fishing, where man can rely completely upon his knowledge and skill, magic does not exist, while in the open-sea fishing, full of danger and uncertainty, there is extensive magical ritual to secure safety and good results."[4] Danger and uncertainty are of course relative quantities, as much a function of a specific cultural viewpoint as any other subjective evaluation. The extensive ritual surrounding Trobriand deep-sea fishing might well find a more convincing explanation in the significance at-

1. I am very much indebted to Mr. J. David Cole for pointing out this and many other aspects of this argument. A somewhat different development of these ideas is to be found in his manuscript, "An Introduction to Psycho-Serial Systems and Systematics."

2. Bronislaw Malinowski, *Argonauts of the Western Pacific* (New York: E. P. Dutton & Co., 1961), p. 421.

3. Bronislaw Malinowski, *Coral Gardens and Their Magic 2: The Language of Magic and Gardening* (Bloomington: Indiana University Press, 1965), pp. 70, 238–39.

4. Bronislaw Malinowski, "Magic, Science and Religion," in *Magic, Science and Religion and Other Essays* (Garden City, N. Y.: Doubleday & Co., 1954), p. 31.

tached to this pursuit by Trobriand society.

The contributions of Levi-Strauss illuminate the matter from an entirely different angle; having dismissed Malinowski's explanation of magic in terms of "practical and affective" ends in an earlier work,[5] he goes on, in *The Savage Mind*, to suggest a theory of magic based on ideal properties and conceptualization. In this view, magic consists of the "naturalization" of human actions, such that magical operations "...present the same necessity to those performing them as the sequence of natural causes, in which the agent believes himself simply to be inserting supplementary links through his rites."[6] Lévi-Strauss's approach resembles the one that I have suggested here in that it regards magic as a conceptual structuring, or mediation, of normally distinct actional spheres; it differs from my approach in that Levi-Strauss specifies the spheres as being those of human action (culture) and nature, and insists that the former is structured in terms of the latter. There can be little doubt that many, if not most, magical rites and formulas could be fitted into the nature-culture opposition; on the other hand, Lévi-Strauss's explanation is completely dependent upon that particular opposition, and upon the epiphenomenal categories "nature" and "culture." Most significantly, then, by focusing his explanation on the *content* of cognitive categories, Lévi-Strauss reduces what might be seen as a *formal* problem to a *lexical* one.

The essential weakness of a lexical definition of magic is not that it underrates the importance of "magic" — for that term is itself of dubious value, an heirloom from an earlier anthropology — but that it diminishes the significance of the modality of human action and conceptualization that "magic" represents. It is this issue, *per se*, that poses the major problem, one that Levi-Strauss has approached far more convincingly in his representation of mythical thought as *bricolage*, a kind of structural improvisation involving mythical motifs.[7]

Daribi themselves construe the metaphoric relationship in terms of concealment and discovery; the juxtaposition of seemingly unrelated causal or experiential fields in a metaphor "hides" the analogy, or thread of meaning, that connects them, whereas this analogy has the potential of resolving the discrepancy, just as the solution to a riddle illuminates an otherwise meaningless proposition. The allusion to two unrelated "fields," generally accomplished by referring to one in the context of the other, represents the "potential" of the relationship, and it is this that the metaphoric link, or analogy, *controls*, bringing the separate fields into alignment. The acquiring or controlling of individuating "power" takes many overt forms in Daribi culture; [8]some are created, as

5. Claude Levi-Strauss, *Totemism*, tr. Rodney Needham (Boston: Beacon Press, 1962), p. 66.

6. Claude Lévi-Strauss, *The Savage Mind*, tr. anon. (London: Weidenfeld and Nicolson, 1966), p. 221.

7. Lévi-Strauss, 1966, p. 17.

8. Cf. Roy Wagner, *The Curse of Souw: Principles of Daribi Clan Definition and Alliance*

magical spells, dancing songs, or mourning chants, others are discovered in the surrounding environment, and yet others are revealed as dreams or omens. Let us consider a set of "innovative styles" in the creation or discovery of such meaning.

THE METAPHOR OF MAGIC

Daribi call magic spells *pobi;* the act of saying spell is referred to by the stem *guru- (pobi gurubo,* "he says a spell"). *Pobi* are known and transmitted individually, and sometimes held in secrecy, although their incantation frequently takes place in semipublic circumstances in the course of gardening and sago-making. Often they are taught to children by their parents in connection with the relevant activities or techniques; before her marriage a girl is told *pobi* for gardening and taking care of pigs. Although many are "standardized," there is a range of alternative, interchangeable *pobi* for any given activity, and theoretically the number of *pobi* that could exist is limited only by the area of efficaceous applications and the inventory of metaphoric expressions permitted by the conceptual system. Individual *pobi* may be tried and discarded on pragmatic grounds, and new spells may be improvised, often reusing or recombining motifs and images found in earlier spells.

Daribi employ *pobi* to effect a favorable outcome in areas whose unpredictability suggests that mechanical techniques alone are insufficient, or simply that a "structuring" of events is efficacious. Spells are intended to ensure success in some individual undertaking, and Daribi will say of a man who seems especially skillful or lucky that he "has some kind of *pobi.*" Magic is particularly prevalent in hunting, gardening, food-processing, and the growth and development of children; certain pursuits such as the clearing of a garden or the processing of sago involve a series of spells that accompany each stage of the work. The relationship of magic to areas of cultural concern is illustrated in Daribi rain magic.

The "control" of weather occasions as much or more in the way of recriminations in Daribi society as its prediction does in our own,[9] for wet weather is a nuisance, especially for those who are committed to outdoor activities. A sudden cloudburst can make one acutely uncomfortable during a journey, rain can spoil ceremonies, and when a day promises to be chill and rainy, most Daribi simply roll themselves in their bark-cloaks near the fire and go to sleep. Generally Daribi attribute all downpours and even extensive spells of rain that are not obviously seasonal to human intervention. People are said to make rain in order to avenge some slight or injury, and in my experience Daribi always

---

in *New Guinea* (Chicago: University of Chicago Press, 1967), chap. 2, especially pp. 47-57; here "power" is referred to as "influence."

9. In this context it matters little whether the experts are believed to actually "control" the weather, or only to predict it; predicting *is* controlling insofar as both have the same social effect, which is to maneuver people into rainstorms that they did not anticipate.

have some motive and some culprit in mind as an explanation for a given drizzle, though different individuals will favor different hypotheses. It is said that "If women make it rain, men feel cold; if men make it rain, women feel cold," and also that the rain made by men is strong and hard, whereas that conjured by women amounts to nothing more than a weak drizzle. At a performance of the habu ceremony at Tiligi' in August 1968, which I attended, and which was dogged by an intermittent, chill drizzle, indignation over the weather ran high. At one point a sudden shower drove a considerable crowd of men into one of the houses, and there was a general grumbling about the rain; one man got to his feet and said "Now that we're here, we might as well talk about who made it rain," and, thumping his fist into an open palm, he added that someone "should thrash" *(haru mainau)* the rainmaker. Bamboo pipes were lit and passed around, with the idea that if the pipe went out while a man was smoking it would prove him the culprit, but the results were inconclusive.

Although rainfall at Karimui does show a seasonal periodicity when averaged over a number of years, and the natives themselves recognize these cycles and sometimes elaborate them on the basis of the ripening of certain crops during the wet season, the actual rainfall at any time is highly erratic. Spells of dry, clear weather lasting days or even weeks can occur at any time during the "wet" season, whereas veritable deluges can occur during normally "dry" months. Table 1 shows monthly rainfall for the years 1961-68 as recorded at Karimui Patrol Post; a seasonal pattern is indicated in the monthly averages, showing the period from September through April as being relatively rainy, and the remainder of the year comparatively dry. The individual monthly figures, however, tell a different story; with the possible exception of the February-March period, which is the most clearly delineated "season" in the native reckoning, most monthly figures are either significantly above or below the respective averages, with fairly little pattern in the deviations. Were we to chart weekly or daily rainfall, it is probable that a similar sporadic configuration would result.

Whatever the ultimate roots of Papuan rainmaking, rainfall as unpredictable as that recorded at Karimui does little to discourage the illusion that the weather is open to tampering, or that someone is tampering with it. Nor is the illusion strictly confined to the natives; one of the patrol officers stationed at Karimui would pay a small sum to local "experts" to keep the rain off while he was on patrol, with reportedly excellent results. In September 1964 I commissioned a downpour for three shillings to avenge myself on an impudent helicopter pilot, and was rewarded handsomely,[10] although admittedly it was a day of unsettled weather.

10. Perhaps thirty minutes or so after the commission, a tremendous downpour came down from Mount Karimui and rained itself out over the airstrip. Unfortunately, the helicopter pilot had left in the interim. It must be assumed that helicopter pilots have *pobi* of their own.

TABLE 1
Monthly Rainfall (in inches) recorded at Karimui Patrol Post

Year	Jan.	Feb.	Mar.	April	May	June	July	Aug.	Sept.	Oct.	Nov.	Dec.
1961	9.21	11.58	*	17.64	12.73	7.03	16.87	12.25	11.62	14.97	10.14	10.02
1962	9.33	12.97	19.73	18.04	11.21	7.16	14.47	9.05	19.71	11.54	8.09	16.27
1963	7.06	5.21	13.62	11.24	5.97	11.87	4.68	18.79	10.89	12.66	4.36	8.96
1964	14.41	12.67	16.01	9.19	6.10	4.57	3.97	7.17	11.78	8.78	19.35	6.20
1965	15.11	11.42	17.12	8.71	14.25	6.25	1.72	2.37	6.69	6.25	7.85	21.42
1966	19.20	19.80	19.59	9.03	13.13	5.77	1.25	4.90	6.81	14.51	9.48	13.80
1967	10.21	17.14	17.45	6.55	12.41	9.07	10.29	7.45	6.73	12.55	7.50	8.32
1968	16.02	10.75	10.77	15.40	3.90	2.84	7.83	6.98	9.06	11.00	6.17	*
Av.	12.07	12.69	16.33	11.98	9.96	6.82	7.64	8.62	10.41	11.53	9.12	12.41

*Figure not available.

The Daribi term for a rainmaker is *turubage sabo bidi* ("rain-taker"). The technique of making rain involves keeping the bark of a certain tree *(turubage ni)* in the house; when rain is desired, the bark is either burnt in the fire or thrown into water, and a *pobi* such as the following is recited:

U   Suạru   dari   Mio   dari   te korogu ugwa
This   Mount Suạru   with Mount Karimui together that   cloak

turugua-sobau.   Te Iwai ta Mawa si,   te   hai'nami   si,
together I sew. They Iwai and Mawa both, those cross-cousins both,

te   pe merabu   te enebodau, te   poi   tabo   tụ enebodau.
that bat-wingbone them   shoots, those urine-passing ways shoots.

Ba' hogwaiabo   gera'   u dari   meni-iabao, me   soborage ba'
[A kind of bird] cries here together   as if,   also [another bird]

gera' urubao. Te   ại   porolia sanama   e   burumaru usuasiru
cry   utters. That river   rising   this flat-place   fills

meniraba. Aie   wẹ harape te   pu iariru-ebo meni-iaba. Tegidari
as if.   Yonder water climbs that mud making   as if.   All

wego   sida   uru   meniraba.
women shouts-utter   as if.

The "cloak" referred to here is overcast; the image is probably meant to suggest a joining of the haloes of cloud that generally crown both of these mountains with identical configurations.[11] Iwai and Mawa are the two cross-cousins who live in the sky, and who "carry" respectively the moon and sun across the heavens. The metaphor here is a complex one; the flying fox wingbone lodged in their penes causes their bodies to swell up with urine, so that the accumulated urine, like rain, will "cover all places." (This image alone constitutes a separate *pobi.*) The single bone also joins the two, "fastening" them together: normally, during the day, Mawa is thought to be carrying the sun from east to west across the visible heavens, whereas Iwai is carrying the moon in the opposite direction "inside" (above) the sky; the "fastening" alluded to here metaphorizes the action of rain clouds, which are believed to "hold" the sun *inside* the sky.[12] *Hogwaiabo* and *soborage* birds are thought to cry before rain. The imagery of the river rising and overflowing its banks, creating mud, refers to the effects of heavy, prolonged rain, and the women shout in fear and surprise at the height of the water.

To cause rain to cease, another, related *pobi* is recited:

Te   somono ba' meni-iabao, te   sore   urura pabaro-sobao, te
Those lorikeets   as if,   that torch lighting   goes,   those

hai-nami   si   bobogaza   te pobau, me ibabade pobau,
cross-cousins both genitals-fastened they leave, one below-at leaves,

11. All interpretations are those of my informants, although occasionally I have added supplementary statements, as here, to inform the reader of the general context.
12. An alternate interpretation, which is not, however, easily reconciled with my informants' explanation, is that the "fastening" of Iwai and Mawa represents the period of the new moon, when, according to Daribi, "the moon has gone to sleep" *(sugua piai)* and rain is likely to occur.

me   ogwabade pobau,   te   sore   te   urura   pabaro-sobau,   te
one   above-at   leaves,   that   torch   [it]   lighting   goes,   those

gi-rape, be'-rape,   te   sore   pabaro-sobau.
gardens, houses,   that   torch   goes.

The birds referred to here, probably red-and-black lorikeets, presage the sun by their brilliant color; the "torch" is the sun, underway once more and visible. The two cross-cousins, Iwai and Mawa, are here unfastened, and go their separate ways, one eastward "above" the sky, the other westward "below" it. The gardens and houses become visible once again, lit by the "torch" of the sun.

Pobi sometimes combine several metaphors, as in the preceding examples, and in such cases the common theme serves to "focus" the various individual metaphors. The way in which a metaphoric "link" or analogy "controls" the action of a metaphor is best demonstrated, however, in a spell that accompanies the setting of a cassowary-snare. The snare itself consists of a sapling that is bent down and tied with a rope to a trigger-stick, loosely caught on the ground. Another rope with a noose on it hangs from the sapling. A small fence is made, enclosing the area into which "bait" is put in such a way that the cassowary must slip its head through the noose in order to reach the bait, so that its neck is caught when the trigger is tripped. As the snare is set, a *pobi* is recited, stating that: "All the men have gone away carrying cargo for the Europeans,[13] therefore Pesquet's parrots, black cockatoos, you come to this road, there is a man here, he will not hurt you, he will tie a pearl shell around your neck." Daribi say that they address the black cockatoo and Pesquet's parrot so as to conceal their true interest in the cassowary, and the latter will overhear, or the black cockatoo will let it know. Actually both Pesquet's parrot and the black cockatoo resemble the cassowary in coloring, and a legend relates how the black cockatoo became the "cross-cousin" of the cassowary by knocking tree fruit down to it while feeding, and thus "sharing food" with it.[14] This resemblance or relationship serves as a metaphoric link directing the spell at the cassowary, who will "know" or "overhear" as a result.

The "man" referred to in the spell is the bent sapling, the "pearl shell" that he will "tie" around the neck of the cassowary is the noose of the snare. The effect of the spell, which is to draw the cassowary to the snare, is achieved through the very kind of deception by which the snare itself operates; through the use of bait the snare is presented as something desirable, and its actual intent is hidden, and the spell,

13. Before European contact the spell began simply "All the men have gone away," or "All the men have gone to Gumine."

14. The cassowary once climbed a *haga* tree, looking for nuts. He was unused to climbing and very nearly broke his neck. The *kuna*, black cockatoo, came by and said "Oh, cross-cousin, what if someone shoots you up there? Go down, in the future I can shake some nuts down for you, and eat others myself." The *kuna's* cry is *"hai' toba duare,"* "Cross-cousin, I'm sorry for you."

TABLE 2:
Metaphoric Effect of Magic Spells

Occasion	Content of Spell	Separate Areas	Metaphoric Link	Desired Effect
felling trees	I am a *sezemabidi*	spirit/human	similar action	to make tree fall
felling trees	using old-style ax	spirit/human	similar tool	to make tree fall
fence-making	grasping small snake with foot	animal/human artifact	small longitudinal object	to shorten necessary length of fence
fence-making	killing Europeans, scattering limbs	human limbs/logs	long, white members	to obtain good fence-poles
clearing garden	claw of megapode	bird skill/human skill	raking brush into mound	to clear ground
sharpening digging stick	sharpening Souw's bone	legendary/human tool	long object	to make stick strong
gardening	men, go away! children, stay!	human/insect	size-effectiveness	to rid garden of harmful worms
weeding	megapode beak, claw, hornbill beak	bird/plant	curling growth	to make sweet potato vines curl
cutting first sago shoot	cutting tail of *dasyures*	animal/plant	(supposed) regenerative power	to make shoot grow back profusely
giving sago chopper to women	this is a hornbill's beak	bird/human tool	chopping ability of bird	to assure effectiveness of tool
filling cloak with sago pith	marsupial skin	animal food/ vegetable food	container of food	to augment sago yield
placing settling basin	python egg	animal/plant	whiteness	to make sago white
squeezing sago strainer	Souw's testicles	legendary/human	producing white milky fluid	to augment starch yield
settling of sago starch	rising of sun, moon	celestial/ domestic	rising above water	to make sago plentiful and white

Occasion	Content of Spell	Separate Areas	Metaphoric Link	Desired Effect
carrying sago to house	Souw's head	legendary/human	giant size	to insure high yield
pig-raising	mushrooms, come up!	plant/animal	growing speed	to make fat develop
pig-raising	cumulus clouds	celestial/animal	visual similarity	to make fat develop
pig-raising	foaming water	natural/animal	visual similarity	to make fat develop
pig-raising	stems of crotons, edible leaves, blow!	plant/animal	movement while attached	to make small pigs stay with their mothers
hunting	thorny vine is snagging leaves	plant/animal	catching forest products	to make dogs catch game
bird-shooting	food, firewood gathered, people expected	human/avian	similar flocking behavior	to bring flocks of birds
snaring cassowary	a yam is put in trap	human taste/ animal taste	desire for food	to draw cassowary to bait
snaring cassowary	young of *kuna*, *kaware* in snare	desire of birds to find food/young	"relatedness" of birds	to draw cassowary to bait
snaring bandicoot	putting salt into snare	human taste/ animal taste	desire for food	to draw bandicoot to bait
washing young girls	*oyutoro* bananas	plant/human	similarity in shape to girls' breasts	to make girls mature
washing young boys	*mogware* bamboo	plant/human	speed in growing	to make boys grow
shooting arrows in warfare	these are bees, wasps	insect/human artifact	wounding	to make arrows find their mark
rainmaking	a corpse is swollen, people come to see	human corpse/ swollen river	superfluity of liquid	to produce rain
leprosy curing	black sky go inside, blue sky come outside	sky/human skin	clearing of surface	to rid skin of sores
when rain threatens	your mother-in-law, sister-in-law are uncovered	natural/human	avoidance	to keep rain away

similarly, conceals the nature of the snare by misrepresenting its action metaphorically. The metaphoric link aligns the technological efficacy of the snare itself with a somewhat anthropomorphic area of motivation, augmenting its dissembling effect. Other Daribi snare-*pobi* metaphorize the action of the bait itself.

Table 2 presents an analysis of thirty Daribi *pobi* in terms of their metaphoric effect. Characteristically, one "area" to be structured by the spell is "given" by the occasion itself, and the other is stated in the spell. Many of the metaphors themselves are understandable only within the context of Daribi culture; the tree-felling *pobi*, for instance, refer to the *sezemabidi*, bush-spirits who live in the trees, are expert axmen, and use old-style axes. Others allude to the supposed ability of the *dasyurus* (marsupial cat) to regenerate its tail, the legendary association of Souw with sago-processing, and the rule of mother-in-law avoidance.

As the foregoing examples indicate, the whole of a metaphor need not be verbalized; part of the meaning may be transmitted by the context or simply encapsulated in abbreviated form as a cultural allusion. Metaphoric relations can, in fact, be entirely nonverbal, as is illustrated in some magical operations involved in the learning of language. These employ objects that are brought into contact with the mouth and that may be passed from person to person in a reciprocal fashion, to metaphorize the reciprocal oral activity of speech. One of these is the bamboo tobacco pipe, which is ordinarily passed around in the course of any conversation; Daribi say that the sharing of a pipe can lead to the sharing of a language, in that those who know the language blow wind from their throats into the pipe, and others inhale this and can learn the language easily.

Another technique is based on the use of *hoborai* leaves; the large leaves that grow near the top of this vine are often folded into makeshift drinking cups. A man who knows the language folds the leaf into a cup and drinks from it; someone who wishes to learn the language then takes the leaf from which he has drunk, folds it inside out, and drinks from it. Then the man who knows the language takes *megebora'* leaves and shakes the water that has collected on them onto the skin of the man who wishes to learn it, and this allows him to learn it quickly. The mediating element here is water rather than breath; the sharing of the leaf-cup parallels the sharing of language, and in the inversion of the leaf, the inside of one man's drink becomes the outside of the other's, so that the fabric of the leaf separates the two, as the knowledge of the language "separates" the two men. In the act of sprinkling water, the man who knows the language mediates the separation by bringing water directly into contact with the skin of the other, and thus structuring the two "separate" discourses.

In the examples discussed thus far, we have seen how the metaphoric link brings two separate fields into alignment, structuring their inter-

action to provide an increment of power for some activity. Such an alignment, of course, is apt to have consequences for *both* fields involved,
and in some cases the structuring in *each* area yields a result that is
useful to man. This can be seen in the magic that accompanies the
preparation of *husare,* a white, granular poison.[15]

Husare is made from a substance called *beseni,* which comes from a
hole in the ground through which water "boils up," at a place where the
earth has been "cooked" red and hard. Youths and children may not
approach the site, and many men are said to be afraid of it. Those who
do approach it are careful to walk on branches laid down for this purpose. Stinging nettle and *gemiano* leaves are gathered, and the *beseni*
is twisted onto a stick and then fastened in leaves. A rack is made, and
the *beseni* is put on it to dry over a fire made of the leaves of wild taro,
togaro, and kinds of stinging nettles. When the *husare* is finished, it is
put into a small bamboo tube; to do this the hands are wrapped thor-
oughly in bark-cloth, with the leaves of stinging nettle fastened to the
outside. As the tube is being filled, the following *pobi* is recited:

> *Tori   nage   eba   burasagazau*
> Cassowary you hither enclosed-take-come
>
> *Huq nage   e   genage-rage   eba   burasagazau*
> Crab   you   this bamboo-section hither enclosed-take-come
>
> *Ozoguane nage   e   genage-rage   eba   burasagazau*
> [An insect] you this bamboo-section hither enclosed-take-come
>
> *Haza   nage   e   genage-rage   eba   burasagazau*
> Marsupial you this bamboo-section hither enclosed-take-come
>
> *Kibu nage   e   genage-rage   eba   burasagazau*
> Pig   you   this bamboo-section hither enclosed-take-come

Informants claim that this spell is recited in order to "pull" or "sing out
for" various kinds of animals and insects to make the poison "eat" or
"bite" the victim, that is, to align the biting capacities of these creatures
with the deadly effect of the poison. At the same time, according to
Daribi, the mention of these animals aids in hunting them; as the alignment of the animals focuses their capabilities onto the poison, so, by
the same token, the killing powers of the poison are focused back onto
the animals. Some of the animals, especially the pig and marsupials,
seem to have been included primarily to facilitate hunting them; others,
like the crab, which are not hunted, are mentioned purely on account of
their biting qualities.

If the metaphoric alignment of fields can be manipulated to provide
an increment of power for certain undertakings, then an inauspicious or
hazardous alignment of this kind is also possible. We have seen in the
preceding chapter that the food eaten by young male initiates is the
subject of concern and restriction. A series of food taboos, called *webage,*
are imposed to prevent the initiates from eating foods that involve harm-

15. See Wagner (1967), pp. 73-74, for a discussion of its social significance.

ful metaphorical alignments, based on some characteristic of the food plant or animal. The taboo food is called *webage-nai*. Some of the taboos remain in force until the initiate is again permitted to eat food prepared by his mother and the other women of the clan, others until he has married or has children.

The tree-fruit called *wa* takes a long time to ripen, and it is felt that if young people eat it, they will take a long time to grow up. The kinds of marita, or pandanus fruit, called *sobe, bemu, huibe,* and *bogi* are taboo for the same reason.

The birds called *teaburu, pomu,* and *wagari* are forbidden as food because their feathers fall out easily after they have been killed, and it is felt that they would weaken the initiates.

Bower birds, *morobari,* are forbidden because "unlike other birds, they make gardens." If eaten, they might cause the initiates' *horoara,* the hair on the base of their skulls, to fall out, and the *horo* (back of the neck, base of the skull) to be bare, like newly made gardens.

Pa grubs are forbidden because they live inside trees and their origin is unknown and unseen. Initiates cannot eat these until they are married and have children themselves. If eaten before this, they might cause the initiates not to have children, since their own origin is unseen and dubious.

The large constricting snakes called *gura', yowa,* and *pini,* commonly used for food, are forbidden to the initiates because they periodically lose their skins, whereas people do not. Should the initiates eat these snakes, or certain kinds of eels, their faces would be subject to a condition called *a,* or *guni-a,* in which the skin peels off.

In each of these cases, the food species is forbidden to *avoid* the influence of a metaphoric link based on some undesirable characteristic, and this usage constitutes a kind of negative instance of Daribi metaphoric magic. This application of metaphoric relations to magic and food taboos represents, however, but one in a series of such applications within Daribi culture.

DREAMS: THE PERCEPTION OF POWER

When I first came to live among the Daribi, one of the most common explanations given to me to excuse the early-morning absence of an informant was that "he had a dream" and had gone hunting. Generally Daribi men regard a good hunting dream as an opportunity not to be missed, and take immediate action on it. Dreams are usually felt to be prophetic and are often mentioned in myths as revealing some secret or hidden danger to the hero.

Daribi say that the soul leaves the body during sleep, passing out, as at death, through the *borabe,* or coronal suture (or, as some informants maintain, through the nose), and travels about, experiencing the action that we perceive as dreaming. The later return of the soul causes the sleeper to awaken, and if awakened beforehand, he will be dull and drowsy until it arrives. The actions performed by the soul while it is out of the body indicate, according to Daribi, a kind of capability or affinity for certain undertakings, which need only be interpreted correctly after waking to bring results, or knowledge. The ultimate origin of this affinity is obscure, an irreducible fact, like the dream itself; the important thing, insofar as man is concerned, is its interpretation.

This interpretation, moreover, must take place if the dream is to be of any help; a literal acceptance of the content of the dream would be useless. According to one informant, "In my dream I took hold of a woman; now I am able to take hold of a marsupial." If, according to this man, he were to look for the woman in his dream upon awakening, rather than a marsupial, he would not find her. Again, in another example given by my informants, if a man dreams of eels, and "sees their bodies" in his dream, he will not be able to get any if he hunts afterward; he will find eels, however, if he dreams of pandanus fruit, pitpit, or manioc. The interpretation of a dream must involve some transformation of its content, and yet Daribi insist that the content of a dream itself represents the actual experiences of the soul, and not some distortion of them.

The seeming paradox is resolved when we realize that Daribi interpret their dreams metaphorically, and that the kind of affinity or capability revealed by a dream is identical to the personal capacity or power that is believed to result from a successful *pobi;* both represent something additional to ordinary abilities, like luck. The correct interpretation of a dream reveals a metaphoric link between the action experienced in the dream and the successful performance of some other activity, such that the affinity and capacities shown by the soul in accomplishing the former can be successfully brought to bear on the latter. A dream in which a man has sexual relations with a woman reveals a particular, fleeting affinity of his soul that will bring success if applied to hunting, and this is presumably why Daribi leave for the hunt immediately upon awakening.

In their interpretation dreams, like *pobi,* involve a structuring of normally separate "fields" or areas of activity. A *pobi creates* capabilities through the invocation of a metaphor that "pulls" two such fields into alignment, whereas a dream *reveals* capabilities that, through metaphorical interpretation, can be effectively exploited; the former starts with the occasion and works toward capability, the latter begins with capability and seeks an occasion.

Formally, the role of metaphor in dream interpretation is identical with that in magic; a link, or analogy, "controls" the alignment of the two areas. On one occasion Kagoiano had a particularly "good" hunting dream, in which he was trying to have intercourse with a woman, but stopped when he saw that her genitals were bloody, realizing that she was in her period. He explained that "the blood in the dream is the blood that a man sees on his arrow when he has shot a pig." Asked whether the penis in the dream is the same as the arrow, he replied that it was. In another instance, Yapenugiai had a dream in which he went with the wife of Hǎgi, a close relative, and cut her head with an ax, causing it to bleed, whereupon she began crying out for Kagoiano. Taking this as a favorable omen, Yapenugiai took Kagoiano hunting with him when he awoke, and, according to the latter, managed to shoot a marsupial above the eye, "just as he had struck the woman in the dream," so that it bled, and he was able to kill it.

As we have seen in the previous chapter, the flesh of pigs and game animals constitutes a significant part of the wealth that is given in exchange for a woman,[16] and can be seen as a kind of "equivalent" of them. Moreover, hunting is as exclusively a male activity among the Daribi as the man's role in intercourse, and women resemble game in that both are the objects of such activity, and, indeed, both are highly dependent on "luck." Yet, of course, hunting and sex, or any sort of contact with a woman, remain distinctly different areas of activity. Dreams that involve aggressive action toward women or the drawing of blood from them provide highly explicit metaphoric links between these areas and are therefore regarded as "good," or auspicious in applying a "knack" for success in one to the other.

Daribi recognize a series of standardized formula for the interpretation of dreams, some of which are analyzed in Table 3. As in the case of *pobi*, some of these are part of general public knowledge in the culture, others have a more esoteric distribution. The capacities and affinities revealed in dreaming, like those manipulated by *pobi*, pertain to normally unpredictable and unstructured activities, with the difference that the former, which are properties of the soul, refer more to personal, internal skills than to technological abilities. As with magic, hazardous and inauspicious alignments are also possible.

Just as new magic spells may be invented, so the practice of dream interpretation allows improvisation, and here, too, the standardized formulas provide models. Specifically, the interpreter uses his skill in metaphorical construction to discover new, hidden "meanings" in the content of a dream along the lines of existing interpretative paradigms. Details of a dream are searched for possible meaning; "If we dream of a woman of Noruai, we go to the bush around Noruai in the morning to find game; if we dream of a Kurube woman, we search around Kurube." A single dream may in fact reveal a single "message," either in simple or in embellished form, or it may include several unconnected "messages." The latter was felt to be the case in a dream that Kagoiano had as a youth, before the coming of the Europeans.

In his dream Kagoiano was walking with Be'togobo, the wife of a clanmate, and she gave him some sugarcane. Then he went to fight an enemy line, possible Daie. He put on a wooden shield, took bow and arrows and a javelin, and walked along the road. The enemy had set an ambush, and he shot two of them. Then he ran from them, climbed a tree, and flew to another place, where he saw a *sigibe'* under construc-

---

16. Pigs, of course, may be substituted for people in general in the exchange system, and in fact a dream in which one kills a pig indicates that one will kill a person.

TABLE 3:
Metaphoric Dream Interpretation

Subject of Dream	Separate Areas	Metaphoric Link	Capacity
intercourse with white woman	hunting/sex	skin-color, male act	to kill *hweabi* (light cuscus)
intercourse with dark woman	hunting/sex	skin-color, male act	to kill black pig, cassowary
intercourse, with blood	hunting/sex	blood, male act	to kill game animal
killing a woman	hunting/inter-sexual act	killing	to kill pig or cassowary
killing a pig	human/animal	exchangeability	a person will die
being attacked by a pig	human/animal	exchangeability, treachery	to be attacked by *kebidibidi* sorcerer
intercourse with *izara-we*	human/spirit	slimy skin of *izara-we*	to perspire profusely
seeing cassowary	human/bird	association of cassowary with sorcery	to get sick
mere (light) pandanus fruit	animal/plant	food, light color	to kill *hweabi* (light cuscus)
pandanus fruit, pitpit, manioc	animal/plant	length, food	to kill eel
picking breadfruit	animal/plant	similarity to egg, fruit-eating habit	to kill cassowary
picking *dora'* fruit	animal/human	similar habit	to kill *hweabi*
planting sago	human/plant	planting male crop	to beget son
bases of "Job's tears" *(sia)*	human/plant	female mourning attire	to beget daughter
cleaning *hamia* Cordyline	human/plant	preparing male rear covering	to beget son
cleaning *harape* reeds	human/plant	preparing female rear covering	to beget daughter
breaking sugar, cutting bamboo	animal/plant	length, food	to kill small snakes
fruit on vine	human/plant	offspring-seeds	to beget (so many) children
ants	human/insect	massed numbers	to have many children
lake	human act/natural feature	dead live beneath lake	to die
being given a pearl shell	animal/cultural	curls around neck	to kill constricting snake
being given a bottle	animal/cultural	acquiring something	to kill wild pig
striking down breadfruit nuts with pig-arrow, woman gathers them	animal/plant food	use of pig-arrow in gathering, male-female cooperation	to kill many pigs
a woman following one, carrying a *tanket*	intersexual act/domestic chore	obedience, *tanket* as fencing material	woman will take good care of pigs if married
climing to top of casuarina tree, playing jew's harp	music/speech	conspicuousness, performance before audience	to be able to talk much, have much to say
being inside house, unable to look out	concealment/house	secrecy, internal effect	to be poisoned

tion, with no roof as yet. About a quarter of a mile away was another *sigibe'*; he went to it and climbed to the men's quarters, but the door was tied shut. He shouted, asking if anyone was there, and Newi, wife of his classificatory brother Suabe, replied that only women were there. He began to play a bamboo flute, and Newi praised his playing, saying it was very good. He held the flute out in his hands and it played by itself. Then he and Newi went back to the house under construction and saw that there was a lake behind it. Kagoiano suggested that they cross it, but Newi warned him that if he entered it he might die. He walked into it, found that he could walk "inside" the water, crossed it, and pulled himself up via a wild taro plant on the other side. He then crossed back in a similar fashion. He climbed again to the men's quarters and was in the process of climbing down again by way of a vine that was tied to one of the poles, when the pole broke, and he felt himself falling. He awoke to find himself twisting his bark-cloth blanket.

Kagoiano's interpretation of this dream was given to me long after it had occurred, and was undoubtedly influenced by subsequent events. He claimed that his killing of the two enemies and his escape indicated that he would take part in fighting but would emerge unhurt. His flying was perhaps an indication, according to him, that he would travel a great deal. The men's quarters, with the door tied shut, and the presence of his brother's wife below, he took as a premonition of the deaths of his brothers.[17] He conjectured that the flute-playing episode could indicate that he would later become a *porigi wabo bidi* (an articulate person, who "talks much, and has a lot to say"). His passage through the lake indicated perhaps that he would perspire a great deal. The "transformation" of objects in a dream into mundane, familiar items experienced by a sleeper upon awakening, exemplified here by the vine in the dream and Kagoiano's bark-cloth blanket, is a matter of great interest and curiosity for the Daribi. Possibly this is because it provides a kind of corroboration for the metaphoric effect of dreams by actually demonstrating a "transformation." Kagoiano once had another dream in which his dead brother gave him an item of wealth, which he clutched in his hands. He awoke holding it and went excitedly to blow on the fire; when the flames sprang up he saw that he had merely dislodged a piece of wood from his sleeping-place.

In some cases, the "transformed" material that "accompanies" the waking dreamer is identified with the metaphoric link governing the effect of the dream. Kagoiano often dreams of the *izara-we*, or underground women, and regards his dreams as a source of knowledge about them. These women are believed to live without men; their skins are said to be very slippery, coated with a whitish substance like soapsuds or saliva. In one dream, again before European contact, Kagoiano

---

17. The deaths of his classificatory brothers (patrilateral half-brothers and first cousins), which occurred in rapid succession, but in various ways, has always been a matter of puzzlement to Kagoiano. They formed a dominant political faction, and their deaths caused a major shift in political control, which was not to Kagoiano's advantage.

encountered an *izara-we* whose skin exuded a peculiar, unpleasant odor. She asked him to sleep with her, indicating that he should lie in the passageway. She sat in the sleeping-place, and he wanted to come near her, but she kept moving away. Kagoiano then awoke, his skin all wet and slippery, and began to blow on the fire. His classificatory brother Suabe was also awake, blowing on the fire, and Kagoiano told him his dream and said that he could still smell the skin of the *izara-we* Suabe brought him a tube of water and told him to drink and rinse his mouth. Kagoiano claims that if he had not rinsed his mouth he would now perspire profusely.

Certain individuals are recognized by the Daribi as good dreamers (*na-iai-bidi*), persons gifted with a talent through the perceiving of power.[18] Some of these are specialists who possess a particular skill revealed to them in dreaming. A man who has removed the bark of *gorogobe* or *hogobiai* trees, which have oil beneath the bark, in his dreams, is often asked to remove the flaking skin and juices of decomposition from a corpse that is being mourned. A man who has seen in his dreams where a dog has hidden an animal it has killed is selected to hold the pole used in divination for *kebidibidi* sorcery,[19] for the pole first leads to the place of killing, and the ability to trace the route of the carnivore in a dream is believed to confer a particular efficacy in following the trail of a human killer. Other *na-iai-bidi*, such as Kagoiano, are felt to have a more generalized ability to foresee future potentialities in their dreams.

The information revealed by such a dreamer is often invested with considerable significance, and his reputation is doubtless established by a series of particularly portentous, or perhaps cleverly edited, dreams. When his line was living at Suguai, Kagoiano had a dream in which Tạre's wife had killed a small pig, and he came to her and said, "You killed this pig, now you cook it." She replied "I killed it, but I can't cook it; you said I should cook it." Then he asked where Tạre was, and she answered that he was nearby. When he awoke, Kagoiano told this dream to Tạre's wife. The next day her baby died, and Kagoiano said to her, "See, I told you my dream." Then he asked where her husband was (to tell him to make a grave), and she replied that he was nearby. Later Tạre's wife, disturbed perhaps by the sense of *deja vu*, was angry with Kagoiano and accused him of having killed her child, but he rejoined that he had merely dreamt the death. To protect her other (and future) infants from the purport of his dream, however, Kagoiano then threw water from a bamboo tube onto her daughter Aị; once this was done, the child could no longer be hurt by the dream, because it had

18. Wagner (1967), p. 49.

19. See Meggitt's remarks on "dreamers" among the Mae Enga, where the significance of dreams and the mode of their interpretation are strongly reminiscent of Daribi practices ("Dream Interpretation among the Mae Enga of New Guinea," *Southwestern Journal of Anthropology* 18, No. 3 [1962]: 220). Unlike Meggitt, I found no particular correlation of dreamers with "big" or elderly men.

been made known. (According to Kagoiano, the water in the tube "hears" the talk of the dream through the mouth of the tube, and carries the knowledge onto the skin of the child.)

On a later occasion, Kagoiano had a dream concerning Pewai's daughter, whose offer of marriage he had refused on the grounds that her father had become a clanmate. In Kagoiano's dream a *neru* vine in her garden bore small fruit that fell to the ground, whereas a vine in his garden had two fruit that stayed on the vine and ripened. He interpreted this to mean that if the woman went to another man, her children would all die (young), whereas if she came to him, her children would live, and that in any case he, Kagoiano, would have two children who would live. (He pointed out to me, as partial confirmation, that his daughter Maruwe had not died in infancy.) When Pewai's daughter married and had a child, Kagoiano went to her and told her of his dream, and threw a tube of water on the child. Again, as in the previous example, this act protected the child and any possible later siblings by making the dream known. Kagoiano claims that he will later ask the mother for compensation for his services.

A dreamer is valued because of his ability to perceive power, or capability, which is revealed to him through a metaphoric link between two experiential areas, and would otherwise remain unknown.[20] In the examples just cited, Kagoiano was able to anticipate the potentiality of two women to lose their children through dreaming of the pig and the *neru* vine in association with them. Although the women were specifically identified in the dreams, their children were not, and thus the potential danger extended to all children of these women. In order to protect them, the dream and its interpretation, embodying the metaphoric link, had to be made known to the children and their mothers. Had this not been done, the danger would remain an unknown potential.

The talents and skills involved in a number of craft specialties, including the decoration of arrow-shafts, the making and playing of bamboo flutes, and the weaving of belts, armbands, and string bags, are all thought to be acquired in dreams. Of course, anyone can try to learn these techniques, but real talent, like hunting luck, can only represent something additional to ordinary effort, and must be obtained through a dream. Thus a Daribi who sees a badly decorated arrow-shaft will conclude that "this man did not have a dream." Like the contents of dreams themselves, the motifs employed in these crafts have a metaphorical character.

---

20. Omens seem to operate on much the same principle. A mistake in speaking, a so-called Freudian slip, is believed to indicate a capacity or capability of doing what the "slip" implies. When a new house is built, fireboxes are slung beneath the floors; first the supporting stick framework is made, banana leaves are put over the sticks, and tree-bark is then laid down. Then a layer of earth is put down, followed by a layer of ashes from the previous house. A fire is then built in the hearth, and banana leaves spread on the ground below. If there is water, particularly discolored water, in the leaves next morning, this means that a man will die in the house (the water represents decomposition fluids); if not, no one will die.

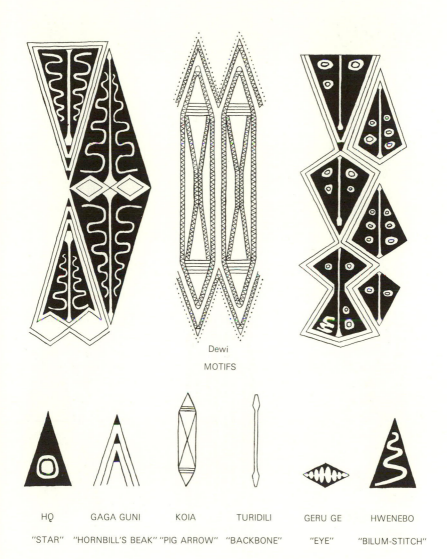

Dewi

MOTIFS

HQ	GAGA GUNI	KOIA	TURIDILI	GERU GE	HWENEBO
"STAR"	"HORNBILL'S BEAK"	"PIG ARROW"	"BACKBONE"	"EYE"	"BILUM-STITCH"

FIG. 1: *Sigaze* motifs and patterns.

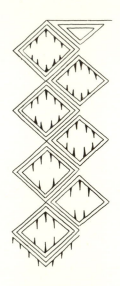

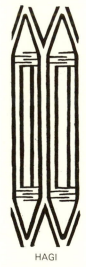

WEBAI   HAGI   IAPENUGIAI

FIG. 2: *Sigaze* patterns.

Daribi call the arrow-shaft decorations *sigi-aze* or *sigaze*[21]; these are incised in the smooth surface of a dried pitpit arrow-shaft, immediately below the tip where the wooden head is inserted, with a marsupial's sharpened tooth. The technique involves keeping a steady pressure on the tool, while moving or revolving the shaft. After cutting, the design is rubbed with a sweet potato leaf, and soot is applied and rubbed into the incisions, producing a black-and-white pattern. A set of standardized geometrical motifs (Fig. 1) are arranged in a wide variety of combinations to produce the complex designs (Figs. 1, 2). The motifs themselves are named abstract representations, with glosses such as "hornbill's beak," "pig-arrow," "star," and "bilum-stitch" (Fig. 1), and thus are partly pictures and partly symmetrical regularities. As such, they take the form of representational metaphors, expressions uniting two different fields of experience (or, as my informants put it, they "imitate something"), as do dreams when correctly interpreted.

When he was young, Yapenugiai did not know how to make *sigi-aze* or to weave armbands; his mother's brother told him that he would have to dream before he could make them effectively. As he was trying to weave an armband afterward, Yapenugiai fell asleep and had a dream in which he walked along a kind of bridge made of spiderweb until he came to the place of a man named Weai, who showed him how to make *sigi-aze* and armbands. Since then, according to Yapenugiai, he has been skillful in these undertakings. There are usually one or more people with this kind of skill in every clan or small settlement, and others bring their arrows to them for decoration, though no payment is asked for this service.

Women, too, must have dreams if they are to weave string bags well; they are taught the skills by the *izara-we* whom they meet in their dreams. Yapenugiai's mother had a dream in which, walking about, she came to the place of an *izara-we*, located in a clearing. Two or three string bags were hanging nearby. The *izara-we* gave her some string, some string bags, some *seza'* (leaf strips used in the process), and a needle with which to make them. Then she showed her the technique of making them, after which, upon awakening, Yapenugiai's mother began making string bags.

The decorative motifs employed in string bags, as well as those used in woven belts and armbands, are stylized, geometrical "metaphors" similar to those portrayed in *sigi-aze;* one string bag pattern is called the "moon-disk," for instance. In the case of string bags, the decorative pattern dictates the working procedure; a spiral design is made in a spiraling sequence. The "star" patterns woven into belts and armbands are even more obviously limited by the techniques (vertical and horizontal woven strips), and, therefore, the dream-revealed procedures, of production. Just as metaphoric dream interpretation brings the capacities

---

21. *Sigi* means "arrow-shaft" (made of a *pitpit* stalk, "*sigi*"), the verb *azebo* denotes the making of incised patterns blacked with soot, and its meaning has been recently extended to include writing and typing.

revealed in dreaming to bear on the occasions of everyday life, so the complex craft techniques of engraving, netting, or weaving, acquired through eccentric encounters (with *izara-we,* etc.) in dreams, resolve into metaphors when turned to the uses of depiction and decoration. The technique is one "field" of the metaphor; perceptible form, represented by the gloss, is the other, and the motif itself becomes the link.

Daribi bamboo flutes, called *ona',* are made of three-foot-long internodes of bamboo, which are open at one end. A small "reed" hole is made near the closed end, and another is made near the open end. The player cradles the closed end on his shoulder, blowing into the "reed" hole, placing a middle finger over the lower hole, and the palm of his other hand over the open end; the sound is modulated by controlling the intensity of breath and by closing or unblocking the two lower openings. *Ona'* are properly played in pairs, in a sort of canonic imitational pattern, each player alternately providing a drone accompaniment while the other echoes the thematic motif. Although smaller, more slender flutes are known, *ona'* are the instruments used in the initiation ceremony, and seem to have been adopted together with the ceremony itself from highlanders at some time in the past.

The flutes are hidden from young boys, and "shown" to them during initiation, when they are expected to try to play them. But it is said that they will only be successful if they have had a dream, which supposedly often happens while they are in seclusion. The technique is learned in the dream; the initiate dreams that he is playing together with a clanmate, and, upon awakening, he seeks out the latter and tries his luck in playing with him. Sometimes the dreamer will also cut and prepare his own flutes. A limited repertoire of thematic motifs is employed, which can be seen as metaphoric in the same sense that representational designmotifs are, for they involve the superimposition of a (dream-acquired) technique upon human oral expression. Flute-calls are sound-metaphors; they combine the articulation of artificially modulated sound, characteristic of speech, with the techniques and acoustic possibilities of the bamboo flute, into a singularly expressive musical form.

Like *pobi* or dream interpretations, the motifs of Daribi flute-playing and craft-representation partake only partially of perceptible reality; they are refracted apparitions, stylized and distorted by the techniques and materials through which they are produced and realized, just as dreams and spells can only achieve their effects through the mediation of two fields. But they also achieve artistic effect through their enigmatic and riddlelike ability to bring technique and object into an esthetic relationship.

THE POETRY OF METAPHOR

Kegena page suguare
Kegena's base moonshone
        —Daribi bạria

In the context of Daribi culture, the distinction between magical power and expressive power is illusory; the facility acquired by the incantation of a spell, the potential realized through a skillful dream-interpretation, and the plaintive effect of bamboo flutes are all additions to the ordinary stock of human capabilities, created through the felicitous use of metaphor. The skill of doing and the facility of saying have metaphor as a common vehicle.

As in the case of magic spells, the metaphors used in Daribi poetry are verbal; they refer to one conceptual area in the context of another, providing a sort of imagistic counterpoint for the latter. But whereas in magic spells the metaphoric link structures capability by "pulling" the two areas into alignment, Daribi poetry uses this relation to control or structure expressive power. The thread of meaning carries the expressive load of a formulation by embodying the relation between the artist's imagery and his subject. Thus metaphor is used to extend the expressive power of language as magic extends the power of human action by projecting its capacities into new realms.

In the quotation at the head of this section, "Kegena's base moon-shone" or "shone as the moon," for example, a metaphor is involved connecting the sheer cliff-face, dead white with limestone outcrop, which haunts the Tua valley near Bumaru, and the shining of the moon. The image assumes a particular eloquence for anyone who has seen Kegena, for its outcrop seems to hang suspended over the valley and the roar of its river, and is seen against dark foliage and an often lowering sky; like the moon's face, that of Kegena is pocked and mottled with dark stains. The lyricism of the passage is especially poignant, too, in that it accompanies a lament for those killed in bitter warfare in the valley, which is the traditional ancestral home of the Daribi. The evocative power of landscape imagery has been typically associated with the poetic traditions of Europe and the Far East, though its currency among tribal societies is probably wider than has been suspected. A brief, piquant reference such as the preceding one, in which the associations of a particular place serve to compress much more into the words than is actually stated, is especially characteristic of oriental verse. Daribi poetry, for whatever reason, also favors this technique, as well as a fondness for landscape. The form recalls not only the terseness of Japanese *haiku*, but also the grand style of Chinese poetry, which for all its richness relies on as simple a skeleton of allusive metaphor.[22]

Daribi call such expressions *baria* or *dobare,* and they take the musical forms of dancing songs, especially those used by women, and mourning chants, or laments, each of which has its own standardized melodic and

---

22. Thus a word-for-word transliteration of the famous couplet by Tu Fu makes good grammatical and poetic sense in Daribi:

war	smoke	blue
boi	*hanu*	*huzhuku*
man	bone	white
bidi	*dili*	*ohai*

verbal idioms. The term *baria* alludes to the real or fancied resemblance of a special vocabulary used sometimes in dancing songs to the language of the Baria people, identified as the Wiru-speakers of Pangia, of whom a group is said to have once lived at Karimui. (Other informants suggested that the language was "Kewa'," the Foraba language spoken to the southwest of Karimui.[23]) Many *baria* of both varieties are traditional, kept alive by memory, but others may be improvised or composed for ·an occasion.

The content of *baria* employed as dancing songs, whether or not improvised on the spot, generally includes some allusion celebrating the occasion. Often, particularly in the case of women's dances, these make use of the vocabulary known as *baria po* ("*baria* talk"), in which, for instance, the word *ue*, ordinarily meaning "vomit," is used as a synonym for "give"; *dina*, which has no ordinary denotation in Daribi, is used for "cuscus" *(phalanger); sora* is used for sago grub; and so on.[24] Thus at the habu ceremony the massed women sing "*dina ma ue*" ("Cuscus now give!") in reference to the smoked game used in the ceremony. At a young men's dance beginning an initiation, a *baria* was improvised proclaming *izara-wego ware menia*, "not the skin of an *izara-we*," referring to a slighting insinuation that the mother of one of the initiates was an underground woman. A more ambitious *baria* is sometimes danced and sung at the habu:

Sizi	*tori*	*paiio re,*	*harogo*	*torigo*	*hoboragi*
Black cassowaries	gone,	[for] brown	cassowaries	to sorrow

iribadi	*weyu meneo re-e-e-e*
they perhaps	work I speak not

"The black cassowaries are gone; brown cassowaries, you have much work, I will hold my peace in sympathy." The black, or mature, cassowaries are the fathers of the present generation; the brown, or immature, cassowaries are the men taking part in the *habu*, whom the women mildly taunt with this song.

Mourning laments are sung over a body day and night as it lies in state, and lamenting is often continued sporadically for weeks or months afterward by aggrieved relatives. The "cry" begins immediately with the news of death, and it frequently has the effect of an almost spontaneous expression of feeling.[25] Daribi sometimes lapse into laments in periods of depression or sentimental recollection.

The style of the laments, like that of the dancing songs, is characterized by an almost telegraphic brevity; standardized allusions are made to the circumstances of the life or death of the deceased, and to

23. I have found no concrete evidence to corroborate either of these suggestions. It may be that Daribi simply intend this to emphasize the strangeness of the language, as in our expression "It's Greek to me."

24. Other substitutions include *haio* for "none," *hwe* for "I don't like," and *kapo kapo* for "run."

25. On the other hand, it seems quite senseless to speculate whether a mourner is "really sincere" or "only shamming"; presumably one could sham for the very "best" of motives, or even sham "sincerely."

the bereaved's relationship to him. A lyrical reference to the country of
the deceased, of his father or mother, is often included, identifying it
through characteristic trees or natural features. This can be seen in the
following lament, in which a man of Noru bewails his brother:

> *Kibu-haza*   *tori-haza*   *torua-serama koabo dogozo*
> Pig-animal cassowary animal   eat-taking   howls [a tree]
> *ama'o*   *ama'o*
> brother-o brother-o
>
> *Karibaii*   *dogozo*   *ama'o*   *bo bo*
> [A tree] [same tree] brother-o
>
>   *Siga*   *iano*   *bidi*   *ogwa*   *ama'o*   *bo bo*
> Breadfruit leaf people's   son   brother-o
>
>   *Siga*   *iano Noru-o*   *ama'o*   *bo bo*
> Breadfruit leaf   Noru   brother-o

The first line of this lament recalls the pleasant days that the singer
spent hunting with the deceased; the howl is that of a hunting dog. The
dogozo, or *karibaii*, tree was said to be characteristic of the deceased's
mother's place. The breadfruit tree is a prominent feature in the landscape around Noru.

In another lament, a woman keens for her dead husband:

> *Buru*   *aze*   *bidi*   *ogwa,*   *hai'*   *ogwa-bidi o bo bo bo*
> Place [of] limestone people's   son,   cross-cousin   youth   o
> *Bidi-o*   *bidi-o*   *bidi-o*
> Husband-o husband-o husband-o
> *Wai'*   *kiri*   *bidi*   *o bo bo*
> Children's father husband
>   *Siga*   *iano*   *bidi*   *ogwa*
> Breadfruit leaf people's   son
> *Burage wanoma bidi o bo bo*
> [A tree] [a cliff]   man

The mention of limestone here alludes to the long ridges, white with
outcrop, that characterize the Noru area, and of which the cliff Wanoma,
near Hobe, is an example; the mention of the deceased man's children
in a "teknonymic" reference adds a poignant touch, for a married pair
with children address each other in this way. Repetition of the "bread-
fruit-leaf" motif in the two laments is typical of the usage in this form.
The possibilities of improvisation within the conventionalized stan-
zaic and rhetorical patterns of this form permit considerable elaboration,
as in the following example. This lament, called *bidi erazama wabo
baria*, the "*baria* that speaks of coming to kill men," was made when
Pebi, of Pobori (Komori) Noru, was killed in warfare against the Foraba-
speakers of Soari Clan, both to bewail his death and to boast of the
vengeance that followed. Because of the richness of allusion, I will

present it with a running commentary.

Bidi dili daninama ho wo-ro
Man bone clawing

Pebi was killed with the characteristic Foraba javelin, tipped with a sharpened, human armbone, like a claw.

Moma ma ho
Moma give!

Mount Moma, a part of Kegena, might be sufficient compensation.

Naba mu, naba mu, hwe-e-e
Head-disk true, head-disk true

Pebi was as the head-ornament of his people.

Kuba kugulibu
Kuba moulders

Kuba was an important warrior of Soạri killed in revenge.

Kuba kugu, Kuba kugu
Kuba rots, Kuba rots

irigo   irigo   irigo o o o
Deceived, deceived, deceived

Kuba and the Soạri brought on the fighting through an act of deception.

Waiba waiba o o wo-ro
[A tree]

The dead Soạri were piled beneath a *waiba* tree.

Degana pobi, degana pobi hwe
Killing magic, killing magic

The Soạri are thought to have worked magic to cause their victims to come unarmed.

Bidirama pare-o
Staying, gone

The Soạri are now dead.

Bidiga ba' wanareo
Lorikeet birds in a line

The dead Soạri laid in lines are likened to red-and-black lorikeets, because of the contrast of red blood and dark skin.

Bidiga ba' pa-are-o
Lorikeet birds gone

The "lorikeets" are dead.

Guni-bazo pareo wo wo-ro
Angry-being gone

The Soạri made "nose-talk" *(guni po)*, or angry talk, and now they are dead.

Yare ba', yare ba' pareo wo wo-ro
Yare birds, *yare* birds, gone

The Soạri are called *yare* birds because they favor the plumage of this bird.

Naba mu, naba mu
Head-disk true, head-disk true

Kuba kugu, Kuba kugu
Kuba rots, Kuba rots

irigo   irigo   irigo
Deceived, deceived, deceived

Pạde ba', pạde ba', wanareo
Close birds, close birds, lined

Many were killed; they are laid in a close line.

Yare ba' wanareo, wo wo-ro
Yare birds lined

The expressive province of the Daribi lament includes all forms of deep sorrow, as death is merely the severest form of bereavement. The other usages expressive of mourning, including self-abasement, covering the body with clay, the wearing of relics, and the amputation of finger-joints, may be similarly invoked. In 1964, in response to a (false) rumor of my imminent departure, two old women of Kurube prepared to go into mourning; and, earlier, a man of Noru, whose favorite pig had been secretly butchered while he was participating in the *habu,* covered his face with mourning clay, hung the pig's jaw around his neck, and walked the footpaths in search of the culprit, crying a death lament as he went.

The following represents an eloquent example of the adaptation of the conventional lament style to an unorthodox theme. It was composed by Kagoiano when he learned that his first wife, after bearing his child, had married another man during his absence at the coast.

Nago idago denege muabe iape paii-hagere piu, nago ena
Your mother's small *muabe* leaves to-go-wishing leave, you me

turiba wabo-iabo
back-to speak-act

Eno aiago siwa iape pinau, eno dano po ware, nage
My father's *siwa* leaves we'll go, my little talk spoke, you

oraredigio
heard-in-vain

Eno aiago sabo-gi tigi tarua si pigisogora, usuigio;
My father's waterfall bank together if-had-gone, it would be well;

kuaibidi we nage dobo-iabo
plateau-people woman you wrong-do

Eno aiago tarua gi-degedu pinau, waredigio, nago ena
My father's together stream-course we'll go, spoke in vain, you me

turiba wa wabo-iabo
back-to bilum speak-act

Nago idago denege muabe pagede ebi-haza izi siripiria,
Your mother's small *muabe* base-at cassowary fire without-sleeps,

sabo-au ego, waredigio, nage ena turiba wa wabo-iabo
thus [we] could, spoke in vain, you me back-to bilum speak-act

Be'bidiwe nage dobo-iabo, ena duagiai po wareda, nago
Clanswoman you wrong-do, I good talk spoke, you

oraredigio Duagiai po waredigi, nago ena turiba wa
heard-in-vain Good talk spoke in vain, you me back-to bilum

wabo-iabo
speak-act

Like the conventionalized dream interpretations and magical formulas, and the sets of geometrical design motifs and flute-calls, the rhetorical devices employed in Daribi laments represent local traditions or "styles" of actualizing metaphoric relations. They constitute limited repertoires, which could presumably be extended or altered by innovation or external influence without noticeably affecting the principles in terms of which they operate. While it is true that they act to constrain or channel the innovative aspects of Daribi culture, they also resemble the artistic, literary, and scientific conventions of our own society in this respect, for even so estimable a pursuit as experimental science must achieve its goals through a limited set of concepts and procedures.

4/ Daribi Naming

*A man is small; when you speak
his name, he is big.*
—Ebinugiai of Peria, Karimui

THE POAI RELATION

The relations embodied in Daribi naming resemble the set of metaphorical relations through which power is structured in that they refer to individual attributes rather than the collective norms and valuations stressed by social ideology. Names are selective and individual; a name distinguishes a person or group from others of the same class, much as the interpretation of a dream or the incantation of a spell is meant to confer success on some particular individual and some specific undertaking. But although both naming and power relations distinguish the individual as against the collectivity of society, they cannot do so in social terms, for social ideology is already committed to the expression of *collective* values. Thus they must necessarily be phrased in terms of "external," impinging elements[1] and take the form of individuating metaphors. In the preceding chapter we have seen how metaphoric relations apply to the structuring of power; now we shall see their significance in terms of identity.

Daribi use the term *poai*, a participle of the verb *poie*, to refer to the relation between persons or objects that share some recognized point of similarity or congruence; persons or objects connected through this relation are said to be the *sabi* of one another. It is often stated that a person resembles his *sabi*, and that *sabi* should help each other. Thus an elderly Daribi acquaintance told me "You shouldn't eat *hweabi* [*Phalanger* species], the *hweabi* is your *sabi*; it has a nose, forehead, and hands just like yours."[2] People and/or animals that share the same skin coloration are said to be *tedeli tigi ware poai*, "one skin congruent."

The *poai* relation also obtains between individuals and the persons, animals, or items for which they have been named, for these at least share the name itself as a point of congruence. The verb *poie* therefore

1. Thus avoiding the predicament presented by the character Major Major in the novel *Catch 22*, in which the Major's personal name(s) happen to coincide with a military rank, which is used much as a name is in address and reference. Major's rapid promotion to Major via bureaucratic error can be seen as inevitable, as such things go.
2. The pinkish skin coloration of Europeans generally suggests to Daribi the pink, hairless skin on the face and paws of the cuscus.

means, among other things, "to name," and those who are *tedeli nogi poai*, "one-name congruent," or namesakes, also stand in the relationship of *sabi* to one another. In this sense the act of naming merely serves to establish or recognize the more general type of correspondence designated by the term *poai;* Daribi naming involves a relation of correspondence between the bearer of a name and its source, and naming itself implies resemblance, just as resemblance or similarity connotes naming.

In a certain sense, all attributes that serve to individuate a person, including his names, affinities, personal characteristics, and details of appearance, can be seen as establishing correspondences that effectively "name" him in a real or potential way. Of course, only a small portion of the vast range of "namings" made possible for any given individual by this system is ever actualized in the form of recognized names, but the totality nevertheless remains, defining a realm of possibilities.

The usages and techniques of Daribi naming have the effect of a selective system, which represents or extends the set of *poai* relations in such a way as to generate identity. A person's names, *nogi,* refer to socially accepted correspondences, *poai* relations, which metaphorize his identity. Like the system of power-relations, the naming system applies a potentially infinite range of metaphorical correspondences to social ends. In magic and dream interpretation, certain advantageous alignments are selected out of a vast range of potential ones by explicit metaphorical means in order to generate or realize individual skill or power. The naming system likewise uses a variety of techniques to produce metaphors, whose metaphoric link, the *poai* relation, represents a person's identity.

The fact that both power and identity systems are structured in metaphorical terms explains why *sabi* should "help each other." *Sabi* are separate individuals, each with his own needs and abilities; the point of congruence that unites them forms a metaphoric link, like that which aligns the separate "areas" of a magic spell, and just as the "controlling" effect of the latter adds the capabilities of one area to those of the other, so the social relationship between human *sabi* prescribes their cooperation. Through the *sabi* relationship, the capacities of one individual may be brought to bear on the needs of another.[3]

As in the system of power-relations, there are essentially two ways in which metaphorical structure can be "generated" in the system of identity. Names can be simply created or imposed, constituting an "addition" to the situation similar to the metaphor that is invoked in a *pobi,* or they can reveal or recognize some attribute of the individual that already exists as a personal trait or an event that coincided with his birth, in the way that dream interpretations serve to reveal and apply

3. My own *sabi,* a friendly, obliging man named Hori, of Meyo, made use of his specific, native capacities to tie up a bundle of arrows that I had purchased so that their points wouldn't be broken. I, in turn, made use of my specific European capacities to provide Hori with some Australian coins.

some innate capacity. Of course, the *poai* relation remains the same, regardless of whether it is imposed or merely recognized, as the "power" acquired in magic is indistinguishable from that revealed in dream-interpretation. As a metaphoric construct, the *poai* relation invoked in naming can serve to "carry" expressive meaning, in much the same way as the metaphors occurring in *bǫria*.

In those instances where a name is imposed on an individual, the metaphor that names him is *created* simply by applying the name of some plant, animal, or other cultural element to him, thus generating a new *poai* relation. Often a parent or some other close relative will choose a "good" name, representing some brilliantly colored bird, popular animal, or sturdy or useful plant or tree, and bestow it on a child to metaphorize a certain kind of excellence. Exotic names, including those borne by members of foreign cultures or words taken from pidgin English, are often selected because of their association with strange-ness and adventure, with Europeans, or with the ideology of progress disseminated by the Administration.

Names "inherited" from a deceased relative, or bestowed in honor of a living person, also have the effect of creating a new *poai* relation, but here the relationship between human *sabi* takes precedence over that verbalized by the name itself. In such cases Daribi say that one is *aga sabi ma poai*, "named again after his *sabi*," so that the bird, plant, or other element signified by the name is actually used as a means by which the relationship between the two people is metaphorized. Of course the *poai* relation between the holder of such a name and the element that it designates always remains in force, but after the name itself has been passed from person to person the reason for its original bestowal is often forgotten, so that the social "value" that it acquires outweighs the metaphoric significance of its content. Such names be-come treasured possessions, passed on as social "heirlooms," and form a "pool" analogous in some ways to the limited sets of "given" names employed in our own culture.

In cases where the bestowal of a name recognizes or reveals an already existing *poai* relation in the form of a personal attribute, the metaphor that names a person is merely developed from that attribute. Almost any one of a potentially infinite range of personal traits or affini-ties, or incidents with which one has been associated, might theoreti-cally be utilized as the basis for a name. In practice, however, names of this sort tend to be selected from fairly standardized series of charac-teristics, or chosen according to some conventional technique.

Names based on personal appearance often refer to skin color, body size, or other outstanding characteristics. Many Daribi are "named" by unusually light skin ("peeled," "red-skin," "light-fellow") or dark skin ("soot man," "dark"), or by tall or short stature ("long-man," "big-fellow," "tree-stump," "pearl shell–fragment," "short-cut"). The name *yape*, "leaves," or "foliage," is often given to persons with "bushy"

heads of hair; *awidili*, "pitpit-bone," is reserved for those with a delicate bony structure, and names like "dirty" and "big-belly" are often
encountered. Behavioral characteristics, or evaluations based on them,
are also used to name people, giving rise to names like *popara*, "talka-
tive," or *pobaze*, "left-handed," as well as *duagi*, "good," *dobo/gwa*,
"bad/fellow," or *dwai/gwa/we*, "worthless/fellow/woman."

An event that coincides with the birth of a child is often used to
name it, so that the metaphoric link is "given" by the simultaneity of
the two occurrences. Thus in many cases a Daribi is named for a particular species of bird whose cry was heard at the time of his birth, or given
a name that represents such a cry phonetically. Others are named for
the species of tree beneath which birth took place, and one girl was
named *Hweaba* because two birds were seen to be fighting near a leaf
of this name at the time of her birth. The name *buipage* ("fight-base")
or *bui/we* ("fight/woman") is sometimes encountered, and refers to
warfare that took place at the time of birth. *Ebi/nugiai* ("cassowary/
name") was given this name because his father caught a cassowary in
a snare when he was born, and *Nogorage* ("hand-cut") was so named
because blood from his father's hand dripped on him. The place where
birth occurred occasionally forms the basis for a name; *Kerauburu* ("cold
place") was born on the ridge Kuraru, *Sai* ("sago") was born in a sago-
processing shelter, and a girl, *Gizugame* ("laughable"), was born in the
sight of many men.

The event that "names" a child may also be one that occurs in a dream
experienced by a parent. *Komeage* was named after a mountain that her
father saw in a dream, *Sere/we* ("root/woman") was so named because
her father dreamt of aerial pandanus roots, and *Wari* ("wind") was
named when her father encountered wind in a dream. The role of
dreams in creating metaphors here resembles that which they play in
the perception of power; in a sense the father "perceives" a name in
the circumstances of his dream that is later applied in the context of
naming his child. A somewhat analogous technique of divination is
based on the child's own perceptive abilities; the mother will ask the
child to bring her a certain object, and if it recognizes the object and
brings it to her, the child will receive the name of the object. It was in
this way that Kagoiano received his name, for he brought his mother the
leaf *(iano)* of a certain variety of bamboo *(kago)*.

A Daribi name consists of a relation between an individual and some
other element, and the techniques through which names are selected
also permit the expressive exploitation of this relation, so that a person
can be said to be "named" by an act of expression. Like the metaphors
that characterize *bqria*, those of Daribi naming are capable of conjuring
rhetorical meaning and power; the naming relation becomes a vehicle
for the expression of a situation, which is then objectified as a person's
identity. A name may consist of pure imagery, like the designation *yape*
for a bushy-haired individual, it may embody a relation between the

living and the dead, as in the case of "inherited" names, or it may convey the plight of its holder, his parents, or his "line."

The name of a characteristic tree species, river, or landform may be given to a child, usually in a spirit of sentimental recollection, to memorialize the home country of its mother, or, perhaps, its father. Names of this sort recall the similar naturalistic allusions employed in mourning-laments. Rivers and mountains are especially favored in the naming of girls. The name *saburai,* "distant limestone," referring in a generalized way to a prominent limestone outcrop, is also typical of this usage, which metonymizes the sorrow of separation.

Names that constitute oblique references to the deaths of relatives, and hence expressions of sorrow, have been termed "metonymical sorrow-names" or *penthonyms* by Strathern in his analysis of Wiru naming practices.[4] Such names occur among the Daribi, but are by no means as common at Karimui as Strathern has reported them to be among the Wiru, possibly because Daribi prefer to "pass on" the name of the deceased directly.[5] The name *sau* ("ravine"), held by an acquaintance of mine, thus refers to the death of his mother's sister, for the entrails of the pigs killed on that occasion were thrown into a ravine. Likewise the name *dani* ("finger") memorializes the death of a sister with reference to the severing of a finger in mourning, and a small girl was named *Duagi* ("good") because her patrilateral cross-cousin, who died, had been well-behaved.

A related practice "names" the individual for the plight of his sibling-group, or "line." Thus a man named his daughter *Dorai* (a kind of mush-room) because, as he put it, his children had died "as mushrooms disappear," and a synonym for "slippery," *berege, genaga/me,* or *penaga/me,* is often used to name a child by mothers whose other children "slipped" from their grasp. Names like *to̜* ("earth") and *puberai* ("buried") are often given to commemorate the extinction of one's siblings.[6] Names such as *siazabo* ("he finishes"), *sirai* ("finished"), and *derigwa* ("single-fellow") express the situation of a "sole survivor" directly, and only implicitly allude to the deaths of others. These particular designations accrue generally to grown men as cognomens, as, in the course of events, they are "named" by the dying-off of siblings or lineage-mates. The fate of a lone survivor is not often a particularly pleasant one in societies of this kind.

4. A. J. Strathern, "Wiru Penthonyms," in *Bijdragen tot de Taal-, Land-, en Volkenkunde* 1 (1970).
5. Thus Strathern reports that "sorrow names" constitute fully 65 percent of the naming-instances that he recorded. (Ten percent of this figure represents "direct-succession" names.) This figure exceeds, but nevertheless approximates, that which I recorded for "inherited" or "direct-succession" names among the Daribi (to be quoted in a later section of this chapter).
6. In some cases, a name may be given *to avert* the fate of the bearer's siblings. Thus a woman of Peria gave her sons "good" names, and they died, and when her last son was born she thought "I will give him a bad name," and called him *ore* (a ground-dwelling insect). This practice suggests the similar "sacrifice" of cutting off the finger-joint of an infant whose siblings have died to substitute the finger for the whole child.

A child may also be "named" by the infanticidal intentions of a parent at birth, so that its identity expresses the emotions and actions engendered by its arrival.[7] Daribi feel that the newly born do not have souls, and the practice of male as well as female infanticide is common. *Huǫbere* ("ashes") was "named" when his father, angry with his mother for bearing a boy, threw ashes on the two of them; the father of *Pagane* ("pig-arrow") said, "We didn't get a girl, we got a boy; let's shoot him with an arrow," and named him. Names such as *sawai* ("thrown away"), *giziga/me* ("finished, but thrown away"), and *pina-ia,* or *pinawai* ("kill it") are common, especially among women.

The fate, or the plight, of a parent at the time of birth may also "name" a child. In effect, the parent expresses his plight, which can be said to "name" him, by "passing it on" in the form of a name to his child, who thus objectifies, and becomes the *sabi* of, the infirmity.[8] A series of names represents the injury of parents in this way, including *nigorai* (*ni-go-erai*, "struck by a tree"), *hwǫgo-erai* ("struck by an ax"), *kibugo-nai* ("bitten by a pig"), and *tṵre-erai* ("killed by the road"). A girl was named *Kuruba'* (a leaf plant) because her mother claimed she had no decent food at the time of birth, and had to subsist on *kuruba'*. A man named his daughter *Auwa/we* (for a variety of sweet potato) to protest his wife's preparation of a despised variety of food, and a series of names signifying "unripe," "uncooked," or "unpalatable" testifies to the popularity of this practice. More poignantly, a much-married woman named her daughter *Bazi/be* ("ginger-name") to metaphorize her situation with the thought "What am I, a hot plant like ginger, that men should all loose me?" Another woman used a punning warning to her husband, a fingerless leper who liked to fight, to name her child; she called him *Eregobe* ("You shall not in future fight!"), which is also the Daribi phonetic approximation for "helicopter," creating a metaphor of flailing arms and rotors.

In keeping with the metaphorical nature of Daribi names, the name given to a child often registers the strongest affective influence occurring in the circumstances of its birth or early childhood that could be seen as "marking" it by drawing it into a relationship. There is always *some* expressive content to a name, although this content may be effectively "hidden" by the metaphor, and its original significance may be lost as the name is passed on. At the same time, of course, names are markers of identity, so that the *poai* relation merges the significance of naming

7. Daribi names referring to the act of naming itself, such as *poie* ("to name"), *poziawai* ("unnamed"), or *bidi/wai* ("person-spoken" or "name-sake"), name a child by expressing the relation between the child and this name itself, so that the form of the name becomes its content. A child is thus named by the act of its being named, or not named. This kind of name can also be an expression of parental actions and emotions toward the child. See D. J. Ryan, "Names and Naming in Mendi," *Oceania* 29 (1959): 109–16.

8. This usage also correlates with the use of teknonymy among parents of a newly born child, who become the *sabi* of the child and each other. Should one of them also be "named" in some other fashion, this "name" could be shared among the others. The name of an infant names the parents as well.

with that of expression; as a metaphor, it can simultaneously accommodate capability (as in the *sabi* relationship), expression, and identity. Although differential circumstances may accentuate one or another aspect of a name, the over-all effect is to transmute the valuations, griefs, joys, and humor of a people into objective designations that "stand for" them, so that the content of life is not wholly lost, and what they *feel* becomes, in a sense, what they *are*.

Because Daribi naming generates *identity* out of the congruences of the *poai* relation, thus representing partial similarity socially as total similarity, it follows that *sabi* should indeed "resemble one another," as Daribi say they do, and also that *sabi* should share *all* of their names. This sharing obtains among human *sabi* as well as between a person and the element that his name designates. A man who is named for the marsupial called *hǫgi*, for instance, is also named *piba*, another term for the same animal, and both are equally his names. For the same reason, a man named *mara*, for a kind of banana, is also named *digaze*, and a man who is named for the tree called *tobaruai* is also named *gibuani*. Likewise a man who is named for several distinct elements, a bird, perhaps, and a tree, may share both names with a human *sabi*, or, when he dies, pass both of them on to the child who is named for him. Thus in a single house at Daie Clan I found two young men, both named *Sorouw/ nugiai* (a kind of grass) as well as *Kanama* (a synonym for *sorouw* grass), and *Pigibidi* ("gun-person").[9] Words are only incidental to names of this kind, which are actually verbally indicated correspondences between a person and an element or between two people *via* one or more such elements.

Just as Daribi names metaphorize identity through the correspondence between person and element, so the name itself, through its implications or associations, may generate further correspondences as additional ("small") names. A man named *Ebi/nugiai* ("cassowary/ name"), for instance, is also called *Buru/bidi* ("bush/person"), because carrowaries live in the bush. *Bunu* ("bee") is called *Gibu/bidi* ("forest/ person"), because bees live in the forest, and a man named *Kụ* ("harpy eagle") is called *Bunu* because these birds allegedly eat bees. Small names are also created by puns or plays on the sound-value of words... A man called *Do* (a kind of bird) is also called *Tesogo* ("that time"), since *do* also means "yesterday" or "tomorrow." Bilingual puns are particularly common, as pidgin loan words are likely to be assimilated into Daribi as homonyms of existing words. Thus *pusi* (a kind of tree) forms a pun with *pusi* or *puskat* ("cat"), so that a boy named *pusi* is often called "*kat*."

Whatever the devices used to generate or elaborate it, and however it functions as a vehicle of expression, the *poai* relation retains its nature as a correspondence, allowing Daribi to metaphorize the diversity of human attribute and experience through the imagery provided by their

---

9. The two were distinguished, insofar as this was necessary, by patronymics.

Table 4:
Daribi Name Referents

Category	No. of Names	Male			Female			Total		
		Trans.	Given	Total	Trans.	Given	Total	Trans.	Given	Total
Exotic Names	98	10	86	96	5	62	67	15	148	163
General Attributes	36	18	16	34	8	7	15	26	23	49
Personal Traits	27	21	10	31	8	13	21	29	23	52
Expressive Names°	34	29	13	42	10	20	30	39	33	72
Valuative Names	12	7	7	14	7	8	15	14	15	29
Attire and Ornament	24	3	4	7	21	15	36	24	19	43
General Cultural Objects	29	13	16	29	9	8	17	22	24	46
General Natural Objects	44	15	9	24	24	24	48	39	33	72
Human Body Parts	20	12	7	19	4	6	10	16	13	29
Kinds of People	9	7	4	11	1	2	3	8	6	14
Diseases	6	5	0	5	3	1	4	8	1	9
General Tree Parts	12	8	3	11	4	6	10	12	9	21
Place Names	43	7	10	17	17	23	40	24	33	57
Nizizibi°°	124	67	77	144	27	55	82	94	132	226

Nizimeniaizibi***	88	30	12	42	42	68	110	72	80	152
Domestic Plants	78	25	18	43	31	58	89	56	76	132
Wild Plants	196	108	50	158	63	87	150	171	137	308
Total	880	385	342	727	284	463	747	669	805	1474

*Including names referring to death, lineal situation, infanticide, fighting and poison, the giving of names, casualties, speech, and food qualities.

**Literally, the "hair lineage"; animals with hair, fur, or feathers.

***The "hairless lineage"; animals without hair, fur, or feathers.

world. We have seen earlier how names that are "passed down" as social heirlooms over the generations tend to "dilute" the metaphoric significance of their content through being used primarily to express social continuity. The inverse of this situation occurs often in Daribi stories when the hero, drawn by his destiny to some ultimate contradiction, renounces his identity by "collapsing" the *poai* relation and turning into the bird, plant, or insect for which he was named or with which he was associated.

DARIBI NAMES: FORM AND CONTENT

Daribi have anywhere from one to three or four names *(nogi)*; a child will generally have only one unless several have been passed on to it by way of single, deceased *sabi*, or unless it has been "named" more than once. As they grow older, men in particular tend to acquire more names as a consequence of the development of distinctive traits of personality or appearance, or through associational "plays" on existing names. Such "acquired" names are known as *pagerubo nogi*, or "basing" names, in contradistinction to those that have been formally bestowed. Although new names may be acquired, the original ones are never really dropped; they may still take precedence, or may simply fall into disuse. A name, given in childhood, which has lapsed in this way, is sometimes spoken of as a *bu nogi* ("infant name"), though Daribi recognize no special category of children's names. Apart from such distinctions, there is no native typology for names.

Because their names are drawn from the lexicon of everyday experience, Daribi explain that special verbal "markers" are used to distinguish the person who is named for a particular object or element from the object or element itself. These markers take the form of suffixes added to the ordinary words employed in naming. They are by no means always used, and they are to some degree interchangeable, although there are certain general regularities in their application. We can distinguish several series of markers. Those that refer simply to the fact of naming include /*nugiai* (an adjectival derivative of *"nogi"*), /*be*, /*bai*, /*ba*, /*ma*, and /*a*, and tend to be used with words denoting objects or species, especially in the case of men's names. Sex-specific markers include /*gwa* (a contraction of *ogwa*, "boy" or "son"), and /*bidi* ("man" or "person") for males, and /*wegi* ("girl" or "daughter"), /*we* ("woman"), and /*(a)me* (or /*(n)ame*) for females. In the case of males, these markers are usually combined with words designating qualities, whereas their female counterparts are used with most other types of designations as well. Markers referring to the act of speech such as /*boro* ("I speak of…") and /*wai* or /*ware* (participial and perfective forms of the verb "to speak") are most commonly used with names given in reference to the act of naming itself, such as *pozia*/*wai* ("unnamed"), but can occur elsewhere. Ordinary grammatical suffixes may also act as name-markers, as in the case of /*ai* (an adjectival-participial suffix), /*aie* (the infinitive suffix), or /*ebo* (the third-person suffix); the specialized inflections given by these forms somewhat tend to remove the stems used in naming from the context of ordinary discourse.

We have seen in the previous section that Daribi draw upon the imagery of their lives and surroundings in the formation of names. Quite apart from our analysis of the name as relation, and of its bestowal, then, we can inquire as to what lexical areas are favored in naming, and whether there is any tendency toward sexual association or specialization in the choosing of names. Table 4 shows the results of a naming census carried out among the pre-adult populations of 23 Daribi clans,[10] as organized into rough topical categories. The columns of male and female names, as well as the totals, are subdivided, listing names that have been "transmitted" or "passed on" and those directly given both separately and as a combined total. Insofar as men's names are generally passed on to other males, and women's names to females, the fact of transmission need not seriously affect our result. The census includes all children born to the present adult generation, many of whom died after being named, though in almost all cases only one name was given per child, so that the instances listed here are virtually all separate namings.

A total of 880 names were employed in the 1,474 namings, yielding an average of one name per about 1.8 individuals. A slight majority, about 55.2 percent of the names, and 55.5 percent of the namings, involves natural species. The remainder includes exotic names, personal attributes, parts of human beings or natural objects, place names, and generalized natural and cultural items. Exotic names (drawn from pidgin or other languages), as well as those referring to generalized attributes, personal traits, expressions of death, generalized cultural objects, human body parts, kinds of people, and furred or feathered animals, tend to be given to males. Names referring to attire and ornament, generalized natural objects, place names, hairless animals, and domestic plants tend to be given to females. In part, at least, these tendencies can be seen to reflect the cultural specialties of the sexes, for it is men who come into contact with exotic cultures, speak pidgin, develop and flaunt personal traits, and hunt marsupials and birds, whereas women are distinguished by net bags and bark-cloaks, frequently wear their husband's pearl shells, fish, and are associated with gardening. (It is significant in this light that 68.1 percent of the names for tree species in our sample were given to men.)

The tendency toward sexual association in Daribi naming can be demonstrated more effectively through a detailed breakdown of instances. Table 5 lists the names in our sample that refer to the Daribi

10. The sample includes whole clans in order not to involve the prejudiced selection of individuals. The clans, in turn, comprise two large, noncontiguous blocks, representing respectively the Daribi of the Karimui Plateau and those of the adjacent limestone country. The clans are: Kurube, Noruai, Kilibali, Sizi, Soboro, Haubidi, Karuwabu, Daie, Maia, Siabe, Waime, Hwea, Irage, Sogo (Di'be'), Sogo (Waramaru), Kebu, Sau Hobe, Nabi Hobe, Hoia Hobe, Pobori, Wazo, Tane, and Hagani. A sample taken among adult males in these clans parallels closely that given here for male children.

categories *nizizibi* (furred or feathered animals) and *nizimeniaizibi* (hairless animals); in each case, the category is subdivided into its constituent subcategories, as recognized by Daribi (though no designation was found for "insects"). As we have seen above, males are more often

TABLE 5:
Sexual Association in Daribi Animal Names

Category	Male	Female
Nizizibi ("hair lineage")		
Haza (marsupials)	26	15
Boro (rats)	3	6
Kibu (pigs)	2	0
Yowi (dogs)	3	1
Bogwa (bats)	1	2
Aru Ba' (decorative birds)	17	3
Tǫ Ba' (ground birds)	2	21
Oro Ba' (other birds)	90	34
Total	144	82
Nizimeniaizibi ("hairless lineage")		
Yogwa (lizards)	2	5
Gereli (frogs)	1	39
Hazamani (snakes)	8	3
Ai haza (fish, eels)	4	16
(insects)	27	47
Total	42	110

named for creatures in the *nizizibi*, females for those in the *nizimeniaizibi*.[11] Within the former, marsupials *(haza)* and birds *(ba')* form important naming series. Whereas male names predominate in both cases, a significant distinction can be drawn between decorative birds, used for personal ornament, which are almost exclusively devoted to male names, and "ground birds" (those that, as Daribi say, "make gardens"), which are largely restricted to female names. Within the *nizimeniaizibi* four significant naming-series emerge, those of frogs, "stream animals" (fish and eels), insects, and snakes, of which the first three are largely devoted to female names and the final one to male names.

Table 6 indicates the consequences of the sexual division of labor for tendencies in naming. As our rough approximation in Table 4 indicated, names involving domestic plants tend to be given to females. Nevertheless, male names predominate by a slim majority in the area of "male crops," although only one significant series, that of pandanus, stands out. Within the area of "female crops," series referring to sweet potato, pitpit, leaf-plants, and ginger appear, the last three of which are important sources of female names.

11. This contrast parallels the cosmological opposition by which males are associated with upper regions and trees (where most birds and marsupials live) and females with lower regions, ground crops, and fishing.

TABLE 6:
Sexual Association in Daribi Domestic Plant Names

Category	Male	Female
Male Crops		
Ta (bananas)	1	2
Waia (pandanus)	10	7
Genage (bamboo)	5	6
(tree crops)	2	1
Sogo (tobacco)	4	0
O (sago)	4	3
Total	26	19
Female Crops		
Kare (sweet potato)	4	6
Boru (yams)	0	1
Q (taro)	2	0
Awi (pitpit)	3	10
Keba (leaf plants)	0	24
Gagi (ginger)	0	11
Gabo (sugar)	0	4
Yuyu (maize)	1	3
Total	10	59
Other Crops		
Burugwa (beans)	0	1
Sia (Job's tears)	0	2
Neru (pumpkin)	1	0
Hamia (Cordyline)	2	2
Miscellaneous	4	6
Total	7	11

The tendencies analyzed here are statistical rather than ideal, but in almost all cases they reflect associations that we have encountered elsewhere in Daribi culture. In general, they reveal an inclination to isolate specific natural series as "appropriate" for naming one sex or the other, and Daribi seem to have relied on general cultural associations to guide them in this. But although they approach our own system of "men's" names and "women's" names in a vague, statistical way, the nature of Daribi names as "correspondences" precludes any possibility of their attaining this kind of exclusiveness, for to become largely "male" or "female" a name would have to lose something of its referential objectivity.

NAME-TRANSMISSION

Daribi say that "It is no good if a name dies," and frequently "pass on" the name of a deceased relative to a newly born infant. In so doing they create a *sabi* relationship between the deceased and the successor to his name, thus memorializing the former. A child who is thus "named again after his *sabi*" simultaneously serves as a repository for the name

itself and expresses the sorrow of its former holder's death. Since, moreover, names have two simultaneous properties, objectively designating
elements (birds, trees, etc.) as well as using these designations to metaphorize identity, the two aspects of name-transmission are in actuality
one and the same; the name itself merges with the identities of those
who have held it. Thus a name that is transmitted acquires a social value,
and in its transmission the sorrow of death and parting is expressed
through continuity, just as continuity is achieved only through death
and disruption.

When a Daribi dies, his name traditionally may not be used in ordinary conversation; he is referred to as *te bidi iziare*, "the person who
died," until and unless his name has been given to someone else, that
is, until he has a *sabi*. When a newly born child is named, its parents
must call each other by its name and so become the child's *sabi;* should
the child die, the name is dropped, and one referring to the previous
child is reinstated. (In the event of divorce, all such terms are discarded.)
The wife of Sari thus called my wife *sabi*, because Sari had named his
youngest daughter Sue in her honor, and Sari and his wife were therefore also "named" Sue.

The recently dead and the newly born, those, in other words, who
have just departed from or entered into society and social relationships,
may only be referred to by way of a *sabi*. In the case of the deceased,
this *sabi* is a *successor;* in that of the newly born, the *sabi* are the parents
who shared the intimate task of bringing the child into the world, its
predecessors, so to speak. In both instances the act of succession, to a
name, or to a line, results in a *sabi* relation between successor and pre-
decessor, as in our own designation of a child's namesake as its "god-
parent." The *sabi* relationship between a child and its parents is also
expressed in the reciprocal use of the kin terms *aia* (father-child) and
ida (mother-child) between them. The effect of the name taboo and the
teknonymic usages is to emphasize social continuity by referring to
society's additions and deletions indirectly by way of *sabi* relationships
with intermediaries who represent living or established members.

A technique of indirect allusion, based on the *sabi* relationship between parent and child, is often used among adults to avoid undue
familiarity in addressing or referring to one another.[12] Actual teknonyms
of the form *kiape agaia* ("Kiape his father") may be used, alluding to
any child of a man or woman, or, in the case of a man, a patronym may
be employed. The latter may simply involve the use of a man's (deceased)
father's name in place of his own, or a suffix may be added, consisting,
as in Scandinavian practice, of a possessive and a form of "son," producing forms like *mazaregwa* ("Maza's son"). A patronym is generally
restricted to only one of a man's sons, who may come to regard it as a
"small name"; alternately, some other small name may be used in the

---

12. See Roy Wagner, *The Curse of Souw: Principles of Daribi Clan Definition and Alliance in New Guinea* (Chicago: University of Chicago Press, 1967), pp. 136–37.

same way for indirect designation.

In practice, a fairly high percentage of Daribi children are named for relatives, although by no means all of them survive childhood. Table 7,

Table 7:
Name-Transmission and Relationship

Category		Male		Female		Total	
		No.	%	No.	%	No.	%
Named	patrilateral	233	31.9	206	27.0	439	29.4
for	matrilateral	97	13.3	39	5.1	136	9.5
relatives	other	61	8.4	54	7.1	115	7.7
	Total	391	53.6	299	39.2	690	46.6
Named for nonrelatives		87	11.9	27	3.7	114	7.6
Name given directly		252	34.5	436	57.2	688	46.1
Total		730	99.9	762	100.1	1492	100.3

based on a sample of 1,492 namings,[13] shows that 46.6 percent of the namings recorded represent the "passing on" of relatives' names; 7.6 percent involve the names of nonrelatives (generally selected because of the sound of the name), and the remainder include names that were given directly. There is a stronger tendency to name boys for others, relatives as well as nonrelatives, than there is to "pass on" names to girls. In fact, a slight majority (53.6 percent) of males are named for relatives, whereas a considerable majority (57.2 percent) of females have been named directly. Roughly 30 percent of all namings perpetuate names belonging to patrilateral relatives, and a smaller percentage involves matrilateral relatives; in the former case there is little discrepancy between the rates for the two sexes, whereas in the latter the difference is considerable.

Table 8, which groups the name transmissions in our sample statistically by kin category, indicates why this discrepancy exists. The largest set of namings (46.7 percent) refer to the first ascending or parental generation, and here the tendency is to name children for the "real" and "classificatory" siblings of their parents, those in the categories *aia, na', awa,* and *paba.* With only eight exceptions (1 male, 7 females, 1.2 percent of the total), the names of male kinsmen are passed on to boys, those of female kin to girls. The percentages for parents' opposite-sex "siblings," the naming of boys for mother's "brothers" *(awa)* and that of girls for father's "sisters" *(na'),* are fairly similar; in the case of parents' same-sex "siblings," father's "brothers" *(aia)* and mother's

13. The sample here is essentially the same as that used in the previous section; the disparity in figures results from the fact that glosses for the meaning of names and information as to whom the child was named for, if anyone, constitute separate "bits" of information, and in some cases one was available where the other was not.

"sisters" *(paba)*, the major discrepancy occurs. One-third of all the male name transmissions honor those in the category of father and his "brothers" *(aia)*, whereas scarcely half that figure is represented in the female names derived from mother *(ida)* and her sisters *(paba,* including mother's cowives).

Table 8:
Name-Transmission and Kin Category

Generation	Kin Category	Male		Female		Total	
		No.	%	No.	%	No.	%
Descending	Ogwa	2	.5	1	.3	3	.4
	Wegi			6	2.0	6	.9
Total		2	.5	7	2.3	9	1.3
Ego's (O)	Ama'	60	15.3	40	13.4	100	14.5
	Ape			2	.7	2	.3
	Hai'	17	4.6	7	2.3	24	3.5
	Mene			7	2.3	7	1.0
Total		77	19.9	56	18.7	133	19.3
First Ascending	Aia	133	34.0	5	1.7	138	20.1
	Na'			61	20.4	61	8.8
	Yage	2	.5			2	.3
	Ida			8	2.7	8	1.2
	Paba	1	.3	40	13.4	41	6.0
	Awa	69	17.7	1	.3	70	10.1
	Aware-we			2	.7	2	.3
Total		205	52.5	117	39.2	322	46.8
Second Ascending and Above	Wai'	107	27.4	3	1.0	110	16.0
	Auwa			116	38.8	116	16.8
Total		107	27.4	119	39.8	226	32.8
Over-all Total		391	100.3	299	100.0	690	100.2

This situation can be seen as a logical consequence of the Daribi social system, which enjoins the retention of a clan's male members and the dispersal of its female members in marriage. A woman's same-sex siblings, real and classificatory, are generally scattered through much of the society by the time she has children, whereas a man's clanmates, whom he calls "brother," form a single solidarity with its own traditions. A father perpetuates the associations of that group in passing on the names of its male and of its out-marrying female members. A mother can best identify and represent her own natal group by passing on the names of its males, who comprise an identifiable, though external, entity. Hence it is that a relatively small proportion of girls are named for maternal relatives. A comparatively high percentage of female namings drawn from the grand-parental generation and above partially compensates for the lower rate in the parental generation. Here too the prevalence of patrilateral namings is greater among females than among males (81.0 percent of the women were named for patrilateral *auwa,* 71.2 percent of the men for patrilateral *wai'),* probably for reasons analogous to those discussed above. The namings representing same-sex siblings *(ama'),* also a significant figure in Table 8, generally memorialize older siblings who have died and are thus similar to the "sorrow-names" discussed in the first section of this chapter.

By far the largest set of name transmissions in the sample is that of namings that honor patrilateral relatives, representing 29.4 percent of all namings and 63.6 percent of all name transmissions. These figures correspond with the tendency among members of a clan, who form a solidarity and often a coresidential group, to perpetuate their traditions and associations by passing on the names of those involved in them. This is particularly true of male names, for their bearers, unlike females, usually remain with the clan. Thus every clan retains sets of male names that are handed down from generation to generation and may represent the lineal "founder" of the clan or phratry, like the name *Para* at Sizi or *Garo* at Noru. Figure 3 diagrams the transmission of four names over a five-generation span within a section of Pobori (Komoru) Clan, of the Noru Phratry.

Although names of this sort inevitably come to take on, and to express, a host of local associations and values, and although they sometimes perpetuate the designations of founders of social groups, they do not become the exclusive property of the clans that transmit them as "totemic" names might. A clan's "stock" of names is always changing, as names are shunned as inauspicious because of the early death of their bearers and as new names are added through the death of others. Nor, except on rare occasions, do such names serve as "markers" to distinguish individual groups; Daribi clans are almost invariably designated by the names of their founders, which take their places in genealogical series, punctuating the incidents of procreation and succession.

In the few instances where Daribi clans are distinguished by contrastive names, these involve the opposition of two units in each case (rather than the whole society) and often refer to the incidents of segmentation. The units called Weriai and Yogobo, for instance, trace their separation from a legendary fight resulting from the stinginess of the ancestor of Yogobo, in which the ancestor of Weriai was blinded.[14] Weriai means "blind," Yogobo means "he is greedy." Another sort of opposition contrasts the Di'be clans living at Orogomaru, near the Tua River, with those living on the ridge Kuraru, a spur of Mount Karimui. The former are called Mama'di'be ("light *Di'be*"), allegedly because of their proximity to the "light" river *(mama' ai),* whereas the latter are

14. See Wagner (1967), pp. 197–98.

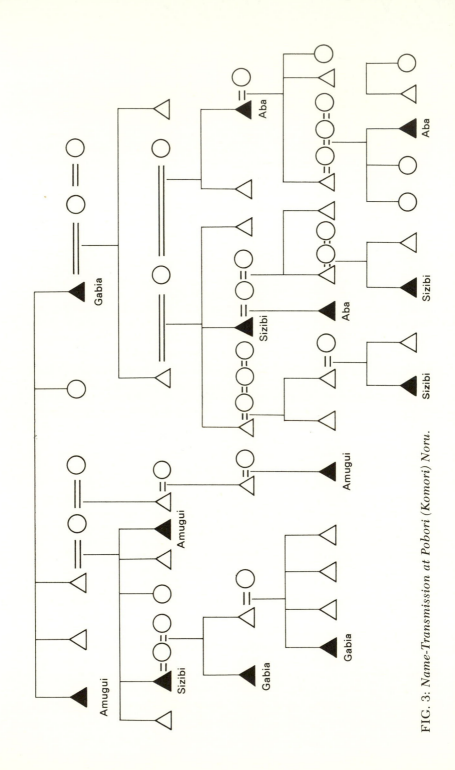

FIG. 3: *Name-Transmission at Pobori (Komori) Noru.*

called Huzhuku ("dark") Di'be, possibly because they live against the "dark" mountain *(huzhuku-buru)*.

The names of Daribi groups, like those of individuals, are developed from incidents expressive of individual associations and proclivities, and not as extensions of preexistent naming-series. Where individual names obtain currency as group "heirlooms," they do so by virtue of further associations—of the name itself with prominent or memorable personalities or incidents—that are "internal" to the group itself. The effect of Daribi name-transmission is to preserve and perpetuate identities as idiosyncracies of the "line" or group, just as identities themselves are generated by the metaphorizing of individual idiosyncracies.

Thus whether we consider individual or group names, and whether we are concerned with the bestowal of names and the relations that this engenders, or with name-transmission, the Daribi naming system emerges as a means through which the individual and the incidental is retained and expressed. As such, it forms the sharpest possible contrast with the collectivities embodied in social ideology, the rules of sharing and equality and the inevitabilities of procreation and death. In this section and in the final section of the preceding chapter we have noted the particular facility with which the metaphorical idiom applies to both the mourning and the transcendence of death. In the chapters that follow, I would like to explore in greater detail the formal means through which this most pressing of all human concerns is conjured and resolved among the Daribi.

2

The Invention
of Immortality

5/Space, Water, and the Dead

Every happy space through
which they move, astounded,
Is child or grandchild of parting.
—*Rilke, Sonnets to Orpheus II, 12*

MACROCOSM

When we consider the human being as a whole[1] rather than as a composite of "elements" or "relations," he becomes an element himself in a wider network of relations, those that distinguish and interrelate various "kinds" of men, including the living and the dead, and human beings as opposed to spirit-people. The individual is cast amid a set of spatial and temporal relationships in terms of which his relations with other beings, and his own life-course together with all the things that bear upon it, become relevant. These relationships are *universalized* in the formulation of norms and ethical codes, which involve the ideal conduct of the human life-course, and also in origin and mortality myths, wherein the characters and plot take on a universal significance.

In our earlier examination of the Daribi origin-stories, we have seen how the establishment of social relationships, the shaming of the hero as an original act of "tempering" the relationship between the sexes, resulted in the curse of human mortality as a reprisal, so that the order of society and the fact of mortality share the same origin. Our analysis stressed the social implications of the account, although society represents only one aspect of its total significance, which concerns man's life-course and his place in the world. Insofar as our present interest is in man's relation to the world and to his destiny, let us briefly consider the Daribi origin accounts in this light.

Regardless of variations in the plot, the central emphasis of the Souw texts is upon human mortality: the irreversible nature of the human life-course and the irrevocability of death. Had the sexually experienced widow responded to the *kaueri's* cry, or had man been able to appropriate Souw's immortal skin before the snakes took it, the result might have been different, but as it is, man must die. The act through which Souw is shamed, which brings about his curse in reprisal, also causes him to wander, to "escape" from his shame, and gives his wanderings,

1. David M. Schneider has introduced the concept of "the whole man" in his writings, beginning with "Some Muddles in the Models" (1965), and his use of it there and in *American Kinship: A Cultural Account* (Englewood Cliffs, N.J.: Prentice-Hall, 1968) have been at least germinal to my application of the idea here.

and his life, direction. In the same way, of course, death and the curse of mortality serve to define man's life-course and give it direction—the span from birth to the grave. In the case of Souw, this directedness takes on a cosmological importance; like Sido in the Kiwai Island tale, and like the great Australian creators of the "dreamtime," his life-course is projected across the countryside, so that its significant incidents become associated with various landmarks. In the course of the story, the temporal order of the plot becomes united with a spatial order, corresponding to the landscape familiar to the Daribi, and it transfers its full universal significance onto this landscape. A cliff or a bend in the river becomes the place where man lost his immortality, and trees, rock-shelters, and watercourses take on a special meaning through association with this and consequent events.

Not only man's life, as a single, bounded destiny with a predetermined end, but also his surroundings, as a definite, identifiable topography, are given meaning by the acts of Souw. The existence of separate spatial and temporal orders is actually illusory, for the topography of his travels is reproduced in the narrative of Souw's adventures, which in turn unites the various features in a single sequence, and the two "orderings" are subsumed in one. From the standpoint of human experience, of course, a temporal interval *is* a spatial interval; time is always expended in moving from one place to another, and it always "passes" in some spatial context, just as space always exists in some temporal sequence. Thus it is largely a matter of representation whether the experiences and life-course of an individual are rendered in spatial or temporal terms or through some combination of the two. The stories of Souw present one such sequence, or vector, associated with the creation of the world and the origin of man's destiny, and the conventionalized Daribi scheme of man's place in the world and his relation to the afterworld represents another.

Significant as these notions may be in Daribi culture, they can only be misrepresented by terms like "cosmology" and "world-view," for such labels impart a false rigidity and abstract quality to ideas that are rather more acknowledged assumptions than articulated constructs. The configuration of the world and the significance of human mortality achieve their greatest relevance during times of crisis or ceremony; otherwise they appear as bits of esoteric knowledge of little or no consequence for everyday life. And yet such ideas are central to our concern, for they form an ideological matrix in terms of which the major ceremonials and mediative acts acquire meaning.

Viewed in this context, then, the Daribi world represents an interval separating the living from the dead, as in fact the lesser subdivisions within the world serve to separate the various "kinds" of people inhabiting it. By the same token, the world-space can be represented as a temporal vector, a kind of life-span, separating the individual from his death. Thus the soul of a sick man is said to follow a "road" (usually identified with a river) to the land of the dead; as long as the soul remains on the road, the man has not died, and should the soul turn back, he would recover. Should the soul actually pass into the land of the dead, of course, the man would die. This conception of space as an aspect of man's destiny is intimately associated with the significance of the sun and the water whose motion "prefigures" it much as Souw himself created the landscape.

Daribi recognize two directions: *ogwaba* or *oboba,* referring to the east or an upward direction, and translated into pidgin as *"antap,"* and *aiaba* or *iba,* referring to the west or a downward direction, and translated into pidgin as *"tambelo."* The former, east or upward, is generally treated as the favored direction. There are no terms for "north" or "south," which are simply referred to as *bogobadu,* "the sides." Right, *doro,* and left, *pobaze,* may be used with respect to a person or a house, but are not applicable to directions as such. (*Doro* carries a favorable connotation, and the right hand is said to be the "strong" or "good" hand, as opposed to the left hand. I have heard the term *pobaze* used in condemnation of sexual misconduct.) The conformation of the world itself can be interpreted in the light of human mortality, as a general westward and downward tendency, exemplified by the sun and the motion of water.

Daribi emphatically maintain that the sun is beneficent, a vital source of warmth and light for man and for his gardens, and the moon, too, is thought of as a boon to man, for it provides clear, well-lit nights for hunting. The sun is called *giliga-ge* or *sia-ge,* or simply *sia* ("fire"), and the moon *porua-ge* or *sugua-ge*[2] (the suffix *ge* in these instances means "pearl shell"). The points of the sun's rising (*giliga-ge-azibomare,* the "place where the sun comes"), and of its setting (*giliga-ge-pabomare,* the "place where the sun leaves")[3] correspond to the two directions and may be used synonymously with them.

The sun and moon are associated with two male beings, who are said to be cross-cousins or, sometimes, brothers, and to carry them across the sky. The elder, or *gominaibidi,* Iwai, carries the moon, and the younger, or *ibadubidi,* Mawa, carries the sun. Their association with the sun and moon is elaborated in the following story:

The two cross-cousins were living together. Their food was bad, and their house was bad, and the whole region was cold and dark, because there was no sun. One night Iwai had a dream in which he saw a distant place. In the morning he left, and, climbing a mountain, he saw a beautiful valley below him; the sun was there, and it was populated by beautiful women. He cut a large sago tree that was growing wild there, but although he chopped and chopped, it wouldn't fall. Then he returned to the house, and Mawa asked what he had been doing. "Come along

2. The phases of the moon are distinguished in a general way. The crescent moon is called a little pearl shell, or sometimes *kege we* ("seek-woman"), the latter possibly referring to the Bokimi story. The full moon is the *moni porua,* or "big moon."
3. Daribi also recognize the meridian, the *giligatomo,* or "sun-middle."

with me, I'll show you something," he replied. The two left, came to the mountain, looked down below, and saw the good thing. Now both of them began cutting the sago tree, and it fell. Then Mawa said "You stay here, I'll go down below and look for this thing. When I find it, I'll come back." He went down and came to the good place, where everything was fine and it wasn't cold. He saw that the food was good. He transformed himself into an insect and found a bamboo tube of water and crawled inside. A young woman who had been working in her garden came by; she drank the water in the tube and also swallowed the insect. After a time she became pregnant. The other women were puzzled and asked how she had become pregnant, but she just said she didn't know. When she was ready to give birth, the other women brought her firewood and water. She made a little house in the bush and bore her baby there. She saw that it was a boy. She was very happy with the child and carried him around, but soon he began to cry. All the women brought things to make him stop crying; they brought sugar, and food, but he wasn't hungry, and kept crying. The mother searched frantically in her net bag for something to give him. Finally she went and brought the sun and the moon, and tied them around the baby's neck; the sun on his back, the moon on his chest. The baby had been crying for these, and now it stopped. Then it began walking around in the garden, then up in the trees, and finally it left altogether. It was Mawa who climbed the mountain and looked down below and saw that the sun and moon weren't there any longer; he had taken them. Then he went to Iwai: "Look, cross-cousin, I've taken them," and Iwai admired them. They walked on and on with them until they came to a tree of the kind called *piguru*, which they climbed. Mawa faced upward and shot an arrow up with the sun, saying "You come up during the day." Iwai faced downward, and shot an arrow down with the moon, saying "You come up at night."

Like Souw, Iwai and Mawa are also credited with being the originators of certain cultural practices such as that of cooking in bamboo tubes. (Previously the whole bamboo stalk, with the internodes removed, had been used; Iwai and Mawa first cut it into sections.) Originally, as the story goes, the two cross-cousins lived on earth. One of them was a hunter, and when he killed a bush-fowl he would eat the meat, giving the bones to the other, who satisfied his hunger with *dora'* leaves. Finally the latter waited for his cousin and clubbed him with a stick, shouting, "What are you trying to do? You always give me the bones." The other said, "Before we didn't fight, now we fight together; let's go to another place where people don't fight," and the two went to live in the sky, where they carry the sun and moon.

The sky is thought of as a solid object, a sort of vault, which touches the earth at the horizon and has an "inside." Clouds are believed to "come out of" and "go back inside" the sky, and after the sun sets it is thought to be carried back "inside" (or as we would say, above) the sky to its point of rising. Daribi say that during the day, when the sun is visible, the moon is journeying back eastward inside the sky, and that at night, when the moon is visible, the sun is moving eastward in this way.[4] Thus the sun and moon are always moving in opposite directions,

4. Since Daribi, like many people in our own culture, associate the moon with night, this theory ignores the fact that the moon is visible roughly as often during the day as at night.

as explicated in the story of Iwai and Mawa. Like many highlanders, Daribi feel that the moon exercises a dispelling influence on rainfall, and the paired seasons are sometimes contrasted as the "rain time" *(be' turubage)* and the "moon time" *(be' porua)*.[5] Rain is also expected at the new moon, when the "moon has gone to sleep."

The sun serves as a point of reference and as a sort of vectoral "operator" within the Daribi world-space. Ideally, a Daribi house should face east so that the rising sun will shine down its central corridor, as my informants explained, and a body should be placed on the exposure-coffin or in the grave facing eastward, "so that it can see the sun when it rises." Dances, ceremonies, and weddings are generally held at noon-day, when the sun is overhead, although delays and other irregularities often postpone such events until late afternoon. Sunset, when the sun has reached the end of its course and shines from the direction toward which the dead move, is an especially foreboding time of day, for it is then that ghosts are thought to be moving eastward up the river gorges. Seances invariably begin in the early hours of evening following sunset.

Daribi say that "the sun and the water go to the same place"; water is thought to rise in the east (although the source of the Tua River is unknown) and on top of Mount Karimui, the various peaks of which are designated as the sources *(gomo)* of the major local streams, and flow westward. It moves to the north of the mountain, gradually accumulating in the Tua River, until it flows away to the west. The fact that the river then turns and flows eastward to the south of Mount Karimui, thus diverging from the course of the sun, is generally ignored or held to be inconsequential.

The Tua River is identified as the "road" on which the spirits of the deceased travel to the land of the dead; together with its system of tributaries it forms a network of passageways over which ghosts are felt to travel in their journeyings between the realm of the living and that of the dead. At a cataract called *igroa* or *parizabo* on the Tua to the south of Mount Karimui, the footprints of *izibidi* can be seen in the sand as, following the river, they descend with the cataract. When the footprints of a pig are seen here, a pig has died; when those of a dog are seen, a dog has died; and the footprints of a man, woman, or child indicate that a person of that description has died. The whistling of the *izibidi* can be heard here, and the foliage of the bananas and other trees is red, as are the snakes and marsupials found in the vicinity. People cannot eat the latter; it is said that a man once killed and ate a marsupial here, and at night as he slept an *izibidi* came and ate his eyes, flesh, and viscera so that in the morning only his bones were found.[6]

5. The "moon time" occurs during the southern winter, when the sun is comparatively low, and the full moon therefore comparatively high in the sky. This may be the basis of the designation, or, more likely, the association of the high moon with the dry season may serve to reinforce the moon-rain opposition.

6. Early explorers in the Karimui area noted many human corpses, in various stages of decomposition, being carried along in the current of the Tua River or washed up on the banks. Leahy reports seeing giant monitor lizards picking at the bones of the latter (see

The place of the dead is called *yazumaru*, or sometimes *yabaramaru*, *dabaramaru*, or *gunumumaru*. It is located "at the place where the sun sets," in caves along the Tua River at a place where steep banks "hold" the river, or in a lake.[7] It is often associated with fine sand, like that found along the Tua, as well as with water, and the dead are said to plant their sweet potatoes and other crops in the sand at the edge of the lake. A lake, or a large pool of still water, represents "dead" water, that which has lost its motion, and hence its direction, just as a cataract, like *parizabo*, represents a sudden quickening of that motion. The lake of the dead, then, represents a place where the world's directionality, its "road," or "way," has come to a halt, like the place of the setting sun. Daribi regard all lakes, no matter how insignificant, with a certain awe, as befits standing water in their land of rushing streams, and many lakes are thought to harbor, or actually manifest, the spirit of some person said to have drowned in them.

Water exercises a certain power over *izibidi*, who seem to be animated by a need for it. They travel along watercourses and live within bodies of water, and the ghosts that come to seances say, "We don't have much water, we have to look for it," and have been heard sipping it noisily from the house-eaves. Bamboo tubes of water are often placed near the grave or exposure-coffin of a relative by those who "think of their relative and are sorry for him"; I counted twenty such tubes, dried, with the stoppers intact, at an old exposure-coffin at Hagani. Water from a tube is also thrown over afflicted persons to remove the possessing ghost; I have seen this done in cases of epilepsy as well as temporary insanity.

The ability of water to "hold" and remove *izibidi* is also applied in a more complex curing practice known as *qi sabo dorobo* ("waterfall curing"), used with small children. In this procedure, the mother, holding her sick child, stands beneath a waterfall until the child's feverish body has cooled, indicating departure of the sickness. Meanwhile the child's father builds a *paii*, a "spirit-fence" of *nawi-bora* leaves, about thirty feet from the waterfall. Then the mother, holding her child, runs from the waterfall and bursts through the *paii*, hiding in the bush on the other side. When this has been done, another clansman, dragging *buni* ("karuga" pandanus) leaves behind him, will rush through the break in the *paii* and off through the underbrush, in a direction away from the mother and child. It is felt that the *izibidi* that has been causing the child's illness will be removed and "held" by the water; when it emerges,

Ian Willis, "An 'Epic' Journey" [subthesis prepared at the University of Papua and New Guinea, Port Moresby, 1969], p. 80). Many of the bodies were undoubtedly carried down from the highlands, although Daribi also dispose of unwanted corpses in this way.

7. Kagoiano saw it in a dream as a place of gardens and decorated paths, separated from the place of the living by huge rocks and an immense log bridge. A man blocked the road with his arm; had he not done so, according to Kagoiano, he would have continued along the road and died. The road to the land of the dead was full of flies that came to people's faces; thus Kagoiano told others they must always brush the flies away from the eyes of a corpse, so that the soul can find its way.

it will follow the trail of the pandanus leaves and thus miss the child. Following this treatment the mother and her child slip away and stay in a small bush shelter with the father for two or three days, to avoid possible rediscovery by the ghost.

A man stands in relation to space as his being stands in relation to its life-course, and the heroes, celestial objects, and streams whose routes metaphorize and circumscribe the world have a universal significance and therefore a bearing on man's destiny. The directionality of the world is that of man's own life, so that sunset and the inexorable motion of water take on the significance of human mortality. The directions recognized by Daribi are charged by the special meaning of this association, orienting man by the very ethic of purpose and continuity that permeates his ideology toward the beginnings of life and of space, eastward and upward.

THE PERIPHERAL PEOPLE

Up the airy mountain,
Down the rushy glen,
We daren't go a-hunting
For fear of little men.
—William Allingham

When we turn to the vertical aspect of the Daribi directional system, distinguishing the upward direction *(oboba),* with its associations of the life-supporting sun, and the downward *(iba),* associated in a somewhat ominous way with water, we find a series of parallel regions, or spaces, differentiated in a rough way by natural discontinuities. These spaces are represented through characteristic types of "people," who differ in various ways from "true" human beings. In addition to numerous legendary peoples mentioned largely in stories, and various monstrous snakes, the major groups of those recognized by Daribi include the *takaru-bidi* ("sky-people"), *buru-kawai-bidi* ("bush-spirits"), and the *tǫ-page-bidi* ("ground-base-people"). Although all of these groups are thought to contain persons of either sex, those situated in an upward direction relative to ordinary human society are generally spoken of as being male, those situated in a downward direction are spoken of as female.

The lives of these "people" are tangential to human society, situated on the margins of man's existence, in the tops of trees or on high mountains, where axmen or hunters encounter them, or in swamps, lakes, and riverbanks, where they occasionally victimize the incautious. Their peripheral existence, which nevertheless parallels human life, gives them many specialties that are useful when brought to bear on human situations, but also surrounds them with an aura of eccentricity and mystery. Hence it is that encounters with them often lead to innovative gains, as when *sezemabidi* are invoked in *pobi,* or when *izara-we* teach women, in their dreams, to weave string bags, but also that people are somewhat frightened of them and seek to avoid them. The association of these beings with mist, cloud, or rain, which conceal, and which men can only produce through magical means, coincides with their ambiguous and peripheral relation to human society. As with ghosts, accounts of experiences with them constitute individual "inventions" within a tradition.

Like many other peoples of New Guinea, the Daribi feel that there is a land above, or "inside," the sky that is inhabited. The *takarubidi*, who live there, are seldom mentioned except in stories, and never have dealings or encounters with human beings. As the Daribi say, "They just make it thunder, and we are frightened." Iwai and Mawa, the two cross-cousins, are said to be among the sky-people, as well as a man called Denigibe and his wife Bokimi, who are responsible for the thunder. According to tradition, Denigibe hunts marsupials and eats their flesh himself, giving only the bones to his wife. When Bokimi tires of this treatment she hides, causing the sky to darken and fill with clouds. Thunder is the voice of Denigibe calling for her, and when he finds her the sky clears and the sun appears again. Daribi sometimes refer to Bokimi as the "mother of rain," and on a stormy day it is said that "the mother of rain is abroad."[8] The story of Denigibe and Bokimi is of course virtually identical with the account of how Iwai and Mawa came to live in the sky, as quoted in the preceding section, and in fact some informants maintain that it is one of these cross-cousins who hides, causing the overcast, while the shouting of the other creates the thunder.[9] Others claim that it is the wives of the cross-cousins who hide.

The sound of thunder is often anthropomorphized as a voice announcing the change of season, generally at the close of the rainy season, through the ripening and rotting of characteristic food plants. The thunder says "Pandanus go, *siburu* [nuts] come!" or "*Siburu* [nuts] come, *haga* [nuts] come!" or "The pitpit is rotting, the pandanus is rotting!"

The *buru-kawai-bidi* include the *urizi*, or *sezemabidi*, and also, for those Daribi living in the eastern part of the plateau, the *uyabebidi*, or "leprosy people." The beings in this category are generally thought to live on the tops of high mountains or ridges and in the tops of trees. Specific groups are associated with particular mountains, trees, groves, or places in the bush. *Sezemabidi* are said to live in the epiphytic growths high up in trees and to move to another tree when their particular tree dies. They are described as dark-skinned, about the size of ordinary people, and wear an old-style *kanda* vine belt, with a stone ax

8. The name Bokimi, in fact, may well represent a transformation of *pǫ-kimi*, "cloud-mother."

9. Since Iwai and Mawa "carry" the moon and sun, the "hiding" of the former during the time of the new moon, which Daribi feel is a rainy period, could well be implied in this version.

thrust into it, and an old bilum tucked in front as a pelvic covering. They are superb axmen and woodsmen and are believed to have the ability to cause mist and rain to descend suddenly and conceal their presence.

Invariably, whenever I asked whether *sezemabidi* were to be found on a certain ridge or escarpment, I received the slow, tardy reply, "No, my eyes have not seen [one]," and then, after interest had begun to slacken, "But the sound of axes has been heard, people have been heard calling out, the sound of flutes has been heard." Other evidences include the sound of babies crying, excrement found beneath trees, lights seen at night, and the discovery of bones allegedly belonging to these beings. Clues of this sort form a necessary adjunct to statements about the *sezemabidi* as a result of the wily nature and powers of concealment attributed to them. Likewise there are accounts of chance meetings and attempts at capture, always concluding with the escape of the *sezemabidi*. Kagoiano's father saw one of them seated, removing fur from a marsupial, and called out to him, but saw him leave. A man named Kabare, of Samia, encountered a *sezemabidi* while hunting. The latter, who was also hunting, had pulled over a sapling to make a platform on which to stand while cutting down another tree, which had a marsupial-hole in it. Kabare wanted to see what kind of man this was; he waited until the *sezemabidi* came down and then seized him. Immediately mist, rain, and darkness enveloped the area, and the *sezemabidi* thrashed about and became very slippery and escaped. Kabare then wanted to return home, but a huge wind and rainstorm prevented him.

The *sezemabidi* constitute a sort of masculine antisociety extrapolated upward into the treetops. It is men who encounter them, when similar tasks or interests bring members of both "societies" into chance contact, and *sezemabidi*, although they are said to include women, show a strong predilection for characteristically male occupations. Indeed, the image of a *sezemabidi* ranging quietly and craftily through the bush scouting for marsupials, cutting trees, or nimbly engineering an escape, amounts to a kind of parody of Daribi male existence. The society of the *sezemabidi* is subdivided into groups, like those of human society, and these have wars and pig-feasts also. It is said that in the pandanus season, when human beings decide to have a pig-feast and initiate their youths, the *sezemabidi* hear the sound of the initiation flutes and have their own pig-feast, though others maintain that it is the *sezemabidi* who have their pig-feasts first and whose flutes are heard by human beings.

Various traditions relate to specific groups of *sezemabidi* in the Karimui area. Some are supposed to live in the ravine cut by the Nami River in the side of Mount Karimui, and there is a peak on the mountain covered with *kunai* grass where they fight. In the past, when separate tall and short races of *sezemabidi* lived on the mountain, they fought here, and the tall ones, defeated, went to live on Mount Suaru. *Sezemabidi* once lived on each of the three peaks of the mountain seen from Di'be Rest House, and those on the two outside peaks, Kebinugiai to the left, and Hoburu to the right, were always shouting back and forth. When the occupants of the middle peak objected, the others fought with them, breaking down their mountain, the Pęwairageburu, to its present size.

Two men once lived in caves to the west of Mount Karimui, one above the other. The man in the upper cave went and found some *dora'* leaves to eat, and the other, who hadn't received any, became angry. The former then gathered sticks and began to beat his neighbor, crying that he should find his own food. Other people heard the fight and joined the instigator in beating his victim. Finally the latter took his possessions and followed the river Yobaze to a place called Wago. Here he planted many *dora'* and blackpalm trees, because the others had attacked him for asking for food, as well as *wiru (Araucaria)* trees. The grove became known as Wago-sili, and when the planter died, his ghost turned into a *sezemabidi* here. The *sezemabidi* who live there can be heard "singing out" when they want to kill pigs; when they initiate their youths, mist covers the area. When they cut up the pork, their voices can be heard calling out the lines that are to receive portions; *"Yogobidi mau, Aberai mau, ubadu Rara-ni mau, Porolibo mau."* They are naming the places where *sezemabidi* live.

The Pawaia mourning lament, with its final choking cadence, is traced to an encounter of the Solida people with the *sezemabidi:*

> Some time ago there were few Solida people, and their houses were scattered through the bush. One of them, Hauba, lived with his wife. When she died, he called out for the others to come, and the *sezemabidi* who lived nearby answered him. He was calling a man of Solida named Tobai, but a *sezemabidi* of the same name heard and came, together with his line. When they arrived, fog covered the place so that even the ground could not be seen. Tobai told Hauba not to cry for his wife, and Hauba just covered himself with his bark-cloak. The *sezemabidi* surrounded the house and gave the Pawaia mourning lament, which had previously been unknown at Solida, and taught it to Hauba. Then they brought food and tobacco from Hauba s garden, cooked the food, called out for the other Solida people to come, and went back to their own place. The other Solida people came and ate the food, and Hauba told them to be quiet, and taught them the lament he had learned from the *sezemabidi.* When his wife was buried, Hauba cried out and told the *sezemabidi.* The Solida people killed some pigs, some of which they ate, and some of which they put down for the *sezemabidi.* When the latter arrived, fog again covered the place, and when the fog cleared, the pigs that had been set aside were gone. The *sezemabidi* have now gone elsewhere, but a clump of "strong" bamboo planted by them may still be seen at a place called Diga.

In this story, as elsewhere, it is the corroborative "evidence" for the existence of the *sezemabidi* that forms the point of contact between the societies. The act of calling out, and the similarity of names, serves to effect communication here, just as the initiation flutes of one society suggest the occasion for a pig-feast to another. Even the excrement of the *sezemabidi* has an application; this is a white, limelike powder found on the top of a cliff near the river Nie, east of Mount Karimui.

Sezemabidi-di is fed to pigs to make them grow, and given to dogs to make them find marsupials easily.

The *uyabebidi,* or "leprosy people," share some characteristics with the *izara-we,* but more generally resemble the *sezemabidi.* They are said to speak Pawaia, and use the lament of the Pawaia-speakers, "who got it from them," and are known mainly to those Daribi who live in close contiguity with the Pawaians. They live in the bush, and have a place of their own called Nilia on the mountain Onaru northeast of Mount Karimui, where they inhabit caves. People have heard them closing horizontal slat-doors, and they have called out to the people of Moio, at Iuro, telling them not to take all the fiber for making string bags but to leave some for them. Others are thought to live near Mount Suaru, and near the Tua River. They are associated with *uyabeburu,* "leprosy places," and people who walk about in these places shortly after eating or having sexual relations are in danger of being burned by their torches and contracting leprosy. Should this happen, a pig would be killed and the *uyabebidi* called upon in order to remove the leprosy.

The *to-page-bidi* include the *izara-we,* or *izaga-we,* and the *sibidi,* or *izara-bidi,* said to be the "men of the *izara-we.*" In spite of this allegation, the two are usually treated separately, and *izara-we* are spoken of as "women alone, without men." The skins of *to-page-bidi* are often described as being slimy, covered with a slippery substance, or even with earthworms. *Izara-we* are sometimes depicted as repulsive hags, but also seem to include young women. All of these beings live underground; as Daribi say, the *sezemabidi* live in the tops of trees, the *to-page-bidi* live down below the base, at the roots.

Izara-we live everywhere under the ground as well as in ravines and in lakes, though not in running water. "Good" or well-disposed *izara-we* live where there is firm ground; "bad" *izara-we* live below muddy places or where there is quicksand, *bege-buru* or *amazi-buru,* in lakes or on the banks of rivers, and are disposed to take people's souls out of jealousy or covetousness. If a man who has recently eaten meat or had sexual intercourse goes to such a place, the resident *izara-we* will smell the odor of meat or of vaginal fluid on his skin and take his soul; they say "come to my house." Similarly, a man who defecates or urinates there, or whose leg sinks into the mud, will lose his soul, and if a man enters a lake the local *izara-we* may cause his testicles to swell or cause him to have huge tropical ulcers.[10]

As in the case of the *sezemabidi,* Daribi cite "evidence" for the existence of the *izara-we;* the steaming of the ground after rain is said to represent the smoke from their cooking fires, which is also said to rise from ravines and form the clouds on Mount Karimui. They are supposed to make a humming sound, *mmmmmm,* beneath the ground, which people can sometimes hear, and Daribi used to find their skulls

10. The term *izara-pabo,* "izara-goes," refers to epilepsy in Daribi, and some informants affirmed the *izara-we* cause epilepsy, although they are rarely mentioned in connection with this disorder.

near Masi, to the south of Mount Karimui, and grind them up to feed to their pigs.

The *izara-we* can be seen as a feminine "antisociety" extrapolated into subterranean regions, an antithetical counterpart of the *sezemabidi*. Like women, they are covetous of meat and jealous of a man's sexual relations with others, and their actions toward human beings show a female possessiveness couched in these terms. The smoke that they produce comes from cooking-fires rather than rainmaking efforts. Thus they caricature the habits and interests of Daribi women.

A person who suspects that he has been victimized by the *izara-we* will take careful note of the circumstances and mark the spot where the encounter occurred.[11] If he becomes seriously ill, relatives or clanmates will go to the spot with a pig or a chicken, play flutes, and call on the *izara-we* to "release this man, he is my brother; all his line are crying for him." Then the animal they have brought is killed so that its blood goes into the ground. When small ants appear, one will be caught and brought back to the victim. The road back is marked with leaves to direct the released soul back to its owner. At night the ant is put on the victim's head and covered with a string bag or skullcap; if it is still alive in the morning, the victim's soul has returned and he will live; if not, he is still in danger. A child who trips in a garden or in the bush and cries may have been victimized by the local *izara-we*, and his parents bring *sizibage* items (bush knives, pearl shells, etc.) and lay them at the spot. The *izara-we* are said to accept the pay, though it is not literally taken. Later on the parents return to retrieve the wealth, and they also collect an ant with which to perform the divination.

The *sibidi* are described as having the same propensities as the *izara-we*, but are rarely mentioned. The origin myth of the Di'be Phratry, which has a tradition of descent from them, mentions them as subterranean dwellers who eat wild foods, communicate by croaking like frogs, and have bodies that are covered with earthworms. There are also accounts of more recent encounters with *sibidi* as well as *izara-we*. Long ago, Hagani and Dogozo clans lived at Yogu, Kanopage, and Sezabia. They found a man living at Kanopage who had short arms and legs; his name was Dogwai, and he said *"Dogwai piiii, ama' piiii."*[12] People did not take the bananas or pitpit at this place for fear of encountering him. Once, however, some women who were ignorant of the situation came to Kanopage to gather pitpit and were routed by the *sibidi*, brandishing a stone ax. He followed them into the house, crying *"Dogwai piiii, ama' piiii,"* and the men there beat him with firebrands and told him to cross the Tua and live in another place. Much later Yapenugiai's father, recovering from an arrow-wound, was living in a bush-house on

---

11. When my leg sank into a quicksand-like area on the bank of the Tua, my friend Geroai carefully scooped up all the sand that had been in contact with my leg and placed it on a rock. In the event of sickness, such sand or mud is rubbed on the body of the victim after a sacrifice has been made.

12. *Ama'* is the term for same-sex sibling, *"piiii"* is meaningless.

a mountain near Sora'. He went off to gather firewood, and when he returned he found a light-skinned girl, a child of the *izara-we,* wearing a white bark-cloak. She had built a fire and was warming herself, but when she saw him she ran off.

In addition to the kinds of people we have been discussing, various species of monstrous snakes are thought to inhabit peripheral areas. A large, two-tailed[13] variety of the *gura',* a local species of python (generally about eight feet long), is thought to live on top of Mount Karimui, and also in swampy or muddy places, in the big bush, or on the edges of lakes and large rivers. Like *izara-we,* these *gura'* are capable of taking the souls of intruders, and when this happens the same procedure is followed as with *izara-we.* Once long ago a man had a dream and went to the summit of Mount Karimui to hunt birds. He built a bird-blind and stayed for a while, but when he wanted to come down, he found the path blocked by a huge, two-tailed *gura'.* Each tail of the snake was coiled around a tree. The man told the snake that he had come because of a hunting dream, and the snake uncoiled one of its tails to let him pass, but as he climbed down the mountain, he fell again and again. When he reached home he was almost dead, and he killed a pig, causing the snake to free his soul.

A more formidable creature, the *bidi-taurabo-haza* ("man-ripe-making animal") is reported to dwell in the small lake located near my house at Hagani. This is a variety of the *teburiape* snake that is white with a trim of red and yellow, with an erectile crest on its head like that of a cockatoo. It lives in the mud at the bottom and sometimes climbs out of the water on a tree, making it shake. When it sees human beings, its crest becomes erect, and it causes anyone who sees it to become "ripe" to die. The skin of people who are thus afflicted turns yellow, and they die after a few days, or go off to fight. Kagoiano's patrilateral cousin Haria died in this way, as did Yapenugiai's wife. In his grief, Yapenugiai paddled a canoe around the lake searching for the snake (for he wanted to die), but was unable to find it.

Ordinary bush-creatures are sometimes given the significance of bush-spirits. Moni Sege, an ancestor of Hagani, had a dream in which he encountered a *horogi* (monitor lizard) at a place called Mogu. The *horogi* told him "When you die, I will come and see you." When he had died and was lying on the exposure-coffin, a big rainstorm descended, accompanied by wind and mist, and a huge line of *horogi,* large and small, appeared with mourning clay on their skins. The people were afraid and put a stone ax and a pig out for them, but the *horogi* left, except for two friends of the deceased, who lingered awhile. Kuiaba of Meyo had a dream in which he came to the house of some *teburiape* snakes, who he saw were really people. They told him that he would die later, especially if he caused trouble, and that when he did they would come to see him. He fought with the Hwanai people, was shot

13. Daribi classify multi-engine jet aircraft as *"gura'-barusi"* because of the twin vapor-trails.

in the knee, and died. At Meyo Kagoiano saw a huge *teburiape* snake come out of the bush and circle his exposure-coffin again and again.

Though perhaps not as ambitious as the cycle of origin myths, or as freighted with significance for man's ultimate concern as the motion of the sun and the water, the tradition of bush-spirits provides a completion of their meaning. Like the Australian aborigine accounts of "bunyips" and waterhole creatures, which they often resemble, these anecdotes and beliefs incidentalize the landscape, evoking a kind of meaning from its details. The peripheral beings represent a realization of the land, with its parallel, contrapuntal spaces and environments, in human terms, not only through the exaggeration of human qualities and characteristics, but also of human fears. The Daribi world-space encompasses this diversity of human possibilities and forms of existence in its breadth of surfaces, spaces, and internal differentiations, as well as the stylized life-course of man in its directionality. Like ghosts, which may also linger in the bush and are often associated with it, the bush-spirits and other peripheral people are spatially and hence cosmologically "separate" beings, and their anthropomorphic form represents a supplementary infusion of extension with cultural significance.

MICROCOSM

The set of directional terms applied to the world at large are also used without modification for orientation within the Daribi house.[14] The direction toward the front of the house, from within, is called *oboba,* which is also the word for "east," and ideally a Daribi house should face east;[15] the direction toward the rear of the house is called *iba,* the word for "west," and this should of course face west. The sides of the house are called *bogǫbadu.* Likewise the upward direction in a house is called *oboba,* and the downward *iba.* Thus whether in a single-story *kerobe',* where the men live in front, or a two-story *sigibe',* where the men live above, the men's quarters are always *oboba,* the women's, *iba.* The central corridor of the house therefore stretches *oboba-iba,* ideally east-west, paralleling the motion of the sun and the water. In a *sigibe',* only the front (eastern) entrance is provided with a ladder; the rear doorway, at the western end of the corridor, serves as a latrine for men and a disposal for refuse and food leavings (Fig. 4). Because a house (like a person) has a "face" and "back" (Fig. 5), however, it is possible to speak of a "right" and a "left" side (*dorobadu, pobazebadu;* see Fig. 4), which are reckoned from the inside, facing forward.

A schematic presentation of the Daribi house is given in Fig. 5, showing structural members as well as areal subdivisions. In addition to front (*mabo*) and rear (*duzuguare*—sometimes omitted) verandas,

14. In fact the word *be'* in Daribi has a similar application; it can mean a weather condition (*be' kurubage,* "rain time"), a house, or a sleeping place within the house.
15. Most of the *sigibe'* that I saw that had been built in precontact times faced roughly northeast, the direction of sunrise in the dry season, when houses are built. Many, however, did not, and more recently Daribi have oriented their *kerobe'* to face the *moni gamani kare tu,* the "big government car road."

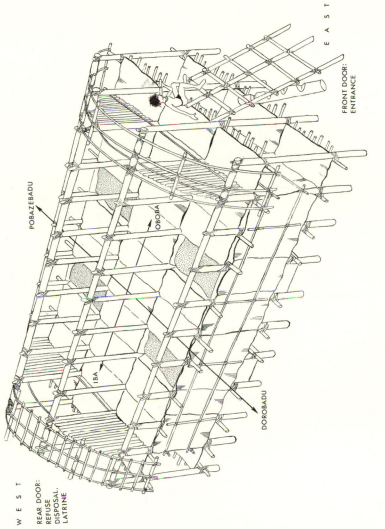

W   E   S   T

REAR DOOR:
REFUSE
DISPOSAL.
LATRINE

POBAZEBADU

IBA

OBOBA

DOROBADU

E   A   S   T

FRONT DOOR:
ENTRANCE

BE'   MESARO   (YARD)

FIG. 4: Orientation of the *Sigibe'*.

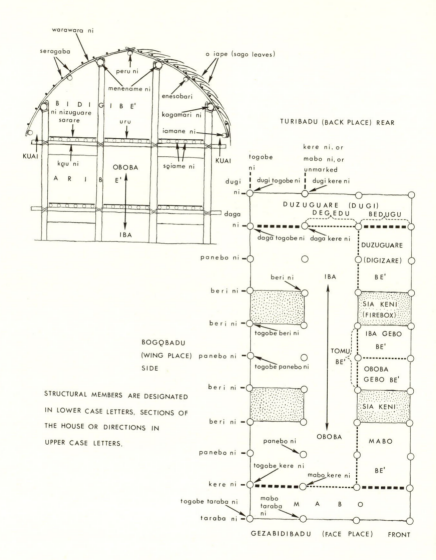

FIG. 5: *Sigibe'* structure and spatial subdivision. Structural members are designated in lower-case letters, sections of the house and directions in upper-case letters.

there is a central corridor *(degedu;* this word is also used for the bed of a stream) flanked by rows *(bedugu)* of alternating sleeping-places *(be')* and fireboxes *(sia keni).* One man generally occupies each sleeping-place more or less habitually, although a number of youths sometimes share the left *mabo be'* among them. A woman occupies a similar space within the *aribe'* together with the small children in her charge; often it is enclosed with bark walls to form a separate room.

In its over-all form and directional orientation the Daribi house suggests a microcosm of the Daribi world-space. The "direction" of life, coming and going, bringing in, preparing, and finally discarding or excreting food, is along the central, east-west corridor. Along the sides fires are built, people talk, sleep, and eat, firewood is dried, and possessions are stored. Men live *oboba,* in the direction of sunrise, the trees, and the *sezemabidi;* women live *iba,* in the direction of sunset, water, the *izara-we,* and the dead. Whether considered in "organismic" terms as having a "face," "back," and a sort of "alimentary" system, or in cosmic terms as an apportionment of living spaces that replicates a larger ordering, the house emerges as a kind of analogic "operator" in the scheme of things. It is neither wholly "like" a person, nor completely similar to the Daribi model of space, but rather amounts to a sort of middle term, which can be extended analogically to either, just as it forms a mediating member between the organic functions of the people it contains and the surrounding space, from which it shields them.

In front of the house is a "yard" or cleared area of bare, packed earth stretching away from the entrance. This is the *be' mesaro,* where much of the outdoor activity associated with the house takes place. It is irregular in shape, and large or small depending on the size and age of the house and the number of its inhabitants.[16] It is bordered with banana trees, tobacco plants, and even in precontact times it was often trimmed with decorative plants. Dances, weddings, and other ceremonies are held in the *be' mesaro,* as well as quarrels, confrontations, and outdoor conferences. A pile of stones off to one side marks the site of the "earth oven," where from time to time food is steam-cooked in a pit dug for the occasion. The rack on which a corpse is exposed is erected along the edge of the cleared area, at some distance from the house, and the shelter built for youths during initiation is usually located in the foliage near the edge of the *mesaro.* When a pig-feast is to be held, the long racks that hold the meat are set up here as well as the sleeping-shelters for visitors.

In addition to a kind of outdoor extension of the house, the *be' mesaro* serves as a staging area from which the house and its inhabitants may be confronted. Parties from other houses or settlements who wish to air their grievances will stand there, facing the house, and address

---

16. The *be' mesaro* is not consciously or purposely "laid out" or "cleared"; it comes into being naturally, as a result of the activities that take place in front of the house, which pack down the earth and render the growth of vegetation impossible. Even so, every house — except perhaps a very new one — has a *be' mesaro.*

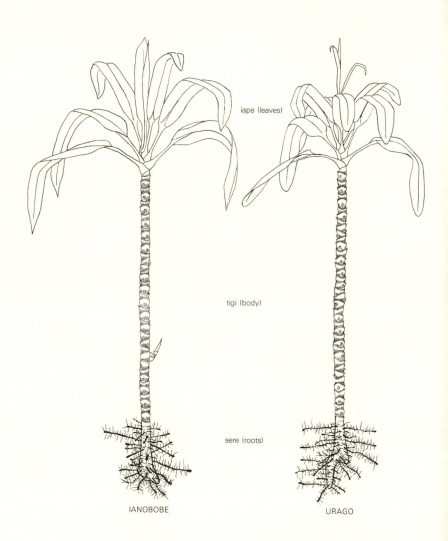

iape (leaves)

tigi (body)

sere (roots)

IANOBOBE   URAGO

FIG. 6: Cordyline varieties used for fencing.

themselves to its occupants, and this position is also taken by residents who wish to harangue their housemates. The opposition is formalized in ceremonies such as the Daribi wedding, wherein the groom and a number of clanmates, formally attired, stand rigidly in single file before the bride's house, facing the door and holding the bridewealth, which is taken by the bride as she emerges from the house. The presence of the *mesaro* testifies to the importance of the front of a house, and of its orientation; even an enemy must encounter it "face to face."[17]

Surrounding the house and the *be' mesaro* is the garden, which may be comparatively new, still bearing sweet potato and other food crops, or old and filled with *kunai* grass, pitpit, and stands of brush. In either case it is crossed by footpaths winding over fallen limb systems and difficult for any but residents to negotiate, and invariably fenced. Since domestic pigs are allowed to roam free in the bush, and wild pigs are about, it is essential to fence all producing gardens securely, and such plots are often fenced off from the house and yard. Beyond the fence lies the bush, virgin or second growth, with its wild pigs, enigmatic spirits, and dangers of lurking *sangguma* sorcerers.

The fence may consist of upright, sharpened stakes tied together, horizontal poles in a frame, or, on sloping ground, logs laid horizontally on a slanted rack. Often, however, it is a "living" fence, made of closely spaced woody plants of the family *Liliaciae,* called variously *Cordyline terminalis,* or *Cordyline fruiticosa* in botanical literature, and *tanket* in pidgin.[18] Daribi use the terms *hamia* and *urago,* referring also to specific varieties, interchangeably as generic designations for plants of this type. Although a number of varieties are distinguished by Daribi (Table 9), most of these are used solely for decoration, and only two, *urago* and *ianobobe,* are made use of in fencing. The two varieties are quite similar (Fig. 6) and differ only in minor characteristics; though other kinds of Cordyline (i.e., *hamia*) may be used as a rear-covering, or for personal adornment, *urago* and *ianobobe* may not be used in this way.

As boundary-markers between garden and bush, hence spatial dividers, these two varieties of Cordyline are respected by ghosts. They may be planted singly to delimit the activities of ghosts and confine them within or outside of a certain area, or they may be planted to fix a metaphorical boundary, to place a taboo on some activity and to "finish the talk" of an opponent. In the latter case the planter invokes ghosts to enforce his imprecation: *"Izibidi,* you look out for this Cordyline, if someone crosses it, you make him sick."[19] The ghosts then are thought

17. Daribi often express acute hostility toward the inhabitants of a house by slashing at the front with axes or chopping down the ladder. In 1964 I slashed at the house of a particularly annoying neighbor in a fit of rage, after which the owner asked "Why do you want to kill me?"

18. Plants of this type are famous throughout New Guinea for their use in fencing, tabooing, and sending messages. See Roy A. Rappaport, *Pigs for the Ancestors: Ritual in the Ecology of a New Guinea People* (New Haven: Yale University Press, 1968), p. 19.

19. The ghosts are invoked as a collectivity; individual ones are not named. The ghosts

TABLE 9:
Daribi Cordyline Varieties

Name	Translation	Appearance*	Uses
urago	"of light, flame" (the dried leaves make good tinder)	glossy dark green leaves with rounded tips	fencing, tabooing
ianobobe	"long leaves"	long, glossy dark green leaves with pointed tips	fencing, tabooing
kauwiri	?	long, dark green leaves, shorter than *ianobobe*	decorative planting
hamia	? (generic term for Cordyline)	green leaves	worn as rear-covering
ago	"of the thumb" (one leaf is always shorter than the others)	yellow leaves	for women's cere-monial skirts (*cf. habu*) if *harabe* reeds unavailable
inobe	?	yellow leaves	decorative planting
kagaruguri	"hornbill" (resembles tail)	white leaves	decorative planting
wegi-hamia	"girl-Cordyline" (delicate in appearance, like a little girl)	white leaves	decorative planting
wesero	?	long, thin red leaves	decorative planting, sometimes worn on head
nogorabo	"hand-scorched"	short red leaves	decorative planting
kabarebogǫ	"Pesquet's parrot wing"	red leaves	decorative planting
nogopuru	"hand-fist"	short, black leaves	decorative planting
toro-hamia	"ogre-Cordyline"	large stem, small leaves	found in bush, old gardens ("people don't plant it, wild men plant it")

*Daribi recognize and distinguish plants by leaf characteristics.

travel in anthropomorphic form; when they approach the Cordyline, they assume the form and voice of a *takezi*.

to "come and look at" the plants in the form of *takezi,* katydid-like in-sects, and the Cordyline itself stands as a testimony to the words of the man who planted it. It is said that those who act contrary to these words are stricken with a sickness by the Cordyline; their hands, feet, or mouths will become crooked like the plant, and their skin will turn dark like its leaves.

The variety known as *urago* is generally preferred for tabooing; if none is available, *ianobobe* may be used. When a man leaves his house for any length of time and wishes it to remain undisturbed, he ties the door shut and hangs the leafy "head" of one of these varieties from the fastening. Alternately, he may simply plant a Cordyline in front of his house. A house, in fact, may be deliberately abandoned in this way if it has been associated with misfortune. When he had lost an infant son, while his wife's other child was sick and he was having trouble with his pigs, Suabe of Kurube suspected the ghost of his father as a culprit. He planted a Cordyline in front of the house, hung several more on the door, painted large patches of red coloring on the outside walls, and abandoned the house, to live in a bush shelter with his family for a month.

Cordyline is especially planted as an expedient against ghosts that are known to be angry or dangerous, and conversely when a ghost-attack is suspected people generally turn to the breaking of taboos associated with specific Cordyline plants in their search for a motive. The ghosts of lepers, or former lepers, are particularly feared, for it is felt that they may infect the living with leprosy.[20] When Pagarabu, a leper of Kurube, was buried, ashes were poured over the eyes of the corpse so that "his ghost would not see those present," and Cordyline was laid over the rolls of bark covering the body before the grave was filled. The area of the secluded grave was bounded by Cordyline, a row of Cordyline was planted in front of the grave itself, and three pairs of the plants were placed to flank the path leading to it. This was "to separate the place that belongs to him from the place that belongs to us."

Two months later Yabare, a classificatory mother of the Buruhuazibi, died after alleged mistreatment by her husband, a member of the opposing faction. Hagi of the Buruhuazibi made an impassioned speech at her graveside to the effect that the lineage of her husband would in-herit no more wives from his own line, at the climax of which he planted a Cordyline plant. After the funeral the aggrieved husband appeared with a stalk of Cordyline that he had expropriated from a chicken-fence and thrust it into the ground in the presence of only the ethnographer, crying that the Buruhuazibi would inherit no wives from *his* lineage

---

20. Snakes and other animals that live near the grave of a leper may not be eaten, for fear of catching the disease, and the smelling of a strong odor nearby is also felt to be danger-ous. If a man eats meat or has intercourse with a woman and then wanders near such a grave, the ghost will infect him with leprosy out of jealousy ("It will turn into a mosquito and cut him with its ax").

either. He returned to the house, but re-emerged shortly thereafter and sheepishly returned his Cordyline stalk to the chicken-fence. On the following day the infant son of this man's brother died,[21] and the morning after that I was awakened by the child's father, who was haranguing the clan. Although his accusations implicated those who had been planting Cordyline in the past few days, he eventually settled on a different diagnosis. As they left for a term of labor on the coast, a group of young men had planted a stalk of Cordyline to enforce their injunctions against adultery while they were gone; the aggrieved father accused Pagarabu's widow of extramarital sexual relations *(pinare)*, and suggested that the Cordyline had killed his child. Later he singled out the ghost of Pagarabu as being specifically responsible for the death. The widow remarried shortly thereafter.

During my absence from Karimui following my initial period of fieldwork, relations between the factions at Kurube were exacerbated to the point of physical separation, and Cordyline was planted to taboo any further eating of pork together by members of the two segments. Nevertheless, in January 1969, after my return, Kurube held a small initiation, including a youth from each segment. On the first morning of the initiation one of the boys, Koio, was stricken with a terrific headache. At first this was attributed to *"habu* sickness" linked with *gerua* boards used at a nearby pig-feast, but it was finally decided that the sickness was brought on by the Cordyline as a consequence of the common eating of pork entailed by the initiation. The most significant of the cures performed involved a "cutting of the Cordyline," in which Koio held the tip of a leaf taken from the Cordyline plant while a relative held the stem and cut the leaf across the middle with a bamboo knife. As he did so, the relative recited the following *pobi*, which is in the nature of a "revealing speech":

Ma we da tedeliba   taruruama kibu   eratugubeo,   augwa
    we to-one [place] gathering pig   shall-not-kill-eat, their

kibu erama tubu, augwa   be'   era tumai-iaibao; ena kibu   da
pig   killing eat,   their   house kill let-them-eat;   I   pig feast

tugu, ena be'de   da   tuibao. Ena doro   azibo   bidi,   ena
do-eat, I   house-at feast will-eat. Me straight coming people, my

be'ba   azibazo,   kibu mawibao. Tiwai po   wai   erarubadi,
house-to when-come, pig I-will-give. Such talk spoken perhaps,

megi ma tarurama kibu e   tubao wiu,   te   gazi   erama,
now again gathering pig here we-eat we-say, that sickness working,

kibu wai'-rape izira-perama, ma   eramo! Megi te   po penare e
pig   child   die-going,   again cease! Now that talk's mouth here

peregebo, geme   pogorama   me   wai' meneo. Hanarima, te
break,   secretly pulling   another child not.   Asking,   that

obao.
I speak.

---

21. These deaths may have been connected with an epidemic of whooping cough, which swept the area at the time.

Whether planted simply as a fence or perimeter for ghosts, or meta-phorically to denote the finality of a prohibition, Cordyline always marks the point where the control of human beings ends and that of ghosts begins. The idiom invoked here is that of spatial separation, of ghosts and the implication of death. When a man plants a stalk of Cordyline he fixes a limit and renders any transgression "beyond" that point unto the trusteeship of ghosts. As an arbitration of "limit" simultaneously among men and between the living and the dead, this metaphorical use of Cordyline brings us to the issue of innovation in the spatial world of man and spirit.

6/Izibidi: The Invention of Immortality

GHOSTS AND THE SOUL

The most profound and universal statement of Daribi ideology is its affirmation of mortality. The notion of ghosts and personal existence after death follows from this as a necessary, innovational completion of its meaning,[1] just as the related notion of the soul represents a similarly innovational expression of personality and volition, opposing the individual to the uniformities of social ideology, as in the case of naming.[2] Upon the death of a human being, the formulation through which his personal uniqueness was expressed as against the collectivity becomes the means through which his immortality and continued existence is invented, or, as Daribi put it, his soul becomes a ghost. Daribi live on precisely because they must die; they are immortal (for the time being, at any rate) through the very metaphor by which they attain individuality, the soul.

Daribi imagine the soul, *noma'* or *bidinoma'*, as the seat of man's volitional, cognitive, and vital faculties, normally resident in the auricles and ventricles of the heart.[3] It develops within a child about the time the teeth appear and the coronal suture, *borabe*, hardens, and the latter serves as the point of egress and re-entry when the soul leaves the body (though some informants maintain that it exits through the nose). Although dwelling in the heart, the soul is closely associated with the lungs and liver, which are seen as extensions of it, "like leaves." Ordi-

1. This opposition does much to explain why the Daribi told me, when I first arrived at Karimui, that "there are no ghosts; when men die they just go into the ground." Similarly, Patrol Officer R. B. Aitken reported on 10 December 1960 that "Daribi-speaking natives claimed that they did not believe a dead body had a spirit. ..." It was at this time too, as well as somewhat earlier, that Daribi were giving "small" or unimportant names to be recorded in the census book. It is likely that under the shock of government opposition to the exposure of the dead and other indications of government and mission disapproval, Daribi preferred to conceal or repress the entire "innovational" superstructure of their religion.

2. Daribi recognize no real or necessary connection between the name and the soul, though their similarity as representations of individual characteristics leads people to associate them. Thus the patrol officer, when he takes the census, is said to be "taking souls" (*noma' sabo*). A picture or shadow may be called a "soul" in the same general, associative way.

3. See also Roy Wagner, *The Curse of Souw: Principles of Daribi Clan Definition and Alliance in New Guinea* (Chicago: University of Chicago Press, 1967), pp. 42–44.

nary breath, *mobo,* as well as understanding, *korizaga,* are produced by the soul acting through the liver, and the word for liver, *homu,* can be used as a synonym for "thought." When a person is angry, his soul is thought to leave the heart and rise into the nose, where it produces the short, snuffling breath called *sebe* that Daribi associate with anger. When this happens, the breath ordinarily used for speech becomes concentrated in the nose, and thus Daribi call angry talk "nose-talk."

Although the soul is thought to leave the body during sleep and at times of sudden, extreme fright, it generally returns, for failure to do so would ultimately mean the death of the person to whom it belongs. The soul of a sick person is said to "sleep" *(noma' ybo)* and to swell up *(moni noma'),* causing the veins and arteries to become engorged with blood. When a person is about to die and has difficulty catching his breath, his liver has almost quit and his soul is about to leave. When the soul finally leaves the body it becomes a ghost, *izibidi, yezibidi,* or *ho* ("whistle").

The ghost of someone who has been ambushed and killed in the bush by *kebidibi* raiders or has otherwise died in the bush usually remains near the place of death. That of a victim of *animani*[4] sorcery goes to the house of the sorcerer; should any member of the victim's clan later go there, ignorant of the cause of his death, and eat with the sorcerer, the ghost will follow him home and cause sickness in the clan. Otherwise, the ghost of a dead person proceeds to the place of the dead. If a pig or a chicken has been killed so that its ghost may accompany that of the deceased, the latter will be permitted to enter; if not it will be barred, and will return to its former dwelling when pigs are killed there. It may return in the relatively harmless form of "a bird or a *takezi* that sings in the house," or it may come as a "whistle" and kill children or make people sick.

Animals, particularly domesticated ones, are also felt to have souls. When a pig is slaughtered, a noose of *kunai* grass is quickly slipped around its snout and removed, held up, and then hung from the rafters of the house. This is to "catch the soul" of the pig so that it does not go among the other pigs and cause them to run wild. As an innovative construct, clothed, like the bush-spirits, in a convincing overlay of corroborative and institutionalized "evidence," the metaphor of the soul is capable of wide extension.

The ideas and practices surrounding the notion of the soul provide an idiom or form for innovative acts generated in dialectic opposition to ideology. Just as the traditions of magical formulation, dream interpretation, or naming serve as guidelines for such individual inventions, and the "evidence" of flute-playing or cries heard in the bush furnishes a matrix of plausibility for the creation of incidents involving bush-spirits, the concepts of ghosts and the soul coincide with a tradition of innovation and impersonation centering around human identity. The actual "invention" takes many forms, for souls may be "taken" by

4. Body substance sorcery; see Wagner (1967), pp. 50–51.

meticulous, furtive efforts of a sorcerer, they may be "lost" or "held" to produce sickness, "recovered" by ceremonial means, and "represented" by a spirit-medium or curer. Events of this sort provide the innovative continuity of Daribi religious life, and the corresponding idiom of "soul," "ghost," and "possession" emerges less as a "credo" or "structured set of beliefs" than as a "style" or mode of innovation.

The creation or invention of a ghost is of course no more bizarre or "unnatural" than the "invention" of a person in his absence, or the "knowledge" or "image" of a person that we build up out of repeated impressions.[5] An "impersonation" of this sort among the Daribi involves the representation of various behavioral or expressive acts, such as aberrations of personality, sickness, whistling, and so on, as ghostly "effects," just as personality characteristics are presented as manifestations of the soul. The impersonation, in fact, *is* the ghost, insofar as a ghost can be no more than the sum of such effects, represented as innovational, and hence metaphorical, impingements of the dead upon the world of the living.

IMPERSONATION AND SICKNESS

All dealings with ghosts, and all events that involve them, take the form of impersonations and are mediated by some individual who is possessed, attacked, sickened, or killed by a ghost. Thus it is that, as my informants explained to me, all they really know about ghosts was learned from the ghosts themselves. A person who mediates in this way, whether against his will or not, becomes the embodiment of an innovative relation, a sort of human metaphor, for he is animated simultaneously by two identities and wills. As is the case with *pobi*, dream-interpretations, and other innovative metaphors, a mediative relation of this kind is potentially very powerful, for it joins the capabilities of the living and the dead. If the impersonator is able to "control" the ghost through rapport, a favorable metaphoric link is effected, and the awesome powers, invisibility, and knowledge attributed to ghosts are at his disposal. If on the other hand the alignment is unfavorable, focusing the power of the relationship onto the ghost, the latter may use the individual to his advantage.

The impersonation of a ghost is always a dangerous undertaking; the relationship is invariably initiated by the ghost, whose capabilities place the impersonator at an extreme disadvantage, always resulting in some degree of sickness on his part. A possessing ghost produces such sickness as a kind of metaphorical death in its victim, an attenuated form of its own state, just as the ghost partakes to some degree in the mortal life of a medium through whose person it is able to converse and inter-

5. Anthropologists have traditionally been wary of the informant who seems to be "making it up as he goes along," but all meaningful activity, and all culture, understood as a productive sequence, is realized and interpreted through invention. It is usually the man who knows his culture well enough to create as well as copy it who has the skill to "make it up as he goes along."

act with other mortals. The advantages of the ghost include its invisibility and incorporeal being, its ability to "see" what other ghosts are doing, to travel quickly, and to "attack" people by "holding" their souls. Ghosts are able to kill children and animals in this way, but are not strong enough to kill adults and can only make them sick. The advantage of the human victim or impersonator is gained through the ghost's former identity and relationships as a human being, which, after all, provide the motives for his continuing involvement with human society. Someone who has known the ghost previously as a friend might therefore achieve rapport with him on this basis, and the motives or identity of an attacking ghost may be revealed to shame him and force him to release his victim.

A sickness whose cause is unknown thus always takes the form of a riddle for Daribi; it represents the uncontrolled form of the metaphor, an inauspicious impersonation of death by the victim[6] whose "cause," or metaphoric link, is hidden. In order to dispel the sickness it is necessary to solve the metaphor by discovering and revealing its metaphoric link in the person and the motives of the possessing ghost. Like a dream, in other words, a sickness must be interpreted and the hidden significance of its innovative effect discovered if the subject is to benefit. The sickness, as an impersonation of death on the part of the victim, threatens to become his own unless it can be identified as the effect, and hence the impersonation, of some specific ghost. This has the effect of "structuring" the unknown, and transforming it into a manageable relation. Diagnosis of this sort may be the result of improvisation and conjecture, reviewing possible motives and culprits and selecting the most likely, or it may be undertaken with the aid of a medium or *sogoyezibidi* and involve further impersonations.

The attack of an angry ghost may take the form of epilepsy, leprosy, insanity, deafness, or some other disorder, but it is often associated with the killing of pigs or the small children of the victim. Old and infirm men often make threats of later ghostly retribution if their wishes are not heeded. When the father of Tạre, of Kurube, was sick, he said, "If you bring me a pig, I won't kill your children or pigs when I die." He was given a pig the first time this request was made, but later requests were ignored. After his death five of Tạre's children died, and when the sixth was born her little finger was cut off as an offering, "so the ghost would not take more." The death of infants, children, or pigs, all too common at Karimui, is generally interpreted in terms of such ghostly "revenge." Precautions against it may involve attempts at placating the ghost or the planting of Cordyline and special burial procedures, as discussed in the preceding chapter.

Epilepsy, leprosy, insanity, and deafness are frequently linked to specific kinds of grievances, which involve the resentment of a ghost

---

6. Hence the pidgin expression *emi dai liklik*, "He's a little bit dead," referring to sickness.

toward relatives who unknowingly eat together with those who have harmed him. The ghost of a man who died of *animani* sorcery is said to attack consanguineal relatives who unsuspectingly share food with the sorcerer, and his attack will take the form of epilepsy, leprosy, or both in series. Sorcery of this kind also takes the form of a "riddle," concealing the identity of its perpetrator, whose possession of intimate bodily products and leavings from his victim allows him to artificially "represent" or "recreate" the soul of the latter and remove it from its possessor. In attacking his relatives, the ghost compounds this riddle with that of his own attack, associating the sorcerer's identity with his own, so that revelation of his guilt will also disclose that of the sorcerer and revenge will be possible. Daribi often make use of this tendency on the part of ghosts in their own efforts to divine the identity of a sorcerer. The clan of the victim will eat with members of a number of suspect-clans in turn; if the eaters themselves or their children take sick following such a meal, the clan with whom it was eaten is proven to contain the culprit.

The attacks of a resentful ghost will often take the form of insanity, which is sometimes even represented by the victim as an act of impersonation. In September 1968 I witnessed a case of temporary insanity in a young man of Dobu Phratry who was visiting among the peoples of the plateau north of Mount Karimui. His insanity was explained as the result of eating with these people, many of whom had taken part in the Dobu massacre of 1960 in which a number of his relatives were killed.[7] Shortly after the attack commenced he was taken into custody by some Dobuans who were staying with relatives at Kurube and tied to a house-post to prevent his harming others. As he was led in, his movements were uncertain and uncontrolled, he would frequently smirk and kick or lash out at others,[8] laugh aloud or whistle aimlessly, and at one point he shouted out a wild rendition of a death lament. Shortly after his arrival Suabe sprinkled water over him and spoke to him loudly and earnestly: "All the people here, from Kilibali to Iogoramaru, they all killed us; we didn't see this, and we ate with them, and now [our] whole line is angry and is killing us." Then he spoke to the ghosts in a "revealing speech": "You are making this man sick; we know this, and you can't make him sick any longer." In spite of these attempts, the attack persisted, and bystanders commented that if those responsible for the killings confessed, it would cease. The victim refused to sleep, insisting that the ghosts of his murdered clanmates were surrounding him and that he could see them, whereas others could not. Later in the evening he asked to be released, and spent the night sleeping in the firepit, like a crippled or very sick man.

The resentment of a ghost is also provoked when its clanmates share

7. Together with other Dobuans who have suffered such attacks, he would have been in his early teens at the time of the massacre, which was by all accounts excessively brutal and as traumatic an experience as one could find.

8. My attempts at befriending him and silencing those who were teasing him were very well received; although I stood beside him all evening I was never once struck.

food with those who have secretly rejoiced at his death, spoken ill of it, or celebrated its death through the ceremony known as *bidi nia sai* ("taking the Cordyline"). Actions and sentiments of this sort are of course concealed, and when the clanmates of the deceased go to eat with those who have expressed them, "The Cordyline [i.e., that used in the ceremony] will go inside their stomachs; the pig and sago that they eat will remain in their stomachs and make them sick." As in the case of an *animani*-victim, the ghost attempts to make his enemies' secret known through metaphorical means; he puts his own hair and finger-nails into the ears of his clanmates "to prevent them from hearing the evil spoken of him" and causing deafness. This is treated by a *sogoyezi-bidi*, who bites the ear and sucks out the offending substances.

Incidental as these attacks may seem, their association with, or inter-pretation in terms of traditional personalities, involvements, and enmities of the community, generally resolves them into a pattern. Thus as "voluntary" or "involuntary" impersonations they become innova-tive acts in the ongoing life of the community, which can be seen as a continuing relation with death through the mediation of the dead them-selves. If the resolution of sickness, as metaphorical death, into the recognized impersonation of specific ghostly identities "structures" this relation and renders it manageable, then the representation of many such incidents as manifestations of a single, ongoing impersonation enhances this control yet further. Even so, the degree of human "con-trol" in such continuing relationships varies considerably, from painful sufferance through the careful collaboration of an accomplished medium to the easy rapport enjoyed by a *sogoyezibidi*.

The relationship of the ghost of Nabia to the people of Hagani takes the form of a possessive, obsessive, and sometimes destructive interest. Nabia had originally stolen a woman who was betrothed to a man of Tane Clan,[9] whose members killed him in retribution. Afterward the woman in question was married to Ogwane, of Hagani, who negotiated an exchange with the Tane people. Following his death, Nabia's ghost established an intimate relationship with the Hagani people through a series of obsessive impersonations by Hagani women. These imperson-ations have often included a "kidnapping" of the woman by the ghost, explained by the latter's desire to "sleep with" (i.e., stay with)[10] her. When a ghost "takes" a woman in this way, according to informants, it "strikes" her and she falls down, her arms and legs twitching. (She may also foam at the mouth.) Then the ghost lifts her up and pushes her from behind. He takes her all around the bush, sometimes for days, takes her up high mountains, and sometimes, according to Daribi, will deliver her to a *kebidibidi* sorcerer.

Nabia's ghost would visit his former wife while she was alive and

9. Tane and the clan to which I refer as "Hagani" here, otherwise known as "Dogwaro," may both be referred to as "Hagani," as in the government census books. Nevertheless they are territorially distinct and have intermarried for some time.
10. Informants denied any sexual interest here.

"take" her in this way; once it kidnapped her in broad daylight and "It was only because [Ogwane] was able to follow her and hold her that she came back." The same ghost had an intimate and possessive relationship with Aruame, the wife of a clanmate. When the ghost first came to her, Aruame became very sick, and only recovered when she discovered its identity. At this time she had to be tied to a tree by the hands to keep the ghost from "pulling" her away. Later on she became an important "mediator" between the ghost and the people of Hagani, but her relationship to the ghost was always somewhat precarious. Early in 1965 I visited Aruame twice in order to interview Nabia's ghost.[11] The first time the ghost did not respond to her "call," since it had accompanied the men of Hagani to a funeral at the Hobe clans nearby. On the second occasion, after the funeral, the ghost was very angry as it came to the house and told Aruame it would like to kill her for "calling out" for it all the time. After a bit of low, whistled conversation, the ghost seized her by the neck and began striking her, and then took her away into the bush. Attempts were made to find her by torchlight, and the people of Waro's house nearby heard the whistle moving through their garden, but she was not located for a day or so.

In cases like this, where there is little control over the ghost, it is said to "eat the liver" of its victim, "because it wants to make a place for itself, since souls live in the liver." Aruame's liver was eaten until "she was nothing but bones," and she died one day in her garden. The people of Hagani who cut her body open later found "no liver at all, only blood." In cases where there is good rapport between ghost and medium, as with a *sogoyezibidi,* this is said not to occur. Following the death of Aruame, Nabia's ghost began visiting her husband's brother's wife.

This ghost's relationship to the people of Hagani, although coercive, is far less sinister than its liaison with Aruame. It is said to resent Ogwane for having married Nabia's former wife, and men sometimes threaten others, saying "If you marry my wife after I die, my ghost will come and eat your liver." Thus far Ogwane has suffered no ill effects, however, and the ghost helps him in hunting by bringing wild pigs to his garden. When the men of Hagani hunt wild pigs, Nabia's ghost helps them by breaking all of a pig's bones and holding it against a tree so they can kill it. The ghost also takes Hagani's part in quarrels; it steals pigs for them from enemy lines and has told them that it will rub the pigs it has stolen with red clay so they may recognize and shoot them. When Ogwane betrothed his daughter to the son of Ṭare, at Kurube, the ghost threatened to kill the girl unless the Hagani men went to Kurube to collect the pig due to them.

Pagarabu, a leper, had made threats to the effect that, if certain of his possessions were touched after his death, his ghost would infect the culprits with leprosy; the precautions taken in connection with his

11. Wagner (1967), pp. 45–46.

burial were described in our discussion of Cordyline, in the preceding chapter. Like Nabia's, his ghost has become the subject of fearful impersonations, and in 1968 it "kidnapped" the wife of my neighbor Hagi, at Kurube, for several days. According to witnesses, the ghost would appear together with the ghosts of four children who had died of leprosy; frequently it would simultaneously possess the two women and two men living at Hagi's house and "cover them like a house." Residents asked me if I would shoot the ghost while it was possessing them, but I declined for reasons of safety.[12]

Ghosts like those of Nabia and Pagarabu represent innovative forces that are only minimally controlled. The "ghostly" half of the metaphor formed by possession is apt to take over at any moment and turn the impersonation into something akin to sickness or insanity, the ghost dragging the medium off to its haunts in the bush or attacking her physically. More frequently, however, the impersonation is fairly well controlled, with the ghost appearing regularly[13] and apparently willing to accept rewards through its participation in the mortal being of the impersonator in return for its assistance to her. Thus the ghost becomes partially "structured" as an innovative force and forms a tentatively negotiable link to the powers and knowledge of the dead.

Insofar as they are represented entirely through metaphorical effects, ghosts are completely dependent upon the "possession" relationship, and through it on the mortal being of the medium, for their interaction with human beings. Their speech, for instance, occurs in the form of a whistled approximation (*ho po,* "whistle speech") of human speech patterns, and they draw their nourishment from the odors of cooked food or the vapors of its cooking. Although fires are allowed to die, and the house is darkened on the night of a seance, it is not difficult to detect that the whistling that is heard comes from the lips of the medium, or that it is she herself who eats the food and smokes the tobacco brought for the ghost. Nor do the Daribi, who are often brought to tears by the whistled messages and the careful "translations" that follow them, or delighted by the disappearance of the food, seem disturbed by this fact.[14] The ghost must necessarily draw its nourishment from the food through its participation and impersonation in the medium, just as it whistles through her lips and, indeed, relies upon her translation of its message.

When announcing its next appearance, a ghost frequently asks its surviving relatives to bring food, which it "consumes" during the course

12. Since many Daribi maintain that a possessing ghost sits on the head of its victim, the feat would be worthy of William Tell (who was not, however, obliged to use a .12-gauge shotgun). Some time later Ogwane requested that I shoot Nabia's ghost at Hagani, but here, too, I was forced to demur.

13. One ghost, which understood pidgin, was in the habit of announcing its next appearance in terms of the days of the week, which Daribi were just beginning to learn in 1968.

14. At one seance that I attended, the medium, an elderly woman, called an acculturated young man, in long trousers and a peaked cap, into the house and presented him with the cooked pigeon that I had brought for the ghost. He devoured it noisily, giving portions to female relatives of the ghost.

of the seance. This is given to the medium upon arrival, shortly after dark. Since a large majority of the ordinary mediums are female, the seance is often held in the women's quarters, with men attending or participating from the proximity of the adjoining men's quarters. Frequently a small crowd gathers, as people come to communicate with deceased relatives, seek help in finding lost or stolen objects, or just watch; I counted twenty women and a good many men in the women's quarters during a seance at Noruai. After an initial period of talking and smoking the house is darkened and conversation dies in anticipation of the coming of the ghost. Then quietly, almost shyly, the sound of whistling is heard as the ghost "arrives" and begins to converse with the participants. Each whistled statement is carefully paraphrased by the medium, although the listeners frequently anticipate its meaning on the basis of context and intonation and speak out on their own.[15] Discussion usually centers around conditions in the land of the dead, the fate of others who have died, and information that the ghost has received about the world of mortals. Occasionally the ghost will take temporary leave of the group in order to investigate the whereabouts of some stolen or missing article, or to gather some other sort of information, but it is seldom absent for long, since ghosts travel with exemplary speed.

A medium characteristically works through a single ghost, who is responsible for initiating the relationship. The association between ghost and medium may develop into a fruitful and long-standing interaction, or it may be terminated by extenuating circumstances. The ghost of Kau, a boy whom I had known during my first period of fieldwork, originally came to a woman of Noruai named Agai. A relationship was about to be established when Agai married at Bosiamaru, after which Kau began an association with another woman of Noruai. There are at most only a few women in each community who serve as mediums, and the desire of aggrieved relatives to get in touch with their deceased kinsmen sometimes obliges a ghost to "bring along" the spirit of the latter, whereupon the impersonation becomes multiple. The ghost of Kagoiano's mother "followed" Kau's ghost to its meetings with Agai in this way, and in its later relationship Kau's ghost appeared with that of Buruhuą, a youth who had died on the coast.

When a ghost is "brought along" and appears for the first time in this way, its whistle is weak and difficult to discern, as it has not yet become used to such communication. One of the major reasons for bringing around ghosts of the recently deceased in this way is to discover the true cause of death, and thus Buruhuą's ghost revealed how he had been tricked by youths of nearby clans into having intercourse with a sorceress, who brought about his death. At another seance that I witnessed in Kurube, the ghost of a young woman claimed that the spirit of a young

---

15. The ghost is addressed by name in a fairly loud voice, as if speaking to someone in the next room.

child who had recently died was staying with her, and explained how he had been killed as the result of a long-standing enmity between Kurube and Ogwanoma clans. While information of this sort may be obtained through the assistance of an ordinary medium, it is available only to personal acquaintances of the medium, and contingent upon her control over the ghost. For curing as well as divination of this sort, however, the services of a *sogoyezibidi,* as dedicated practitioner, are preferred.

THE SOGOYEZIBIDI

The *sogoyezibidi* ("tobacco-spirit"), or *yezi-buai-bidi* ("ghost-filled-person") is a kind of shaman, a person who has attained a long-term relationship of rapport with a ghost such that it may be called upon at will to assist in curing or divining. Anyone may consult with a *sogoyezibidi,* who charges a fee for services rendered. In contrast to the ordinary spirit-medium, whose activities are informal, often temporary, and seldom widely known, the *sogoyezibidi* occupies a distinct and respected social role. The technique of the *sogoyezibidi* represents a completely controlled innovative "style," a structuring of the metaphoric relation with death to render it negotiable.

A *sogoyezibidi* is almost invariably elderly, and, like an ordinary medium, is usually, but not in all cases, female. In 1964 my informants were able to name a total of eleven living *sogoyezibidi,* of whom seven were female, from among the five thousand or so Daribi- and Pawaia-speakers to the north and west of Mount Karimui. Even allowing for some inaccuracy, this yields a ratio of approximately one *sogoyezibidi* to five hundred people, seemingly much lower than that for ordinary spirit mediums.[16] Consequently not every community has its own *sogoyezibidi,* and patients must often travel to see one, or, if too weak, send for one.

Unlike other mediums, the *sogoyezibidi* uses her[17] powers exclusively for diagnosis and curing, and her specialty can be regarded as an application of the metaphor of possession to this purpose. The presence of the possessing ghost, who can "see" other ghosts and comprehend their motives, provides an innovative augmentation of her faculties, so that ghost and human being act as a single unit, aligning the capabilities of the living and the dead and bringing them to bear on the task of curing. This effect is also produced in the metaphor formed by ordinary possession, but there, however, it is at the mercy of the ghost's "whims" and the medium's rather tentative control. In the case of a *sogoyezibidi,* the relationship is completely controlled and constitutes

16. Because Daribi are somewhat hesitant in discussing mediums and their activities, and because their role is not as permanent or well-established as that of the *sogoyezibidi,* it would be difficult to compute the ratio of mediums to the population. I would estimate it to be about 1:100.

17. I will use the feminine gender in referring to the *sogoyezibidi,* in deference to the fact that the majority of them seem to be women. They are depicted as men in stories, however.

FIG. 7: *Sogoyezibidi.*

a structuring of power similar to the metaphor invoked in a *pobi*. The ghost accompanies a *sogoyezibidi* as she travels about in her curing activities, and the state of possession is brought on at will by excessive smoking.

The *sogoyezibidi's* relationship with a ghost, like that of an ordinary medium, is initiated by the ghost itself, and the novice must undergo the trials and discomforts common to all spirit-possession. Someone may tell a close relative or clanmate, "When I die my ghost will come to you and make you a *sogoyezibidi*." Afterward, when the person who made the promise dies, he will appear to the one he has "marked" in a dream and present her with a bamboo tobacco pipe, signifying the fulfillment of his promise. The ghost is said to choose "a strong woman," or "a person who speaks and thinks well," someone, in other words, with good judgment, for otherwise the *sogoyezibidi* might abuse her powers and "go around making people sick." The *sogoyezibidi* is portrayed in Daribi stories as a person of exemplary moral character, who is treated with considerable respect.

After the person who has "marked" her dies, and perhaps appears in a dream, the "whistle" will come to the novice. It is said that the novice must "die" or go into a deep trance (with her "liver still working") before she can become a *sogoyezibidi*. She begins to smoke heavily when the "whistle" appears, and it strikes her unconscious, so that she lies, inhaling always through the mouth, while the other people present continue to smoke and wait for her to regain consciousness. The novice is generally sickly, suffering from diarrhea; she is not allowed to walk around, but must sit and smoke a great deal to make the spirit come. Rain is not permitted to come into contact with her, and she may not touch or drink water, "so that the spirit does not go away." A piece of string is tied to her hair, and the other end of it is tied to a tree; *pusi-iape* and *hogobi'a-iape* leaves are tied to the string. This is to guide the spirit to the woman—it is said to "come to her" along the string.

My informant Sari once saw a woman at Nekapo becoming a *sogoyezibidi*. At first she began to yawn a great deal; people asked her what she was doing, and she replied that she did not know, perhaps she was getting sick. Later she covered her face with a bark-cloth while smoking a bamboo pipe and waved a white leaf up and down. She was "marking the roads," along which she would later travel, to familiarize the spirit with them. The novice puts the bark-cloth over her head "so she can see the spirit," which sits on her head. The ghost approaches from behind, and a slight feeling of heaviness betrays its presence. The ghost is said to instruct a novice in the ways of divination and curing. Afterward, when she begins to perform successful cures, people will take notice and remark "she is a true *sogoyezibidi*."

Although extensive, the capabilities of a *sogoyezibidi* are not unlimited. They center around the diagnostic skill provided by the presence of the ghost. Thus the *sogoyezibidi* can determine whether

a particular illness has been caused by a ghost, or through the *kebidibidi* or *animani* sorcery, but cannot establish the identity of the *kebidibidi* or the sorcerer himself. Nor can she cure leprosy, or the *habu*
sickness caused by *gerua* boards. If a ghost is the cause of the illness,
the *sogoyezibidi* will learn its identity from her spirit and tell it to the
patient, shaming the culprit and causing it to "let go." She can also cure
sickness resulting from *nia sai* and suck out the hair and and fingernails
put into the patient's ear by a ghost to cause deafness. When the *kebidibidi* is involved, the *sogoyezibidi* can determine whether the illness is
merely transient, caused by the "strong" gaze of a *kebidibidi* intent on
killing, or whether the patient has been actually victimized. This is
done by sucking blood from the liver; if the blood is "cold and bad," the
kebidibidi has achieved his purpose, and the patient will die; if it is
"hot and good," he will recover. The *sogoyezibidi* can also detect the
road on which the *kebidibidi* encountered a victim by examining dirt on
the victim's skin.

In the case of *animani,* the *sogoyezibidi* can remove sorcery materials
from the belly of the victim, for "the soul of the sorcery goes into the
belly." This is done by sucking the sorcery materials wrapped in leaves
from the abdomen of the patient.[18] *Husare* poison is also removed in
this way. The removal of sorcery materials by suction does not end the
sorcery, or the sickness, it merely provides evidence, in the form of the
"soul" of the sorcery *(animani noma')*, for the clanmates of the victim
who will investigate the matter. The *sogoyezibidi* Maruwe diagnosed
the affliction of an elderly woman of Kurube as the result of *animani;*
she claimed she could see the soul of the *animani tomage,* or sorcery
bundle, but not the bundle itself. Maruwe smoked, and her soul went
out of her body to find the *animani tomage;* when her soul found it,
it reached out and took the "soul" of the substance and carried it back
to Maruwe, dangling it at arm's length. When Maruwe saw it returning
with the *animani noma',* she took a stick and knocked it out of the soul's
grasp, then retrieved it. It was sent to Kurube suspended from a string,
the middle of which was wrapped around the bundle and the ends held
by the courier. When it arrived at Kurube the bundle was unwrapped
and found to contain a pandanus seed, a length of bark-cloth, a banana
peel, and a leaf of stinging nettle. This was used as evidence at a sorcery
inquest.

Before the *sogoyezibidi* begins a treatment, she familiarizes herself
with the particulars of the case and its social context. Then she will
smoke heavily, sometimes covering her head with a bark-cloth, and in
some instances she will open her mouth and chant in a falsetto, and the
whistling of the ghost will be heard. After this she will treat the patient
with leaves, and also bite parts of the body and suck blood. Finally she
will explain the cause of the sickness and comment on the patient's

18. According to my informants, "We don't know how it got there, the *sogoyezibidi* tells
us it did, that's all."

chances for recovery.

Early in 1965 I witnessed the treatment of Tare's infant son Saza by the *sogoyezibidi* Sidawi. Saza was suffering from *sozogo* (a cough or cold), and Tare had asked Sidawi to come to Kurube' and treat him. She came to Tare's house in the morning and sat eating some pandanus fruit while a number of mothers with ailing children began to congregate in the doorway. After she finished eating, Sidawi began to smoke, blowing the smoke over Saza. Then she told the other women who had gathered there with their children to leave, so that only she, Tare's family, and I were present. Tare and his wife began telling her the details of the sickness as well as their suspicions regarding its cause. Sidawi then took a *hogobi'a* branch and plucked off the leaves, which she divided into two bundles. She took one of these, divided it in two, and, holding one packet in each hand, she crept toward the child's mother from the direction of the door. When she reached her she quickly clapped the leaves onto her body and pulled them strongly and slowly over the skin toward the head, where she clutched them together and twisted them as if trapping something. She placed these leaves in the fire, and, taking the other clump, passed them over the child's body. Then, taking the first clump, which had been heated in the fire, she brought them from back to front over the middle of the mother's body and did the same to the child with the second clump. The purpose of these acts was to trap the ghost who was responsible for the illness in the leaves and burn it in the fire.

Sidawi then lit another pipeful of tobacco and blew the smoke all over Saza, and bent down and sucked at his body in many places—on the abdomen, the chest, at the corners of the eyes, at the throat—and blew quantities of smoke in the ears. She did not bite and draw blood, as *sogoyezibidi* usually do, because Saza was just an infant. Then she explained the cause of the illness to Tare. Two ghosts, those of Eribi, of Kurube, and Saza, of Samia, a *hai'* of Tare and namesake of the child, were responsible. Three weeks earlier the child's mother had eaten pork together with some people of Meyo, and Eribi, who is thought to have been killed through *animani* performed by Meyo, was said to be angry. Saza's sister had been the wife of Pagarabu, and after his death two men of Kurube developed a sexual interest in her, which was frustrated by her marriage. Accordingly, when Saza was drowned in the Tua River, these two spitefully laughed at him because of this, and thus caused the anger of the ghost.

After her treatment, Sidawi said, "Now that I have looked at this child, he will not die." She had discovered and revealed the identities of the ghosts who were making the child sick, transforming the unknown illness into an understandable "impersonation" of the two ghosts, and thereby shaming them. In return for her services Tare paid Sidawi four shillings, which I had contributed as a "bribe" for the privilege of watching.

Sickness and ghosts are intimately related for Daribi, as inverse consequences of the incorporation of the living and the dead within the same body. Ghost and medium both participate in the same metaphor of possession, the medium as a metaphorically "dead" person, the ghost as a metaphorically "living" one, so that there is no ghost without a medium and no medium without a ghost. The act of curing or controlling an infirmity takes the form of identifying it with someone else's death (for death is really the source of all infirmity). But in order for the dead to be identified in this way, they must be imbued with "life," a metaphorical life through the infirmities of others. Thus the dead live on through man's afflictions, and these afflictions owe their origin to the dead.

7/Habu

MOURNING

The mourning of the dead constitutes the most powerful ideological expression in Daribi culture, comprehending within a single gesture the whole significance of the curse of mortality, the "blight man was born for." It infuses this proposition with the immediacy of loss and the finality of personal death; Daribi say they mourn "because we will not see the dead person again: his face will disappear." If the impersonation of ghosts controls the danger and fear of a "nameless" infirmity by "personalizing" it and identifying it with a specific deceased individual, then mourning uses the occasion of individual death to express the grief of collective mortality by universalizing the sorrow it produces. Mourning sounds the emotional and meaningful depths of social ideology.

The act of mourning takes the form of an obsessive and repetitive confrontation with the facts of death, feeding one's grief on the memories and relics of the deceased. Demonstrative outbursts are not uncommon; mourners may attack others or in extreme cases sink into a state of withdrawal. More often, however, they are content to lose their voices in the chorus of wailing that continues, day and night, around the body. Possessions of the deceased, dried relics taken from his body, and finally his bones themselves are treasured and sometimes worn by the mourners. My descriptions of the cremation practiced by the Dani people of the Baliem Valley, in West Irian, horrified the Daribi. One informant said "it would be like killing the person a second time," and Kagoiano felt that cremation would make the bones soft and crumbly and difficult to preserve.

The articles worn during mourning, which Daribi call *yei,* are said to have been "thrown down" by Souw when he cursed mankind with mortality. These include strings of *sia (Coix lachryma-jobi)*[1] beads, and wet clay or ashes, which are smeared on the face and body. Like the relics of the dead that are worn sometimes, they are decorations of sorrow: "They are not like ordinary ornaments, we wear them when we are sorry." Together with the crying of the death-lament, they are

1. "Job's Tears" grow as a commensal at Karimui; they are never deliberately planted, but spring up where old mourning-beads have been discarded.

assumed by the spouses, parents, siblings, and children of the deceased as well as other close relatives and clanmates upon his death. Mourning may continue for an indefinite period, depending upon the mourner and the situation. When a person is extremely ill and expected to die, as well as during the period when the body of the deceased lies in the house and is actively mourned by the clan, no ordinary "work" of any sort may be done. Laughter anywhere near the body or in the context of mourning is discouraged and resented, since it suggests a mockery of the deceased or might be construed as such.

General mourning begins at the moment the fact of death is perceived or learned, regardless of the time of day or night. If a person dies in a garden house or bush-shelter, or at another clan, the body is carried to the main house of the deceased, wrapped in bark-cloth and slung beneath a pole. If the death occurs in the territory of another clan, its members will send a small compensatory payment along with the body, generally a few pearl shells and some trade cloth.[2] In a *kerobe'* the bark partition between the men's and women's quarters is removed and the body is laid out between the two areas; in a *sigibe'* it is simply laid out in the men's or women's level. The body rests on its back on a bark-cloak, often with a few valuables arranged on it or placed beside it. A small group of female mourners, including close relatives, usually surrounds the body, fondling it, adjusting its position, and brushing away flies. Male mourners tend to be more demonstrative at first, straddling the body and looking down at it while crying or striking out at people or objects, but soon retire into the background to smoke and chat with others.

News of the death is sent to the *pagebidi* and other close consanguineal relatives of the deceased as well as to the affines of a man, and groups of them begin to arrive during and after the first day. Their attitude is traditionally one of bitter reproach toward the clanmates of the deceased, who are accused of negligence in allowing him to die. Customarily they vent their anger by cutting down food-bearing trees, especially bananas, growing near the house, and they often do a thorough job of it.[3] They may also chop at the house with their axes, break their own bows or walking sticks upon entering, or attack members of the deceased's immediate family. People are often beaten with sticks on this occasion, and, before government control, many were slashed with axes. In 1964, while attending the mourning for a young woman of Kurube who had been estranged from her husband, I witnessed the opposite of this confrontation. As the senior cowife who had been responsible for the estrangement entered the house, a factional leader

2. The only payment of this kind that I witnessed, at Kurube in 1964, consisted of seven pearl shells and a length of trade-cloth. This was reciprocated in kind by an identical payment, among whose contributors the initial payment was divided.

3. In 1964 vindictive affines cut down three stately banana trees in front of Hanari's house, and in 1969 I watched an angry maternal uncle completely decimate a large stand of papaya trees near Suabe's house. Both cases involved outstanding grievances on the part of the visiting mourners. Pandanus trees and sugarcane are also favorite targets.

of Kurube seized a bow and arrow and rushed at her; disarmed by others, he snatched an ax and menaced her with it until restrained.

Lamenting continues through the night,[4] punctuated by fresh outbursts as new parties of mourners arrive from related or neighboring groups. Sometimes small groups of men, draped in bark-cloaks and holding axes or walking sticks, will do a shuffling dance called *horiabo* before the body, crying a lament as they do so. Many mourners drop off to sleep toward morning, which is the quietest period of the day. From time to time local residents will be seen gathering and steam-cooking quantities of vegetable food for the visiting mourners.

The evidences of bodily decomposition, which become more and more pronounced as the mourning progresses, are taken for granted and largely ignored. I have seen small children mimic them in play. The odors are apparent, but generally masked by those of wood smoke and tobacco. Before the advent of the Administration and the three-day limit that it imposed on mourning, bodies would be kept in the house for six or seven or sometimes even ten days after death. Close relatives would attempt to keep the body in the house against the objections of their clanmates, and sometimes fights would break out over the issue. As the body reached an advanced stage of decomposition, the arms and legs would have to be tied together to keep it from premature disintegration. Often the skin would begin to peel, and a man who has learned the skill in a dream (see chap. 3) would be asked to remove the skin and juices of decomposition[5] before the body's removal from the house.

While the body is still in the house, parts of it, such as the hands, feet, or scalp, are occasionally cut off as relics. These are dried over the fire and then pressed beneath a sleeping mat, after which they are worn around the neck as an expression of sorrow. Horobame, of Kurube, wore the dried skin of her son's footsole in this way "because she couldn't see him anymore, he couldn't walk around anymore." Such relics are worn for a while, then interred with the body of the next clan member to die. Articles of clothing and sometimes the bones of the deceased may also be treated in this way.

Following its removal from the house the body was either exposed to "control" the process of decomposition and obtain access to the bones as relics or disposed of by burial in the ground. In either case the skin was usually removed beforehand and placed with the body "so that the juices would go down." Since the coming of the Australian administration, however, patrol officers have insisted on deep burial in all cases within three days of death. Prior to that, graves were apparently shallower, but otherwise they do not seem to have changed. The grave consists of a small "room" made by erecting a framework of poles in the bottom of the shaft, or in a small chamber dug off to one side, and

4. The polyphony resulting from many individual voices singing their separate laments over and over acquires an ethereal, almost Byzantine effect when one awakens to it from a deep sleep.

5. This would be done with an old and stiff piece of bark-cloth.

roofing it with split logs and sheets of bark before filling it in. Before Australian control, burial was reserved for those whose death was a fairly insignificant event, such as elderly women;[6] the bodies of most others were exposed on the *ku*.

This structure, the "dripping pit" or "exposure coffin," permits the rapid decomposition of the body in controlled and protected circumstances, and easy recovery of the bones. Similar devices have been reported from other parts of the Papuan interior, the central highlands, and parts of aboriginal Australia. At Karimui, as in other areas, the recovery of the bones represents an additional and necessary step in the ongoing mourning of the dead. A pit, about three feet deep and as long and as wide as the person, is dug; above this, supported by four corner-posts or Cordyline plants, a slightly sloping rack, or platform is lashed, from four to six feet above the ground.[7] Slats of "karuga" pandanus are tied beneath two side-poles, with openings between them, and few are placed as a "headboard" at the raised end, and a "footboard" at the other. The whole structure is fenced with close-set, sharpened stakes, or sometimes these are tied horizontally between the supporting poles to form a "wall." A child's shallow grave, filled with leaves and wood-chips and fenced with three-foot stakes, described by J. H. Mater in 1956, probably served the same purpose as a *ku*.

Individual fears of death are sometimes responsible for changes in these techniques, as survivors are usually willing to comply with "last requests" and avoid ghostly retribution. Some ask, as Kagoiano has, that their bodies be merely abandoned in the bush after death and not buried at all. Others, fearing the confinement underground, request that a bamboo tube with the nodes removed be inserted as a pipeline between the burial room and the surface, "so that they can get air after they die," or "so they can see the light, and it is not all dark" in the grave.[8] Near the present Noru Rest House, Yapenugiai showed me the four Cordyline posts, now grown ancient and gnarled, that had supported a half-pitch roof over his father's brother's exposure coffin. The latter had requested that this be erected, since he had a fear of rain falling on his unprotected remains.

Because of the moratorium on work observed by clanmates of the deceased, his *baze* or other affines are obliged to dig his grave or build

6. One informant told me of a situation in which the people of Meyo, anxious to get to a pig-feast at Iuro, hastily buried an old woman who was taking a long time to die. "She was all dead except for this thing [the heart], which was still working."

7. Patrol officer J. H. Mater, on patrol through Karimui in 1956, described them as being six feet from the ground, with gourds of pig-grease or pandanus oil hung from the surrounding fence. The few exposure-coffins that I saw in 1963–64 were lower, about four feet at most.

8. One informant felt that the tube was inserted to permit the soul of the deceased to exit together with his breath, and that if the tube were not installed after having been requested the ghost might break through the ground and kill the children of his clanmates. While it serves to explain the cracked, caved-in soil above graves (which very likely results from the collapse of the burial chamber), other informants criticized this theory, pointing out that the soul leaves the body directly at death and not after burial.

Plates

1. *Hwębo:* wrestling between
   the *habubidi* and the *be'habu.*

2. "Young cassowaries, you have much work": women dance to taunt the men.

3. Snakes for the *habu:* pythons
   killed on the morning of
   the procession.

4. Raising the loaded bilum.

5. The *habu* procession.

6. "These hand-fastened men have been making you sick": the dried marsupials laid out along the house-corridor.

his exposure coffin. Failing these, the task is performed by an allied clan or even a remote segment of the deceased's own clan. When the body is ready, it is ceremonially carried to the *ku* at midday. The body itself is decorated with Cordyline, and seven or eight men cover their bodies with soot, wear cassowary plumes or decorative Cordyline on their heads, and carry the body out of the house.[9] One man carries the head, two each the shoulders, hips, and knees, and one or two others the feet. As the men carry the body, they walk with a "wiping," tiptoe step called *saga daza sabo,* and give the "habu cry," *brrraa-e-e-e,* beginning with the burring sound made with the lips that is used to frighten the ghosts of those whom the deceased (or her husband, in the case of a female) has killed in his lifetime, and in whose deaths he rejoiced.

When the body is to be placed on the *ku,* the face and scalp are removed and dropped into the pit below. If the flesh is to be eaten, the body will be removed again at sunset and dismembered,[10] to allow recovery of the portions considered edible, after which the intestines, genitals, and other unwanted, perishable parts are dropped into the pit and the remains are returned to the rack. When the body is finally left to decompose, whether dismembered or not, it is covered with trunks of banana trees, followed by a layer of *tarowai* leaves, and finally a sheet of bark, all of which is securely tied down. This is to hasten decomposition. A species of horror story is often told in which the body, reanimated, rises from the *ku* and menaces its former clanmates.[11]

In the evening, after the body has been buried or placed on the *ku,* the fires in the house are allowed to die as for a seance, and all conversation ceases. A friend or close relative will go to the door of the house and call to the soul of the deceased in a deep, penetrating voice, either shouting his name or calling *mena bidibauwe-e-e,* "Where are you?" If the voice of the ghost is heard answering in the distance, this is an indication that the deceased was the victim of *kebidibidi* practices and the ghost is at the place of killing. As an experience I found this "calling of the dead" both unsettling and deeply moving.

The final stages of mourning, involving the process of recovering the bones from the *ku,* are celebrated in two mortuary feasts, which closely parallel the somewhat more elaborate series of mortuary feasts described by F. E. Williams at Lake Kutubu.[12] The first of these, *Yape Dagabo,*

9. As in many cultures, the body is always carried out of the house feet foremost, though Daribi were unable to supply a rationale for this.

10. This process was meticulously described by informants, who had participated in it, but I did not witness it myself. The head is first removed, then a circular cut is made, across the upper abdomen, down past the groin, around the rectum, and back again, and the whole area, with its contents, is taken out and dropped into the pit. Then the hands and feet are cut off at the wrists and elbows, the breastbone is severed and the rib-cage broken back to reveal the upper viscera, which are sometimes eaten. Most of the preferred meat is taken from the muscle tissue of the arms and legs, which is spread into sheets and steam-cooked.

11. Roy Wagner, *The Curse of Souw: Principles of Daribi Clan Definition and Alliance in New Guinea* (Chicago: University of Chicago Press, 1967), p. 206.

12. F. E. Williams, *Natives of Lake Kutubu, Papua,* Oceania Monograph No. 6 (Sydney: The Australian National Research Council, 1940), pp. 123–28. Brief and incomplete though

"removing the leaves," takes place when decomposition has stripped the bones clean, and the banana trunks, leaves, and sheet of bark are removed. A pig is killed, steam-cooked, and shared among the clan-mates of the deceased, and the pig's bones are burned near the *ku* "so that the smell goes up" to the bones of the deceased. When the leaves have been removed, the bones are allowed to lie on the rack and dry for a while. Then a small, elevated *dilibe'*, or "bone house," is constructed of pandanus leaves, about eight feet above the ground, and the bones are collected from the *ku* and placed inside.[13]

When the *dilibe'* begins to fall apart, the feast called *dili sabo,* "taking the bones," is held. A party of men goes off to the bush and kills ten to twenty marsupials, which are brought back to the house. Vegetable food is collected and steam-cooked together with the meat, and the food is distributed to members of the clan as well as those of other clans who sometimes also attend. The bones of the marsupials are burned beneath the *dilibe'*, again "so that the smell goes up to them." After this last "sharing of food" with the deceased, his bones are taken down from the *dilibe'* and put into a new string bag, which is hung in the central corridor of the house near the sleeping-place of a close relative.

Much later, when the string bag begins to disintegrate, the bones are removed and deposited in a burial cave or rock-shelter. In some cases the deceased had indicated before his death where he wished his bones to be deposited, and these wishes are usually respected. Otherwise the bones are placed in a traditional burial cave. I counted twelve skulls in such a cave near Noru; in older caves many of the mandibles were wound with string, put there "to keep the teeth from falling out" when relatives had worn them. If no burial cave is available, the bones are buried in the ground.

The period after which the mourning materials *(yei)* are discarded varies; traditionally this is done when the bones are taken from the *dilibe'*. On the other hand a widow who wishes to remarry wears them for only a short time (perhaps ten days), after which she burns them and goes to her new husband. If the widow has no desire to remarry, she should burn the materials at the next pig-feast and go to live with her children. If she were merely to throw the materials away in the bush, without waiting for a pig-feast, this might provoke the anger of the ghost.

THE ANTIFUNERAL

The expressive power of the usages associated with mourning, as the ultimate realization of bereavement, renders them particularly suscep-tible to metaphorization. When invoked or reenacted in a context other than that of mourning they can be used to create a metaphor, an "im-personation" of the forms of mourning, that links its significance with

---

it may be, I regard Williams's Kutubu monograph as one of the finest examples of ethno-graphic writing to come out of New Guinea.

13. These houses were observed by Patrol Officer H. S. Pegg, who likened them to bird-houses, at Bosiamaru in 1954, and by Patrol Officer J. H. Mater in 1956.

that of the context, forming a new expressive meaning. We have seen in Chapter 3 how a man of Noru went into "mourning" in this way to demonstrate his grief over the secret killing of a favorite pig, and also how two old women of Kurube were prepared to mourn my departure. In April 1964 seven men of the Dobu community marched into Kurube, covered with mourning clay and wailing a death-lament. They were "using" the forms of mourning to demonstrate their demands for compensation from Kurube, which had participated in the massacre staged at Dobu a few years earlier.

A more formal example of the metaphoric application of mourning practices is furnished by the *bidi nia sai* or *bidi wia siu* dance. This amounts to a ceremonialized rejoicing in someone's death, a sort of mock funeral held to celebrate the killing or reported death of a known enemy. Before the imposition of Administration controls on warfare, it was performed when warriors returned in triumph from a raid or massacre or when news was received of the death of someone who was marked to be killed in retribution. Essentially the dance takes the form of a joyous parody of the solemn ceremonial carrying of a corpse from the house to the *ku*, a teasing rather than somber "farewell" to the deceased. It is also intended to frighten the ghost of the latter from the premises and persons of its mockers, and for this reason red, rather than black, is used for decoration, as Daribi feel that ghosts cannot bear the presence of red.

Men prepare for the ceremony by applying juice of the red *hora'* bud to their faces and bodies, wearing *wesero* Cordyline as a rear-covering and also in their hair, and placing the magnificent flamelike *koia* vine flower (about 15–20 inches in diameter) on their heads. Women wear the *harabe* reed skirt and place leaves of *wesero* in their hair. The women spread their arms out and moan, singing of axes and arrows to frighten the ghost. The men clasp hands, intertwining their fingers, two by two, and dance about in a procession, using the tiptoe, "wiping" step, *saga daza sabo*, employed in carrying a body to the *ku*. As they dance they also give the *"habu* cry," to frighten the ghost, and sing *"nage iziare usura, nage hoburu tuau, hawa tuau, busurai tuau..."* ("You're dead, good! you must eat *hoburu*, eat *hawa*, eat *busurai*..."), naming the undesirable tree fruit a forlorn ghost might be forced to subsist on. Sometimes they dance with axes and bows, turning from side to side, snapping bowstrings, and singing "You are a worthless man, I killed you with this bow, with this ax. ..." At the conclusion of the dancing, the house is decorated inside and out with *wesero* Cordyline and *koia* flowers. The performance is kept secret from the clan of the victim, though every clan can be said to have its *nia sai bidi*.

The concept of an "antifuneral" is met with again in the *etai* practiced by the Dani people of the Baliem Valley in West Irian. Like the *bidi nia sai* dance, it is an expression of jubilation at the killing or reported death of an enemy; unlike the Daribi celebration, however, the *etai* does not involve the metaphoric "borrowing" of mourning procedures. It is simply a formalized rejoicing with the intent of calling the death to the attention of the group's own ghosts, a way of saying "Look what we have done for you! Now leave us alone."[14]

HABU

The name *habu* derives from the burring sound, made by rapidly flapping the lips, that is used to frighten ghosts as well as pigs — a distinguishing feature of the ceremony. The *habu* is performed when the women, children, and pigs of a clan are sick and there is reason to suspect that a ghost is the cause, particularly when this involves the ghost of someone who has died unmourned in the bush. The purpose of the ceremony is to "bring the ghost back to the house." The *habu* seems to be comparatively old at Karimui; incidents relating to it are found throughout the traditional history of the Daribi, and it is not unlikely that the ceremony has undergone some formal changes over the years. According to one account, performers once wore the whole skin of a cassowary over their own and danced with the *waianu* headdress, which has since been discarded.

Like the *bidi nia sai* dance, the *habu* can be seen as a metaphoric adaptation of part of the mourning sequence. Here, however, since the ghost is to be mollified rather than mocked, it is the *dili sabo* mortuary feast whose forms are "borrowed." The metaphorization can be seen most clearly in the *doziano habu,* or "little *habu,*" a lesser version of the ceremony, performed "if only one child is sick." The essence of the *doziano habu* is a simple transformation of the *dili sabo* feast. Whereas in the latter men hunt marsupials in order to burn their bones as an offering to the ghost of the deceased and to prevent attacks upon their children, the hunters of the *doziano habu* blame the sickness caused by the ghosts on the marsupials they shoot. Thus they "offer" the marsupials to the ghost in a metaphorical way, as scapegoats for its own culpable presence. In the *doziano habu* three to five men go off to the bush, where they spend the day hunting marsupials and snakes. In the evening they return and, after a mock fight with those who remained behind,[15] take the dead game to the sick child. The men who have remained in the house then point to the game and say to the child, "These are the men who were making you sick." Then red or yellow clay is smeared along the arms and legs of the sick person, to frighten the ghost, and in a few days he recovers.

The "large" *habu,* or *habu* proper, follows essentially the same sequence as the *doziano habu,* except that here the emphasis falls on the opposition between the men who go off to the bush, the *habubidi,* and those who remain behind, the *be' habu.* In opposition to the *be' habu,* the *habubidi* undertake an impersonation of the ghost that is

14. Robert Gardner and Karl G. Heider, *Gardens of War: Life and Death in the New Guinea Stone Age* (New York: Random House, 1968), p. 101.
15. This "fighting" is probably undertaken as "proof" of the ghost's exculpation, opposing those in the house who had blamed it.

responsible for the sickness and is "brought back to the house." (In the *doziano habu,* no ghost is brought back to the house.) Thus the whole force of the innovative dialectic, the antagonism between the unmourned ghost and its victims, the "mourners" of the house, is incorporated within the ceremonial division of the *habu.* The social incorporation of this opposition facilitates its "control" and eventual amelioration through the working out of the ceremony. We have seen in the preceding chapter how sickness is overcome by resolving a "nameless" impersonation of death into the impersonation of some identifiable ghost. In the *habu* the "parts" of ghost and victim are taken by different segments of the society, and the antagonism between them, the "force" of the ghost's attack, is absorbed socially in the conflict of these segments. Rather than being identified with the ghost, the sickness is blamed on a "third party," the marsupials killed in the hunt, which are then cooked and eaten by the hungry participants.

The *habu* is traditionally associated with a plant called *kerare,* which is either identical with, or closely related to, *Piper methysticum,* the kava plant of Polynesia. The *hogobi'a* plant, whose leaves are used by the *sogoyezibidi* in curing, appears to be a related form. *Kerare* is thought to be "perhaps a kind of poison," and is feared for its capacity to make people sick. It is used in questioning suspected thieves and adulterers; the suspect is asked to hold a branch of *kerare* while being questioned. If he lies, "his neck will become crooked, and his arms will be crooked and turn backward," like the limbs of the plant itself. Likewise, a stalk of *kerare,* wrapped in a tobacco leaf, may be handed to a person who is shouting angrily, to still his tirade on pain of sickness.

More importantly, *kerare* is linked with luck in hunting. Pigs, cassowaries, and pythons have allegedly been found unconscious or dead near the base of the plant, although no one would touch them for fear of sickness. Sometimes a small length of *kerare* will be carried, wrapped in a tobacco leaf, as a hunting charm. Hunters are said often to carry a branch with them to ensure their success, but game killed in this way must be steam-cooked at the base of a *kerare* plant, for if cooked at the house it might make the inhabitants sick. The association of *kerare* with hunting brings us to the myth of the *habu,* which, like that of the very similar *piaka gwabu* ceremony described by Williams at Kutubu,[16] concerns this plant.

A *kerare* plant used to grow at a place called *Yawarame,* on the road from Bumaru to Hagani, and people passing by would see it. A *hogo'bia*[17] bird frequently sat there, and when it cried marsupials were sighted

16. Williams (1940), pp. 115–21. Like the *habu,* the *piaka gwabu* involves the collecting and smoking of game by a party of men, who then bring it in procession to a cult house (*piaka aa,* or "*piaka* house"), where some of it is burnt as an offering to ghosts. Another ceremony, the *usane habu* (pp. 31, 105), apparently has to do with curing, but is not described in Williams's monograph.

17. The significance of the similarity between the name of this bird and that of the *hogobi'a* plant, which Daribi associate with the *kerare,* is not at all clear.

near the *kerare*. People concluded that the ghost of a dead man had turned into this bird and was "showing them" the marsupials. At first, when people hunted and ate the marsupials that came to the *kerare*, they and their children became sick. Later, when people learned to do so, they gave the *"habu* cry" as they shot the game, and the sickness did not occur.

The *hogo'bia* bird, the *kerare*, and the *habu* cry are all elements in the communication between the *habubidi* and the ghost to be "brought back to the house." Normally when people are sick it is thought to be the work of *kebidibidi* sorcery. When pigs and children are sick, and the cry of the *hogo'bia* is heard, however, the ghost of someone who has died unmourned in the bush is felt to be responsible, and the *habu* is performed. The ghost is thought to turn into a *hogo'bia* bird and stay around the house, causing sickness in the pigs and children. The appearance of this bird thus serves as a metaphorical omen for the performance of the *habu*, for it was just this kind of bird, and just this form of the ghost, which "showed" people the marsupials at the *kerare*. It simultaneously resolves the "unknown" sickness of the pigs and children into a known form, and indicates what is to be done about it: namely, to find marsupials, and thus provide the unmourned ghost with a "mortuary feast," in the metaphorical form of the *habu*. The cry of the *hogo'bia* is answered by the *habu* cry, to acknowledge this "request."

In addition, the *habubidi* carry branches of *kerare* with them when they hunt, to help them find game. Married men cannot carry these, however, for fear of making their wives sick, and in fact many of the *habubidi* are young, unmarried men. The *habubidi* may not associate with women or engage in sexual activity, probably for the same reason. The *habu* cry serves to maintain contact with the ghost; it is given not only when the *habubidi* leave for the bush, to let the ghost know they are leaving and "take it with them," but also whenever a marsupial or other animal is shot, to make the ghost aware of the fact.

Although a large proportion, often half or more, of a clan's male population go off to the bush as *habubidi*, there is no clearly defined means of selection. Generally it is the younger men who go, with perhaps two or three older men accompanying them as supervisors (Table 10). Each house-group of a clan, and each clan of a community, is usually represented; in 1968 (Table 11) the clan Tiligi', which had lost a man who was killed by a tree being felled in the bush, and the clan Tua, a member of which was carried off by the river, provided the large majority of the *habubidi*. It was said that the ghost of the Tiligi' man had killed four children before the *habu* was performed.

The first effect of the departure of the *habubidi* is to take the ghost along with them so that it will not remain near the house and continue to make people sick. As the *habubidi* leave, giving the *habu* cry, the *be' habu*, who remain behind with the sick people, beat on the inside of the house with sticks in order to frighten the ghost into leaving. The *habubidi* carry with them some vegetable food steam-cooked for them by the women. Traditionally, the *habubidi* form into several parties, corresponding to the various clans participating, and each party builds a *habu be'*, a bush-house, of its own where its members will sleep and smoke the game they have shot during their stay in the bush. At the *habu* in 1968 there were three *habu be';* one was occupied solely by Tiligi' men, one was shared by Tiligi' and Denege, and the third was shared by Tua and Yogobo.

TABLE 10:
Participants in the Habu at Hagani (1964) by House Group (With Approximate Age Indicated).

House Identified With	Be' habu	Habubidi
Waro	Hweabini (40) Nuabe (35)	Waro (40) Haiama (35) Orabe (25) Hainugiai (20)
Wabo		Wabo (35) Haru (40) Turidai (10) Borudai (10)
Serai	Serai (40)	Suabe (35) Yogwa (30)
Kiru	Kiru (50)	
Ogwane	Ogwane (30)	Mogwabe (25) Maziki (25)

TABLE 11:
Census of Tiligi' Community Participation in the Habu (1968), by Clan.

Clan	Be' habu	Habubidi
Tiligi'	19	32
Tua	11	9
Denege	1	5
Bobc	18°	
Yogobo°°	15°	2
Total:	64	48

°Based on Administration census figures.
°°Strictly speaking, Yogobo is not part of the Tiligi' community.

The *habubidi* spend their time in the bush hunting and smoking game. Pigs, marsupials, birds, and snakes are all taken, although marsupials and snakes seem to predominate. The hunters range through the bush, hunting at various places, which are recalled and recited later. It is said that the ghost helps the men to find game, for otherwise they would not find any, and that it thinks "Now they know about me, they

are killing game." To assist the ghost in this knowledge, the hunter gives
the *habu* cry when the game is sighted, and he also blames it for the
ghost's actions:

Gazi	iriruare	badi	nage	ena	megi	suareda,	megi
Sickness	having deceived	perhaps	you	I	now	saw-indeed,	now

tama	te	gazi	tagaraza	pa.	Nage	tama
therefore	that	sickness	taking away	go!	You	thus

iriruare-dau.
having deceived indeed.

The dead marsupials are cut open ventrally and disemboweled, then
spread out flat by skewering them to a stick with two crosspieces. Then
they are placed on racks in the rafters of the *habu be'* to be smoked.
Large snakes are sometimes smoked, but more often they are kept alive,
trussed up in woven cages until the feast.

The *habubidi* remain in the bush for perhaps a month or more, until
a large amount of game has been collected. Then two or three of them
go to the place in the bush where the man is thought to have died and
cry: "We have all the marsupials now, and we are going back to the
house." The ghost comes then in the form of a big wind accompanied
by rain and a whistling sound and follows the *habubidi*, and the smell
of the marsupials, back to the house. At Hagani, in 1964, the ghost was
said to be "really bad"; it turned into rain and wind, broke the limbs
of trees, and caused the marsupials to rot.

At sunset or dusk on the evening before the *habubidi* return to the
house, two of them will sneak up to the house and throw a stick at it,
then hide and run away. This is to notify the *be' habu* of their coming.
On the following day, the first party of *habubidi* arrives "at the garden,"
and the men build a *habu be'* there, where they will stay until the *habu*
is finished. At this point, and indeed until the conclusion of the ceremony, the *habubidi* are very dangerous, to themselves as well as to
anyone else. They are engaged in a collective impersonation of the ghost,
which has accompanied them during their stay in the bush and followed
them back to the house. The ghost is said to be "on their skin," and to
"remove" it they must take part in a kind of ritual wrestling called
hwębo.

The impersonation of the ghost by the *habubidi* consists of taking
over its role and becoming its "advocates," as it were; they must therefore attack the house-people for their neglect of the deceased, and also
exculpate the ghost by showing that the dead game was responsible for
the sickness. The "control" of the *habubidi* over this impersonation
depends on their playing the role effectively; if they fail to "fight" with
the *be' habu,* or place the blame on the smoked marsupials, they will
lose control over the impersonation, which then takes the unfavorable
form of sickness. If the *habubidi* should fail in their role, the ghost
would also resume its attacks on the pigs and children of the clan, since
the attempt at placating it would have failed. On the other hand, the

successful performance of the *habubidi* discharges the role and the purpose of the ghost and causes it to leave, thus "removing it from their skins" and ending the impersonation. It is therefore essential that those taking part in the *habu* engage in *hwębo* "fighting"; the first party of *habubidi* to arrive at the garden must take on the *be' habu* in this way, and successive parties must fight the *habubidi* already assembled there. Groups of visitors arriving from other clans are also obliged to fight the *habubidi*. At Tiligi' I was told that I would get sick unless I joined the *habubidi* in fighting the visitors from other clans, for I had been sleeping in the *habu be'* during my stay there. The "*habu* sickness," caused by the ghost, is characterized by weakness and slack, dirty skin.

When the *habubidi* emerge from the bush, they assume a characteristic costume, consisting of soot rubbed over the face and body and a black cassowary plume worn on the head with large, silvery-gray *moru* leaves (*Olearia* sp.)[18] attached to the front, over the forehead. This is worn until the closing of the ceremony. As the first *habubidi* appear, a sham "argument" is contrived to provide a "motive" for the fighting, and this also precedes all subsequent bouts as a regular feature of the *habu*. The *be' habu* shout, "We have taken care of your women, now give us some meat," and the returning *habubidi* reply, "Wait, later you can eat," after which the two sides fight. When the next party of *habubidi* appear, they call out to the first arrivals, "Why did you leave us in the bush?" and the battle is joined. Banter of this sort sometimes leads to rivalries; the Tua and Tiligi' men had upset a banana tree while fighting at an earlier *habu* at Hagani, and in 1968 they expected retribution from the Hagani men. A man of Tiligi' had been injured in that fighting, and the Tiligi' hoped to even that score. On occasion the sham fighting takes a serious turn, and many generations ago an important segmentation within the Noru Phratry resulted from bitter fighting following a quarrel as to which party of *habubidi* should arrive at the house first.

Hwębo ("striking") is a form of body-wrestling, in which the use of hands or feet is not permitted. Two participants crouch with their shoulders opposite one another, then suddenly leap and strike their shoulders together, each one trying to knock the other off balance. Friends of a participant may assist him by holding his "outside" hand, to steady his balance, but may not otherwise interfere. The action consists of crouching, leaping, and bracing oneself on spread legs, and it should continue until someone is knocked down. Often it turns into a confused struggle, with newcomers rushing in and throwing themselves at the original contenders. Several pairs of wrestlers, each surrounded by a crowd of supporters, are engaged most of the time, but at intervals the two sides will fall back and regroup, only to rush at each other again and subdivide into groups of contenders and supporters. From time to

18. Ian Hughes, *Some Aspects of Traditional Trade in the New Guinea Highlands*, a preliminary report, paper given at the 41st A.N.Z.A.A.S. Congress, Adelaide, Australia, p. 12. Hughes mentions this leaf as having been worn by Wiru and Metlpa peoples in pre-contact times as a substitute for baler shell.

time, especially when a participant is downed, someone will begin the *habu* cry, which is taken up by the whole group.

On the evening following the return of the *habubidi*, the *be' habu* dance in the men's quarters of the main house. Four tree-limbs are cut, leaves are tied around them, and they are placed around a house-post in the center of the quarters. One man stands by this post, holding a lighted torch, while five others, decorated in white cockatoo feathers, dance at each end of the passage. The pole is inspected carefully, for the ghost that has been brought back may appear there in the form of a firefly, indicating that one of the *habubidi* will later die.

Hwębo is an exclusively male activity, and in fact women are forbidden to see the final procession of the *habubidi* to the main house, or to eat any of the game that is brought back. Women participate in the *habu* as antagonists of the *habubidi*, taunting the celibate, antisocial role of the latter by dancing in transvestite costume and singing songs in which they disparage their masculine abilities and beg for meat. As a kind of intersexual equivalent of *hwebo*, the women "raid" the *habu be'* at night and hurl peeled banana trunks like spears through the door, [19] and this is reciprocated by the *habubidi*. The antagonism of the women is in fact as necessary to the essential meaning of the *habu* as the *hwębo*, for it serves to heighten the social force of the conflict and thus sustain the *habubidi* in their role. Women of the Tiligi' community as well as visiting women danced every day of the Tiligi' *habu;* they wore men's decorations, pearl shells and cassowary plumes, as well as the traditional women's skirt, or bustle, of long *harabe* reeds.

The "fighting" and antagonism that are so essential to the success of the *habu* are carried forth in an atmosphere of challenge, counterchallenge, and reciprocation. At about 5:30 in the afternoon on the day after the *habubidi* had returned to the Tiligi' community, while the *habubidi* were decorating themselves, a group of eight women arrived in front of the *habu be'* in full panoply. They began to dance in pairs, with fingers interlaced, singing, "All the real men have gone away, there are no men here." After about ten minutes two men emerged from the *habu be'*, dressed in cassowary plumes and shells, with blackened or painted faces. They danced in place, with a bow and sheaf of arrows in one hand, using the other to snap the bowstring, and making a rhythmic *brrr brrr brrr* sound with their lips. After them ten or twelve other men emerged, similarly decorated, and followed in a line, snapping bowstrings, *brrr*-ing, and sometimes circling around each other.

Followed by the women, the men danced from the *habu be'* down to the *kerobe'*, which was serving as the "main house." They danced up and down in front of this house a few times, with the women dancing along the sides. Then the men quickly returned to the *habu be'*, re-

---

19. The banana, for Daribi, is a real, classical "fertility" and phallic "symbol." A Daribi term for the erect penis is *tą*, "banana," and the verb "copulate" merely adds a verbal suffix to this. But Daribi say that banana trunks are used because sticks would be too heavy (and dangerous?) for the women to wield.

moved their decorations, and assumed the *habubidi* costume of soot, cassowary plumes, and *moru* leaves. They picked up a pole, about fifteen feet long, which had been prepared earlier, and, holding it high above their heads with both hands, danced down to the main house, giving the *habu* cry. They danced past the women, who had remained there, singing, and up into the house. There they danced to the back of the house, broke the pole along lines previously scored, pretended to join it, and danced out again holding the "pole," whose pieces they then discarded. This was a challenge to the *be' habu* and the visitors to engage in *hwębo* wrestling.

At about 7:00 that evening the challenge was taken up, as some *be' habu* of Tua and Tiligi', together with visitors from Maina, Masi, and Di'be, assembled in front of the *habu be'*. The "fighting" started amid a great deal of competitive shouting, and the intermittent ringing of the *habu* cry. Challenges were cried out such as "You Anobai never come when we have a pig-feast, but you come now: let's kill them." Now and again someone would shout, "You fight like women, grabbing hands and pulling hair," and the fighting would break up and the sides separate. A few people were injured, though slightly, and they wanted to rejoin the fighting immediately and "get back" at their opponents. Friendly bystanders held my watch and glasses while I took part, but I was continually interrupted by the necessity of having to treat cuts and minor injuries incurred by other participants. By 9:00 it was generally conceded that the *be' habu* had had the better of the fighting, though this was far from obvious to me, and the men began to disperse. A final suggestion that another pole be carried down to the house of the *be' habu* as a challenge to further fighting was declined on the grounds that no one was there.

While the *hwębo* was in progress, women were dancing at peripheral houses all around. Afterward, at about 10:30, when most of us in the *habu be'* were half asleep, a group of them "attacked" the house, throwing banana trunks about three feet long through the door. Against my objections the *habubidi* posted a "guard" at the foot of my sleeping-bag, and others, from the Tua *habu be'*, gathered up the banana trunks and staged a counterattack on one of the houses where the women had been dancing. The women counterattacked in turn, and a party of men took the bananas down to throw at the women for a second time before going to sleep. In the morning, however, we awoke to find the passageway of the house littered with banana trunks from a final, retributive raid of the women.

In its final phase, marked by the procession of the *habubidi* and their load of game into the main house, the *habu* is said to *darabo*, or "come to a head."[20] The *habubidi* generally stay in the *habu be'* for four or five days before this occurs, while the "ghost is removed from their

---

20. When a stream is dammed, the water is likewise said to *darabo*.

skins" in bouts of *hwębo*. Afterward, the exculpation of the ghost and the main feast of the *habu* take place.

Early in the morning the snakes that have been kept alive in woven containers, eight-foot-long *gura'* pythons and the shorter *pini*, are taken out and clubbed to death, after which they are hung temporarily from the side of the house. Somewhat later the *habubidi* begin to fill with game the huge string bags that will be carried in the procession. Two of these bilums, about 3' x 3' or 4' x 4' square when empty, are filled in succession. The lip of each is held open by fastening it between four equidistant posts, and banana leaves are cut and placed inside as a lining. Then the *habu* cry is sounded as the bundles of smoked game are brought out of the *habu be'* and undone, and it is given again when the meat and the freshly killed snakes are placed in the bilum. As each bag is filled, a strong, braided rope is tied to the straps and passed beneath it to help support the weight, and the straps themselves are tied to a stout pole to facilitate carrying. At Tiligi' one bag contained the game brought in by the two Tiligi' parties, while another held that of the Tua party.

When the bilums have been filled, the *habubidi* assume their costume of cassowary plumes, soot, and *moru* leaves as well as, in some cases, shells and other decorations. Late in the morning, at about 10:00 or so, two of them emerge from the *habu be'* dancing as a pair, leaping and snapping bowstrings. The other *habubidi* file out after them, and prepare to carry the bilums. In each case two *habubidi* slip their heads and shoulders between the bag and the pole, clutching the latter in the crooks of their arms, and strain to lift the bilum, with the help of young men and boys, who support it from behind. The *habubidi* form a procession of dancers two abreast, snapping bowstrings and making a constant, rhythmic *brrr brrr brrr* sound with their lips, with the two bilums, supported by four to six men each, in the rear.

At Tiligi', a section of the tree trunk that had killed one of the men whose ghost was being "retrieved" was carried behind the bilums as a further addition to the procession. A length of vine was tied to the log, a short length of incredibly dense wood, as a handle, and it was carried by a clanmate of the deceased and followed by his true brother, crying a death lament. The section of the trunk that had struck the victim's head had been brought in, since the men felt it would be bad to let it lie in the bush, and it was carried in the procession as evidence, "to show that he had not been killed by the *kebidibidi*."[21]

The procession dances from the *habu be'* to the main house, where it circles the *be' mesaro* a few times before entering. At Tiligi' the bilums and the log were placed in the corridor of the house, and one of the *habubidi* placed his right foot on the log and made a speech, in a state

---

21. The victim had been looking for insects and was warned to move away, because a tree was being cut. He shouted back that he was no child, and could look out for himself, after which the tree fell and killed him.

FIG. 8: The *waianu*, a former Daribi ceremonial rite.

of considerable excitement. He explained that his brother had been killed by the tree and that he had brought the log to the house to show that this was so, and the death was not the work of the *kebidibidi*. Then he called out the names of the places where the game had been killed. He spoke of a woman who had lost many children. He said that some people had claimed they had been working the *kebidibidi* in the bush, but that this was wrong, they had been working the *habu*. They had done this because many children were sick.

Within the house the smoked game is removed from the bilum, and a short speech is made blaming it for the sickness:

Bidi gazi iruare bidi e ebao nogo duani bidi
People sick having-made people here I do hand fastened people

megi pesagana sobau.
now dividing take.

Then the animals are laid side by side in a column down the central passageway of the house. The game from the Tiligi' bilum, 25 marsupials and 2 snakes, was placed in a line from the center of the house to the front door; that from the Tua bilum, 30 marsupials and 9 snakes, was laid out from the center to the rear door.

In the afternoon the men begin their preparations for the feast, and the women gradually assemble in areas near the main house, singing their teasing songs and preparing for their final challenge to the men. The men break firewood and heat stones for the steam-cooking. The large snakes are fastened by their heads to poles; water is poured from bamboo tubes into slits cut into their necks, and men pull at them, constricting the bodies to force the water through the digestive tracts. As the men work, the women dance about in their male ornaments, singing short *bạria* such as *nogobeo, ena nu muao* ("You don't cook, put a little for me"), or *subao, awe awe* ("I see, oh yes, oh yes"). [22] The women are "looking for banana trunks," and from time to time a group of them will raise a long, peeled central stalk above their heads and dance up to the main house, thumping it against the walls. They are "rehearsing" for their part in the closing of the *habu*. Otherwise they may gather in large groups to sing and dance, and I was told that a man who approached would be picked up and thrown about, although I was not mistreated when I wandered near to watch.

Finally, in the late afternoon, the women dance up to the main house, holding the long banana stalks over their heads and carrying them down to the central corridor of the men's quarters, just as the *habubidi* carried the pole in their challenge to the *be' habu*. As they move down the corridor, the men, *habubidi* as well as *be' habu* who line the passage, give the *habu* cry. When they reach the rear door (the central partition being removed in a *kerobe'*), the women try to hurl the banana stalk outside, while the men attempt to prevent them. It is said

22. The first of these means roughly "You never cook any for us, I want just a little," the second, "Oh yes, I see the activities of the men."

that if the women should succeed in throwing a stalk out, the souls of the *habubidi* would go with it, and it is this that the men try to prevent. Traditionally they do this by holding a wooden body-shield across the opening, but they may also clutch the ends of the stalks. Four successive lines of women entered the house at Tiligi' in this way, each abandoning its banana stalk in the house after failing to throw it out. At last the men took up all of the stalks and carried them out through the front door, giving the *habu* cry. They carried them down to the end of the *be' mesaro* and back, after which they cut them up with axes and threw away the debris. With this ceremonial alignment of the *habubidi* and *be' habu* against the women, reinstating the more usual opposition, the *habu* comes to a close.

The aftermath of the *habu* is the domain of that same god of anti-climax who presides over the ends of our own outings and rained-out picnics. Beneath a banked, threatening, late afternoon sky, the huge crowds of people who have assembled, unable to make anything further of the situation, begin to collect their food, possessions, and children. The air is full of that bustling about that people seem to produce unconsciously in the presence of something that is finished and complete in itself.

THE GERUA AT KARIMUI

The innovative "creation" of meanings through which the cultural dialectic operates may take place through the inventive realization of possibilities inherent in the system, as in the formulation of *pobi* and the impersonation of ghosts. It may also take the form of an inventive *interpretation* of novel incidents and elements, as we have seen in the cases of dream-interpretation and naming. Actually, since the interplay of invention and incident is continuous in human experience, the effects of these two modes of innovation are often indistinguishable, and to a certain degree it matters little whether a given creation had its origin within or outside of the society. Nevertheless, the innovative potential inherent in an exotic usage or object, and the metaphoric "power" realized through the incorporation of such elements, does much to explain the prevalence of cults in Melanesia. The "cargo-cults" and other millenarian movements reported from many parts of New Guinea seem to involve innovative applications of mission or commercial ideology in a manner recalling that of the earlier religious cults.[23] Of course the novel and often catastrophic force of such cults is a function of their impingement upon the society, and much of it is lost once they have been "structured into the system."

Many of the specific elements of Daribi religion that I have discussed undoubtedly owe their origins to innovative "introductions" in the form of cults. Some, perhaps including the *sogoyezibidi* and the *habu* itself, have found a place within the dialectic as "styles" of innova-

23. F. E. Williams's description of the Taro Cult among the Orokaiva offers a striking corroboration of this *(Orokaiva Magic* [Oxford: University Press, 1969], pp. 3–101).

tive production, so that the significance of their original impact is relived again and again. Others may enjoy a vogue of widespread application in the years after their introduction, only to be dropped later or relegated to the status of insignificant paraphernalia. The fate of such introductions, and the position that they ultimately come to occupy, depends largely on the degree to which they articulate and "contain" the dialectic, or can be made to do so.

Daribi religious "history," like that reconstructed for the Orokaiva by Williams,[24] consists of a sequence of creative and recreative innovations of a cultlike nature. Whether the original impetus is internal to the society or exotic, in the form of "borrowed" or "diffused" elements, the significance of such a cult must always be a product of the cultural dialectic, for novel or exotic elements acquire meaning only through interpretation. The Daribi are in fact able to trace many cultural elements back to exotic "introductions," though in some cases the attempt at genealogical "dating" exceeds their abilities. Thus the bamboo initiation flutes are said to have been brought either from the south Chimbu peoples at Yuwi or from the Gimi speakers to the northeast "in the time of Para and Mese" (legendary phratry founders). Their adoption, together with some of the present initiation procedures, seems to have occurred in the last century.[25] In the early years of this century a rite called *waianu*, featuring a feathered, *gerua*-like headdress and cheekpieces fitted with marsupial teeth, was adopted from the region of Mount Suạru, to the northwest. The *waianu* was discarded in the 1930s, when the *gerua* took its place. During the late 1930s and the 1940s Karimui was shaken by a series of cults involving the coming of the Europeans, comparable in many respects to the "Vailala madness" of the south coast.[26]

A new rite or technique represents a source of unfocused power, which, in order to be effective, must be "controlled" and brought to bear on some specific task. As in the case of dreams, this "focusing" takes the form of metaphorical interpretation; a "link" of similarity is created, aligning the capabilities of the "new" element with the context of its application. The "interpretation" of introduced cults in this way usually involves "fitting them" into existing ceremonial situations, such as initiation or the pig-feast. In the case of the Daribi, the *gerua* board, which was introduced within the memory of my informants, might serve as an example of this.

The *gerua* or *geru* board is a ceremonial element found among many peoples of the east-central highlands, where its dissemination appears to have been relatively recent.[27] Ethnographers have described its use

24. Williams (1969), pp. 7–16.
25. Some aspects of the initiation, which closely resemble that of various eastern highlands peoples, may have arrived later, (also) via the Gimi people.
26. I hope to describe these cults elsewhere.
27. Ian Hughes, personal communication, 1968.

among the Siane, Gururumba, and Wahgi Valley peoples.[28] Its ceremonial significance, as well as the appearance of the artifact itself, seems
to vary considerably from place to place, although it is generally associated with lavish displays of food and the honoring of ancestral spirits.
Often several kinds of *gerua* are made in connection with a pig-feast.
Salisbury has described the ceremonial "impersonation" of the *gerua*
by a dancer in the Siane pig-feast, and his accompaniment by women
who "are" *korova*, or spirits.[29] The Siane also make smaller *korova*
gerua.

The *gerua* reached Karimui by way of the Gimi-speaking peoples
to the east and spread westward through the area from the Pawaian
settlement at Iuro, where it was first adopted. According to informants,
it had penetrated only as far as Iuro at the time of Leahy's and Dwyer's
visit in mid-1930, but had spread throughout the Daribi-speaking area
by the time of Champion's arrival in late 1936. The people at Iuro
encouraged the spread of the *gerua* as a replacement for the *waianu*,
denouncing the latter as worthless. The *gerua* was first brought to Waramaru, where Kurube was living at the time, by Kagoiano's patrilateral
first cousin Suabe, and Haria, another patrilateral first cousin, took it
to the Noru and Hagani peoples. The cult spread to virtually all clans
in the region, with the exception of the clans of Dobu Phratry, which
for some reason never accepted it. When first adopted by Kurube, the
gerua was "held" by six men of the clan, who took charge, as "cult"
members, of making and painting the boards. Such "knowledge" of the
gerua can only be passed on to a true brother, and cannot be purchased.

Daribi say that the *gerua* was "strong" and effective when it was first
adopted, and could "kill" people, but that now it has become ineffec-
tive. The *waianu*, too, is said to have been a mere decoration at the time
it was discarded. When the *gerua* was new its innovative "power" was
put to many uses. Since it could "kill" a person, it could be used to
taboo things. When Kagoiano was a child, Suabe placed a *gerua* board
in his sugar-cane field, to keep out thieves. Kagoiano came across the
board while stealing sugar and collapsed in a dead faint. He was
"brought back to life" by Suabe and others, who performed the cure for
gerua-sickness. The *gerua* was also useful in divining and combating
sorcery. A man who felt that sorcery was being worked against him
would ask the suspected sorcerers, one by one, to paint a *gerua* with
him. If the paint on the *gerua* turned watery and ran, the sorcerer had
been found. A sorcerer who had the temerity to paint a *gerua* board
would be infected with leprosy by the *gerua* itself.

The adaptation and interpretation of the *gerua* at Karimui seems to
have involved a syncretic dovetailing of the traditions accompanying
the cult with elements of Daribi ceremonial practice. Daribi can quote

28. R. F. Salisbury, "The Siane of the Eastern Highlands," in *Gods, Ghosts and Men in
Melanesia,* ed. P. Lawrence and M. J. Meggitt (London: Oxford University Press, 1965),
pp. 66–69. P. L. Newman, *Knowing the Gururumba* (New York: Holt, Rinehart and Winston,
1965), p. 69. M. Reay, *The Kuma* (Melbourne: University Press, 1959), pp. 95, 139–49.
29. Salisbury (1965), p. 68.

a brief myth that they say was learned when the *gerua* was first adopted: it relates that the first *gerua* were made by the *dononi*, a small flying phalanger, and the *warawi*, a larger, related species. The *gerua* of the *dononi* was small, that of the *warawi* was larger, and when they were finished the animals did a dance. Two women heard the dance and took the *gerua* from the animals, after which men preempted them, and now *gerua* must be made within enclosures so that women cannot see them. The use of the *gerua* is reminiscent both of the practices recorded by Salisbury and of the *habu*.

The *gerua* is made "when pigs die," to force possessing ghosts to "let go" of them, when people are sick, or when a pig-feast (and, usually, an initiation) is held. Like the *habubidi*, the *gerua turuai bidi*, those who hold or make the *gerua*, run a grave danger of sickness, for the ghosts that have been making the pigs (or the people) sick remain with them in the enclosure. Thus their task is hedged about with restrictions; women and children may not see the *gerua*,[30] and men who have recently eaten frogs, snakes, or human flesh should not attempt to make them. As the *gerua* is being cut and painted, the men sing *ooooo*. When the *gerua* are finished strips of pig-fat are put in the hair of the *gerua turai bidi* to protect them from sickness, and this is done again when the boards are lodged in Cordyline at the conclusion of the ceremony.

The actual technique of removing the ghosts involves impersonation and a ceremonial "offering" made to them, as in the *habu*. Each *gerua turuai bidi* makes two *gerua* boards, a large and a small one, both cut from wood of the same tree. The large, or "true" *gerua* is for the pig-feast; the small one, which no woman may see, "belongs" to the ghosts, and is given to them. At sunset on the evening before the pig-feast the men emerge from the enclosure carrying the small *gerua*. Two bowmen wearing black cassowary head-dresses, their bodies smeared with soot, impersonate or "turn into" ghosts and menace the *gerua*, whirling in front of them and snapping bowstrings, alternately charging and retreating. Like the *hwębo* in the *habu*, this "combat" has the effect of exorcising the ghosts from the *gerua turuai bidi*. Then the small *gerua* are hidden in the bush for the ghosts, who "go to their own place." On the following day men dance with the large *gerua*, and sometimes a repeat performance of the "impersonation" is staged. Finally, the large *gerua* are lodged in Cordyline near the house to taboo any further sickness of the pigs.

It is not surprising that the technique of the *gerua*, recent as it is, should resemble that of the *habu*, for both involve the same afflictions, the sickness of men and pigs, as well as the same agents, namely ghosts. On the other hand, the fact that the *gerua* has not been totally assimilated to the *habu* is probably a result of the cultural context. The *habu* stands in a metaphorical relation to the traditional mortuary feast, with its practice of hunting marsupials in the bush. The *gerua*, associated

---

30. Just as in the *habu;* if women were to see the marsupials being brought to the house, or to eat them, "new ones would have to be collected."

with the highlands "pig-complex," occurs in the context of the pig-feast, which has long been involved with initiation.

Daribi say that "the ghost knows that people are performing the *habu* to keep their children from being sick." The *habu* and the *gerua* are not to be understood as simple-minded frauds worked upon gullible and naïve spirits, but rather, as metaphor is the vehicle of meaning, as complex, empathetic "inventions" or communications between the living and the dead. At the very core of these inventions, and their deep concern with sickness and the dead, lies the dialectical paradox of mortality and continuance, which we met with so often in the legends of Sido and Souw.

8/Conclusion

And we; always and everywhere
spectators,
Turned toward everything, and
yet not outward!
It sates us. We order it. It decays.
We rearrange it and decay
ourselves.

Rilke, Eighth Duino Elegy

THE PRODUCTION OF MEANING

We do not know how or when human culture began. But we do know that it continues to grow and develop, and that such development always proceeds by a kind of extension of what was produced, given, or "borrowed" in the past. We need only to reflect upon the creativity that has infused every known human culture to perceive that the creation of human society is still in progress, however remote in time its inception may have been. Every extension of culture embodies a kind of invention or discovery that must bear a close kinship to the very first transformations, cognitive or physical, that man wrought upon his surroundings, the only difference being in the quality of those surroundings, which have by now come to consist largely of man's own works. Thus creation has come to assume the form of transformation, and transformation to embody the very essence of culture.

In the preceding chapters I have examined and articulated, by way of the usages of Daribi culture, a number of linked conceptions concerning the production of meaning in human society. Within the limitations imposed by the subject matter, I have tried to present my argument in a gradual though comprehensive manner. Let us now review, as a set of systematic conclusions, the substance of the position I have assumed.

I shall begin with what I hope is a reasonably self-evident postulate, to the effect that the propositions and meaningful elements of a culture all bear some sort of relationship, however indirect or contradictory, to one another. From the standpoint of meaning, in other words, culture can be considered as a set of relations, and any meaningful innovation introduced into the culture automatically extends and participates in those relations. Relationship to the propositions of a culture is in fact an intrinsic property of meaning. It follows from this that nontautologous meaning is constituted through the formation of a determinate and non-arbitrary relation between signifier and signified, for if the act of making something meaningful involves bringing it into relationship with the tenets of culture, then this relationship must be embodied in the signification itself.

A signifier that bears a determinate and nonarbitrary relation to the signified is a metaphor; a metaphor presupposes a contrast (distinguishing signifier and signified as separate elements) as well as at least one point of similarity or analogy with the thing it represents. In ordinary lexical signification the relation between the signifier and signified is supplied by convention alone, hence it is formally arbitrary and cannot be said to convey meaning except in a tautologous sense. Such a signifier becomes meaningful in a nontautologous sense only when it is extended to form a metaphor, that is, when a word that already signifies some element is used to signify another, thus creating (mediating) a relation between the signified elements. Thus a lexical signifier refers to a specific element, but a metaphor signifies a relation.

The extension of signifying elements to form a metaphor has an innovative effect upon the meanings and lexical signification of a culture; it fuses formerly established elements into a new relation, which simultaneously draws upon their "accepted" denotations for its force and adds the force of its own creation to these. As long as the metaphor remains in use it retains this innovative interaction with the elements it metaphorizes; when, after prolonged usage, the relation between signifier and signified comes to be taken for granted, the expression collapses into one of lexical signification, which can of course be incorporated into a new metaphor. The interchange between signification and metaphorization, wherein each draws upon the other, produces a situation in which meaning is a function of change as well as of formal signification and in which the creative aspect of change is metaphoric innovation. Any meaning that impinges upon, or "opposes," a central cultural tenet or proposition must take the form of an innovation upon it, a metaphoric expression involving the tenet itself, and in fact metaphorizing it.

The central tenets or propositions of a culture, however, are also expressed in metaphorical form, so that an innovation upon one effectively metaphorizes a metaphor, using a relation to produce another relation. The result is a dialectic relationship in which the relation signified by one metaphor becomes the context of the other, and therefore the meaning evoked by each is achieved at the expense of the other. Metaphoric innovation thus produces and exploits contradictions among the meanings of a culture, exemplified by those of social collectivity and individuality or of human mortality and the existence of ghosts in Daribi culture. But not all of the meanings produced by a culture contradict one another, and not all of its metaphors oppose each other in a dialectical relationship. Metaphors of a culture may either exist in a *complementary* or a *dialectically innovative* relationship to one another, and the respective meanings may be either consistent or contradictory.

A set of metaphors whose relationship to one another is complementary, since they refer to different and nonconflicting aspects of the same cultural domain (such as social relations or names), constitutes an ideology. The meanings of an ideology are consistent with one another, for they do not conflict at any point. Ideologies, in turn, may be subdivided into component ideologies existing in a complementary relationship, as we might speak of Daribi procreation ideology and Daribi gardening ideology as being complementary components of social ideology. An ideology whose metaphors bear an innovative relationship to those of another ideology, however, stands in a dialectical relationship to the latter, and the respective meanings of the two contradict one another. The creation of a new meaning automatically places it in a complementary relation with some ideological aspects of the culture, and a dialectical relation with others.

It is not only man's words, signs, and gestures that are meaningful, but also his actions, styles of life, and relationships with other people. Kinship, friendship, and courtesy roles metaphorize the specific acts of individuals in cultural terms, so that one "becomes" a father, friend, or a good host by "acting like" one, hence by impersonating the role. Impersonation is the equivalent of metaphorization in the realm of social role. The ultimate generalization of all the "normative" roles of kinship and human interaction is the idealized human life-course, with its beginnings in procreation and its irrevocable conclusion in death. Mythically, Daribi articulate this inevitability through the story of Souw's curse; cosmologically, they dramatize it in terms of the motion of the sun and moon across the sky and of the waters across the earth; but their most powerful and telling expression of it is in the mourning laments and practices.

Just as magic, dream-interpretation, and identity achieve their meanings as innovations upon the collectivities of social ideology, so the concepts of religion attain significance as innovations upon the doctrine of human mortality. What I have called "the invention of immortality," the impersonation of the dead in the form of ghosts by spirit mediums, *sogoyezibidi*, *gerua* dancers, and the *habubidi*, draws its force from this sort of "metaphorization." A ghost is powerful because it has transcended the limitations that characterize men collectively, and the impersonator is powerful because, in the act of impersonation, he has added the ghost's capabilities to his own.

From the native standpoint, of course, there is no distinction to be drawn between the symbolic elements (such as the ideas of procreation) that enter into the conceptualization of kinship and the role of a kinsman or between what I have called metaphorization and impersonation, for this distinction is the product of analysis. In this respect the highly "condensed" (to use Freud's term) mythic and cosmological symbolizations examined and explicated in Chapters 1 and 5 probably retain the closest fidelity to native Daribi apprehensions, but by the same token they probably diverge most widely from anthropological convention.

Otherwise, the explication of Daribi religion in this book embodies a necessary and unavoidable compromise with the presentational styles of anthropology, if only in the interests of communication. The account of social ideology presented in Chapter 2, for instance, resembles very closely the chapters on social "rules" characteristic of standard structural-functional ethnographies. Because of this it is necessary for me to emphasize that Chapter 2, and this book as a whole, is about meanings and not about rules. This is not to deny the relation of "thought" to "action" in human culture, but only an assertion of my feeling that "rule" amounts to a poor articulation of this relation and that innovation and impersonation register its nuances and potentialities in a far more comprehensive way.

In fact, it might be said that an individual learns to "use" his culture, to perform operations upon it, by "breaking" rules, that is, by extending words and other learned signifiers beyond their defined areas of signification. We exist as personalities through the *impact* we make on our culture, the way in which we individuate ourselves through particular styles and modes of extension. A brilliant or creative man, a good talker, a poet, or a jokester is always someone who has mastered the art of effective, controlled innovation; a masterful politician or a skilled shaman is often a true artist in this respect. These people have learned how to invoke and compel the power that "new" meaning represents through the creative displacement of "given" meanings.

Cultural continuity is attained through the learning and transmission of innovative styles that, in their dialectical interdependence, form an integrated whole. Of course these styles themselves undergo change, and the delimiting of styles within a given culture or time period is always arbitrary and subject to the prejudices of the observer. An individual personality can be seen as a style, or rather a refraction into the many styles through which it is articulated, and personal style can be recognized in the works and acts of artists, intellectuals, and statesmen. Such individuating style always partakes to some degree of the expressive and individuating force realized otherwise in the form of totemic or other naming practices.

Style in fact represents the innovative imitation, or repetition of metaphorical constructs, often permutated through a number of individual or incidental variants. A style retains its coherence through the dialectical tension that gives it cultural relevance; extreme departures lose credibility through distortion of the meaningful content of the original formulation. Imaginative applications of a style are often imitated and proliferated into a range of derivative styles, giving rise to the versatility exhibited, for instance, in the Daribi naming system. It is this dimension of stylistic plurality and variability that often distinguishes a culture "on the ground" from even the best ethnographic description.

TRANSFORMATION AND CULTURE

Religious practices and institutions often involve the incorporation of innovative relations as social roles, so that the metaphor of simultaneously "being" human and ghost, or human and god, permits the working out of esoteric power relations in purely social terms. The efficacy of such undertakings is directly dependent on the degree to which the participants are able to assume their roles, and create the metaphor by "becoming" the spirits that they represent. If the roles are maintained, the dual and mediating significance of the performance is realized; if not, the performance becomes a parody, a betrayal of man and spirits alike. The performers become human embodiments, like the Daribi medium or *sogoyezibidi,* of the relation between human and spirit, insofar as their persons represent the "metaphoric link" between the two roles they simultaneously play. Hence it is that they themselves are often thought to embody a *mana*-like power as *foci* of the alignment between the human and spirit worlds, and it is this power that creates the potential of sickness for the Daribi *habubidi* and mediums. As an artifact of innovative force, this power is analogous to that which is conjured by *pobi,* except for the fact that it is embodied socially.

The impersonation of divine or ghostly beings through a "transformation" constitutes the central feature of many religious systems. It is found in the *katcina* dances of the American Southwest, the Balinese drama of Rangda and Barong described by Geertz, and in the Christian Eucharist. Wherever it occurs, the test of faith or credence for the performer as well as the "laity" is a commitment to the ultimate validity of the metaphor. Thus it was that the teachings of the great medieval grammarian Berengar of Tours, who held that the Eucharist is merely symbolic, were branded as heresy. The characteristic doctrinal countermeasure to skepticism of this sort, and the mark of the kind of "control" exercised by the Daribi *sogoyezibidi,* is the notion that impersonation is achieved through a kind of complicity on the part of the being who is impersonated. The impersonation is therefore presented as an act of communication or "communion" between human and spirit. This is indeed true of the Eucharist, and we find it again in the Daribi ideas concerning the *hogo'bia* bird, the *kerare* plant, and the *habu* cry, which serve to maintain the communion between the *habu-bidi* and the ghost. The "meaning" created by this kind of metaphor is not simply another element in a communicative sequence; rather it *becomes* the communication itself, and human beings are the vessels of its innovative power.

For all the sanctity of such impersonations, and for all the stress that is laid on their metaphoric "validity," they must, nevertheless, remain impersonations. The dancers never *actually* become the demons they are portraying, the wafer and wine are never *really* Christ's substance (and this is perhaps what Berengar meant), and the *habubidi* are certainly not ghosts themselves. If indeed such a transformation were to take place, the metaphor being collapsed into an equivalence, then the mediative link between human and spirit would be lost and the ceremony rendered useless. A metaphor depends on both contrast and similarity to sustain meaning; if one or the other is lost, the expression falls out of its dialectical relation with, and hence its relevance to, the society. The *habubidi* are men, like the *be' habu*, but they assume the role of the ghost through their costume, their association with the bush, and their antagonism toward the house people. The fact that they are men allows the ceremonial control of the whole undertaking, the fact that they "become" ghosts, or at least take their roles, assures its ultimate effectiveness.

This fact of impersonation holds true for all of man's culture, as we have seen, from the forms of his social life to the imagery of his rhetoric and the modalities of his spiritual fulfillment. Little as we know of the origins of human culture, it is not difficult to believe that the forms through which it transforms and renews itself are related to the way in which it first came into being. This in turn suggests that culture, as an innovative sequence, is all one thing, however we may choose to subdivide and dissect it through our distinctions of behavioral and ideal, or physical and mental. Man is the great "borrower" of nature; he takes the deer's meat for his food and its hide for his clothing just as he takes its name for his identity. His ingenuity always consists in assimilating the external, creating meaning and power from its novel impingement on the "given." The fact that he must do this in a physical sense, to make his living, whether he hunts for bears or berries, fashions chert tools, husbands the growth of plants, or extracts fossil fuels, is so important and so obvious that we often overlook the conclusion that such acts are no more or less "cultural" than dream-interpretation or religious ceremonial. Activities like drilling for oil and hunting marsupials, quite regardless of their results, are only conceivable because they have meaning, whether this has to do with progress or profit, or perhaps with the health of one's pigs and children.

The simple premise of innovation, that culture exists only through growth and transformation, underlies much of what seems basic in human activity, from the "incest taboo" to the forms through which meaning is created. Technology is only a special case of this, as are naming, artistic creativity, and the practices that we call "religious." Whether we "borrow" power and meaning from nature itself, from the forms and designations of our own culture or from those of exotic cultures, the significant factor is the mode of borrowing and transformation, not the content of that which is borrowed. The ethnographic content of a culture is thus merely a result, a cumulative historical increment of its transformations and a continuing "context" for the formation of new metaphors. The life of the culture, its creations, revelations, activities, and strategies, is carried on through innovational styles.

The blazing feathers, grotesqueries of ornament, and flamboyant naming and totemic systems of "native" peoples often seem to suggest the existence of bizarre and ineffably felicitous cultural idioms wherein act and gesture automatically assume the force of expressive poetry. Most of this must unfortunately be dismissed as individual projection and a romanticizing of the myth of "natural man," if not simply the result of poor translations. Nevertheless, the exoticism and often the stark expressiveness of his subject matter offers the anthropologist a reprieve from his own age of tired metaphors and collapsing idioms, and from a scholastic tradition in which "understanding" becomes increasingly contingent upon cultural elaboration and the manufacture of complexity. Far from being a mere nuisance, exoticism provides a potent means of drawing analyst and reader alike out of their own culture, and the Rousseauist myth becomes a significant factor in its own dispelling. And if transformation is the work of culture, and innovative "borrowing" the form of man's creativity, what better way of transforming the insights of the native into our own than by borrowing the expressive force of his own idioms?

Bibliography

Arndt, W.
  1965   "The Dreaming of Kunukban," *Oceania* 35, No. 4.
Austen, L.
  1932   "Legends of Hido," *Oceania* 2, No. 4.
Baal, J. van
  1966   *Dema.* The Hague: Martinus Nijhoff.
Bateson, G.
  1958   *Naven.* Stanford: Stanford University Press.
Cole, J. D.
  n.d.   "An Introduction to Psycho-Serial Systems and Systematics,"
          unpublished manuscript.
Franklin, K. J.
  1968   "Languages of the Gulf District: A Preview," in *Pacific Lin-
          guistics*, Series A, No. 16.
Gardner, R., and Heider, K. G.
  1968   *Gardens of War: Life and Death in the New Guinea Stone
          Age.* New York: Random House.
Geertz, C.
  1968   "Religion as a Cultural System," in ASA Monograph No. 3,
          Anthropological Approaches to the Study of Religion, ed. M.
          Banton. London: Tavistock.
Glasse, R. M.
  1965   "Leprosy at Karamui," *Papua and New Guinea Medical Jour-
          nal* 8, No. 3.
Haddon, A. C.
  1908   *Reports of the Cambridge Anthropological Expedition to
          Torres Straits*, Vol. VI. Cambridge.
Hughes, I.
  1969   "Some Aspects of Traditional Trade in the New Guinea High-
          lands, A Preliminary Report." Paper given at the 41st
          A.N.Z.A.A.S. Congress, Adelaide, Australia.
  1970   "Pigs, Sago and Limestone," *Mankind* 7, No. 4.

Landtman, G.
   1917   *The Folk Tales of the Kiwai Papuans*, Acta Societatis Scien-
           tarum Fennicae 47. Helsingfors: Printing Office of the Fin-
           nish Society of Literature.

Levi-Strauss, C.
   1962   *Totemism,* tr. R. Needham. Boston: Beacon Press.
   1966   *The Savage Mind,* tr. anon. London: Weidenfeld and Nicol-
           son.
   1969   *The Elementary Structures of Kinship,* Revised Edition, tr.
           J. H. Bell, J. R. von Sturmer, and R. Needham, Editor. Boston:
           Beacon Press.

Malinowski, B.
   1954   *Magic, Science and Religion and Other Essays.* Garden City,
           N. Y.: Doubleday & Co.
   1961   *Argonauts of the Western Pacific.* New York: E. P. Dutton &
           Co.
   1965   *Coral Gardens and Their Magic, 2: The Language of Magic
           and Gardening.* Bloomington: Indiana University Press.

Meggitt, M. J.
   1962   "Dream Interpretation Among the Mae Enga of New Guinea,"
           Southwestern Journal of Anthropology 18, No. 3.
   1964   "Male-Female Relationships in the Highlands of Australian
           New Guinea," in *American Anthropologist* 66, No. 4, Part 2.

Newman, P. L.
   1965   *Knowing the Gururumba.* New York: Holt, Rinehart and Win-
           ston.

Rappaport, R. A.
   1968   *Pigs for the Ancestors: Ritual in the Ecology of a New Guinea
           People.* New Haven: Yale University Press.

Reay, M.
   1959   *The Kuma.* Melbourne: Melbourne University Press.

Rivers, W. H. R.
   1904   *Reports of the Cambridge Anthropological Expedition to
           Torres Straits* 5. Cambridge.

Ryan, D. J.
   1958   "Names and Naming in Mendi," *Oceania* 29.

Salisbury, R. F.
   1962   *From Stone to Steel.* London: Cambridge University Press.
   1965   "The Siane of the Eastern Highlands," in *Gods, Ghosts and
           Men in Melanesia,* P. Lawrence and M. J. Meggitt. London:
           Oxford University Press.

Schneider, D. M.
   1968   *American Kinship: A Cultural Account.* Englewood Cliffs,
           N. J.: Prentice-Hall.

Simpson, C.
   1962   *Plumes and Arrows.* Sydney: Angus and Robertson.

Strathern, A. J.
   1970   "Wiru Penthonyms," *Bijdragen tot de Taal-, Land-, en Volken-kunde* 1.
Wagner, R.
   1967   *The Curse of Souw: Principles of Daribi Clan Definition and Alliance in New Guinea.* Chicago: University of Chicago Press.
   1969   "Marriage Among the Daribi," in *Pigs, Pearlshells and Women*, ed. R. M. Glasse and M. J. Meggitt. Englewood Cliffs, N. J.: Prentice-Hall.
   1970   "Daribi and Foraba Cross-Cousin Terminologies: A Structural Comparison," *Journal of the Polynesian Society* 79, No. 1.
Williams, F. E.
   1940   *Natives of Lake Kutubu, Papua*, Oceania Monograph No. 6. Sydney: The Australian National Research Council.
   1969   *Orokaiva Magic* (reprinted). Oxford: Oxford University Press.
Willis, I. J.
   1969   (unpub.) *"An 'Epic' Journey."* Subthesis prepared at the University of Papua and New Guinea, Port Moresby.

Index

of life-style of, 118; and costume in *habu*, 158; and opposition to *habu-bidi*, 158–59; and role in conclusion of *habu*, 162–63
Work: male and female, 43–45; tabooed at death or crisis, 146

Yard. See *Be' mesaro*

Zibi: and sharing of cooked food, 47; and restrictions of sharing wealth, 50; and marriage reciprocity, 53